Remaking Democracy in America

Bear Kosik

Remaking Democracy in America

Print ISBN 978-1-941071-79-3
ebook ISBN 978-1-941071-80-9

STAIRWAY PRESS—APACHE JUNCTION

Cover Design by Guy D. Corp
www.GrafixCorp.com

STAIRWAY PRESS

www.StairwayPress.com
1000 West Apache Trail #126
Apache Junction, AZ 88120 USA

Dedication

To my father, Hugh E. McNeelege,
passionate student of knowledge…

and

…to my stepfather, Samuel O. Teague,
decorated defender of freedom.

Preface and Acknowledgments

I WAS GOING to call this part "Prescription Insert," because I gather my writing ought to include some information about its molecular structure, appropriate uses, side effects, warnings, and contraindications. And I know prefaces are often not read. If you are reading this, bully for you!

This book's structure can be understood from the table of contents along with the additional note that the chapters move from the heavens of theory and ideas to the hell of current politics in the USA. Since readers know where they are headed, perhaps they will take their time getting there. With any luck, it will be an interesting trip.

The intended uses of this work are for the arguments, ideas, and suggestions to be comprehended, considered, and contested in the real world. The side effects readers may experience certainly include drowsiness, giggles, energy, irritation, and confusion. In rare cases, readers may experience ennui, disorientation, and dander. If your left arm starts feeling numb, it is not a heart attack. Use your right arm to hold up the book for a while. Always read sitting up, neck aligned perpendicular to the floor. Chiropractors ain't cheap!

Reading this book is contraindicated if the reader does not wish to gain knowledge and confront illogic. The greatest failing in the USA since 1980 has been the relentless whittling of expectations and ceaseless weakening of challenges in schools and colleges. As will become quite clear, remaking democracy requires restoring the kind of education that had developed prior to the 1970s. That means nothing gets "dumbed down." Anyone with a desire to learn anything can fulfill that desire with sufficient dedication, time, and, when needed, assistance. That is the mantra of developmental education; it really must be fully embraced in this country.

The contents use comparative analysis of historical, ideological, and political evidence to understand terms, ideas, and views relevant to political discourse. Readers are warned that this requires explanations of and references to a great number of individuals, events, and philosophies that may require further research to understand. In other words, the book is packed with factlets and factoids, Easter eggs, and a few plot bunnies from the author's fiction, but the entire work is most definitely non-fiction.

The rhetoric may seem difficult, even too difficult to merit the effort of working through this preface. English syntax is as malleable and valuable as gold. Using the different ways to construct sentences makes writing less of a chore and reading less of a bore. Our language has a sizeable and uniquely mongrel vocabulary. All of our words exist because they have been introduced into the language by someone, from William Shakespeare to Matt Groening (yes, *The Simpsons* remains on the air solely to keep English fresh although the author would have preferred that task had been taken over a few years ago by *Futurama*).

Much of that variety and variability in English owes to King James I of England commanding the compilation of a new translation of the Old and New Testaments. The Holy Bible, the most popular book in the USA, is a greater challenge to understand in any of its English language versions, even The Action Bible, than this book.

Our words ought to continue to be used as fully as possible because they are a blessing. No other language has come close enough to warrant making a thesaurus since Sanskrit's *Amarakosha*. Although the word "thesaurus" sounds like a survivor of the Cretaceous-Paleogene extinction event, it was adopted into English from Greek via Latin by Peter Mark Roget in 1852. Amazingly, its meaning as "treasure" is quite close to the meaning of the Sanskrit title but otherwise it really doesn't have any good synonyms. That is a shame, but not too remarkable for a word defining a specific kind of reference book. Feelings, actions, and attributes are more in need of nuances and shades of meaning that may require searching for the treasured right word. If the right word is obscure, does it matter? Almost no one any longer needs to stand, walk to a bookshelf, pick up a three-pound dictionary, find the correct page, read the definition, reshelf the dictionary, walk back to the chair, sit, get comfortable, and try to remember where to begin reading again. Did you ever notice how pedometers came into vogue once everyone had remote controls for televisions?

Roget was a physician and natural theologian, two professions that often encounter multiple words with the same or similar meanings. Significantly, he was a member of the Society for the Diffusion of Useful Knowledge, an unsuccessful effort to publish materials explaining science and other subjects. Mid-nineteenth century England was hardly the place to attempt to convince the working and lower middle classes to build on whatever education that they had received.

The Society closed down in 1848 due to lack of interest within its target audience, most likely as a result of its failure to explain why scientific knowledge was useful to workers who were never called upon to demonstrate their understanding of the physical world. The American counterpart founded in Boston lasted 99 years longer but had no more success. Henry David Thoreau presciently and jokingly suggested a Society for the Diffusion of Useful Ignorance in an essay entitled "Walking."

Rupert Murdoch and many neo-conservative commentators seized that idea with vigor in the 1990s. A void had been created and they took advantage of the opportunity to create what is now the large base of support for Donald Trump.

Writers a century ago could feel free to use allusions to many ancient, medieval, and early modern texts because everyone reading their work would have had essentially the same education in the classics and approved canon.

Even a quick biographical note about a Greek hero or two-line intercalation explaining the significance of an event was unnecessary. They even sprinkled in French phrases without needing to include a parenthetical definition afterward. *Ah, le bon vieux temps!* Most of the short Latin terms like ex post facto, reductio ad absurdum, et cetera were long ago adopted untranslated into English dictionaries. Thus, we could speak of common knowledge because so much knowledge actually was common to everyone who completed grammar school or high school or college or even summer Bible school.

Except we were ignoring a great bit of equally fine work that provided the added benefit of opening our eyes to the perspectives of a world of creative, perceptive authors who were not pinkish or not equipped with penises or both. The Information Technology Age has made English the global lingua franca and made many native English speakers unable to define "lingua franca."

For very sound reasons, education at all levels has become greatly diversified. For somewhat less sound reasons higher education has largely eliminated the liberal arts degree in favor of subject-specific majors. The formerly reasonable assumption that almost all readers who had attained the same level of education broadly had been exposed to more or less the same materials and methods is no longer reasonable in the slightest degree.

As a result, pretty much everything referenced in a work like this must be explained to some degree. Fortunately, the author enjoys explaining things, to the point that students often have breathed a sigh of relief at the end of a forty minute discussion when all of the explanations finally are pulled together and they see the connections. The great thing is the students are the ones who see the connections rather than the connections being pointed out to them. Now that's what we called education!

Some of that method of teaching is idiosyncrasy, some a hazard of comparative analysis, and some the need to provide the background for students who learned other important things. The explanations use language that may be disputed, but the essential facts have been checked and rechecked.

Careful readers can tell when something smells truthy, but casual readers deserve not to be misled. When the information may have questionable reliability or may be reliably questioned, it is noted. I have always warned classes and participants in workshops I have conducted that I answer questions as fully, honestly, and accurately as I can; if I don't know the answer I will make up something that is plausible. No need to worry about that here as I have been posing the questions to myself. When I am the student, I insist on verifiable information from reliable sources cross-checked against other reliable sources. All of the research and writing has been completed solely by the author. Accordingly, the author owns sole responsibility for all inaccuracies and accuracies contained herein.

I was baptized into the Disciples of Christ. In their tradition, a child must be old enough to understand the faith he is accepting. After declaring his faith, he strips naked, dons a white smock that becomes see-through when wet, is water-boarded in a waist-deep pool behind the altar, and given a thimbleful of wine and a miniature chowder cracker that have not been transubstantiated.

I was then baptized a second time four years later to be "Born Again." Given those intentional actions and my firm agreement with and daily efforts to practice the teachings of Jesus of Nazareth, I am a dictionary-definition Christian. I accept that a man whose name in Greek is Jesus probably died to redeem the sins and be the savior of mankind sometime around 30 CE; that is not sufficient to make me a Biblical-definition Christian. I also follow the precepts of Daoist philosophy and recognize the accuracy of widely-accepted scientific theories as determined by scientists in their fields of study.

I hope readers will see, despite some sarcasm and criticism herein, my faith and reason both affirm that we are made of the same elements as everything else in the universe and every member of our species is unique, equal, valuable, and gifted. When we act solely or principally in our own interests, we typically help ourselves and possibly others. When we act firstly in the interests of other people, creatures, or our planet, we invariably help ourselves and others even more.

Self-interest is poisonous to humans in all but the smallest amounts. Others around us may become ill from our ambition, but the greater suffering is felt by the one who attends too much to him or herself. These are moral and ethical precepts that may coincide with religious teachings. The beliefs of any religion cannot inform laws or government in any society unless the people agree to create a theocracy or accept theocratic influences.

Individuals have provided encouragement, assistance, and care to the author without which this book would not have been completed. I thank Kenneth Dudley, K-lee Klein, Marilyn Locci, Suzanne Stanton, and Mary Teague for their compassion and support.

Please turn the page and enjoy!

Contents

Chapter 1—Political Change and the Role of Participation

WHETHER WE LIKE it or not, political change happens. Change is the one, universal constant. Living things placed in stasis of some kind, like insects in amber, change at an immeasurably slow rate. Just because we can't measure it or sense it does not mean change is not occurring. No matter how little we do, no matter how much we try to stop it, change happens. Indeed, even our efforts to stop change create change. The question will never be do we want our political system to change. The question will always be do we want to consciously guide how our political system changes. The answer is always yes for politicians and other engaged citizens like activists, political pundits, and donors of time and money to political campaigns. Everyone else typically answers no and remains disconnected from or tenuously connected to the public sphere unless they become motivated to act.

Why would anyone become motivated to move from apathy or disinterest to active participation? Someone or some event sparks within them the recognition that their needs and interests are not being met but should be. Usually the problem does not warrant too much effort and the individual can sink back into the so-called silent majority. One of the more frequent forms of political participation is to help someone else in dealing with local government. Friends, neighbors, or relatives generally will lend a hand of support.

Only rarely does one problem become three. Three become eight. Eight become disaffection for how the political system operates. Whether these passive citizens realize it consciously or not, the bargain they have with society no longer works. The politicians and other engaged citizens no longer act for the benefit of society as a whole. The time comes when the unengaged see that they must act either to assert their rights under the bargain they have with society or negotiate a new bargain they hope is less likely to deteriorate.

This book provides a thorough enough understanding of politics for anyone to grasp the consequences of remaining disconnected from or tenuously connected to the public sphere. It demonstrates the importance for all citizens to participate now and in the future in the political sphere. It describes some of the paths that can be taken if enough citizens participate in a united movement to change the political system of the United States of America. It explains why it is necessary to restore the noble principles of the Founders of the Republic consistent with the knowledge, wisdom, and experience gained in the last two hundred forty-odd years. It recommends the establishment of a new social contract that strengthens the ability of the citizens to conduct their own affairs while guaranteeing all residents equality under the law and equality in accessing opportunities to improve their lives. This book is the water. Readers are the horses. Drink or don't drink.

In the rhetoric of politics and civil society the sliding scale of change runs from glacial to explosive. To let everyone else know where we prefer to stand on that sliding scale, we create ideologies. Ideology initially prioritizes issues. Then ideology indicates just how rapidly we want change to occur depending on the issue in question. Both priority and rapidity link to the changing conditions around every issue. The difference is like that of driving a car versus flying an airplane; the former only requires the ability to navigate in two dimensions while the other requires three. Given the number of issues societies deal with air traffic control has its hands full.

Unfortunately we are not very good at recognizing when implementation of our ideologies alters the pace of change until it becomes inconsistent with what we said we prefer. Nor are we all that good at monitoring how implementation changes the conditions in which we are operating. We wait for events to catch up with us or find events get out of hand. We take snapshots of data at specific points when we need to be videotaping how the process is unfolding or wind up with reams of film that take hours to edit down to a coherent story. Even people who claim they want to call a halt to change or turn back the clock to the circumstances and values of a "better" past find out that what they want requires doing the opposite of what they want.

An ultraconservative wants as little change as possible and would be delighted if we put everything back the way we had things before. Even if we can pinpoint "before" it is impossible. Everything has changed and we cannot go back. The less intelligent ultraconservative does not understand that the way-back machine has not been invented except in a clever cartoon created way back that entertained and educated. She tries to force everyone to behave as though the present is the past, violently if necessary. She issues laws identifying anyone who has changed as a heretic. She starts looking for everyone who has changed, starting with the Archbishop of Canterbury Thomas Cranmer and the other architects of making the Church of England more Protestant. Queen Mary I transforms from being the older half-sister to become Cinderella's stepmother, cutting off her subjects' toes and heels to fit them into the slipper, which hopefully can be cleaned of the blood between fittings. Why? Because she cannot conceive of a world in which her sister marries a prince or worse yet revels in becoming a Virgin Queen who will not peer into the hearts and souls of men. Not only does she find her efforts unsuccessful, she has now done quite a bit of harm to her own people and will only be remembered as Bloody Mary.

The more intelligent ultraconservatives recognize that returning to the past is impossible. Instead, they try to replicate the past in the present as though no change has occurred. No force required. They will just pretend the French Revolution and Napoleon Bonaparte never happened. They will all meet in Vienna in 1815 just like everyone met in in the Westphalian cities of Osnabrück and Münster in 1648. They will draw up treaties that will establish a long and prosperous period of relative peace in Europe. As long as another Louis XIV of France doesn't show up and try to annex the Low Countries or place his relatives on other thrones, everything will be fine. If rebellions break out to impose liberal democratic governments in Spain, Naples, or Russia, there is no need to worry. The peasants have rebelled before. The regiments have rebelled before. The nobles have rebelled before. Who the rebels are or what the rebels want is irrelevant. Nothing new to see here. Nothing new to do here. Just crush the rebels and go back to listening to the beautiful classical music being composed in every royal court.

Restoration is obviously far less disruptive than reaction. Generally speaking the public sphere much prefers evolution over revolution. Conservatives can't even be satisfied with evolution. The fundamental inconsistency of any conservative philosophy—ultra, neo, or traditional—is the desire to act on things in order to preserve them or return them to a previous state. There are two irreparable flaws in attempting to maintain or restore a society much less react to a new one. One, the actions required to do so necessarily have the opposite effect. Every single action results in change. Two, we cannot go back or stand still. Physical law prohibits us.

Many people nonetheless firmly believe and desire that Humpty Dumpty can be pieced together again. The results of restorative actions actually may recreate a semblance of what was. The repairs to Michelangelo's *Pietà* after it was damaged by a hammer-wielding assailant were so well done the human eye cannot tell the marble was ever repaired. Judging by appearance alone, anyone would say the restoration work was completely successful. Only the records that the statue was damaged and repaired tell us changes occurred. Paradoxically, these records of the facts can never change. In situations like this, even our interpretation of the facts cannot change.

That is not always the case. In every moment that passes new facts appear. Sometimes they relate to older facts and require us to reevaluate our interpretation of the earlier facts. Newer facts can even tell us that the information we had known for centuries was scandalously false. When the bones of King Richard III of England were dug up in a car park in Leicester in 2012, the world discovered a few months later that Shakespeare and Tudor-era painters all depicted a man bent and dark not by nature or the wicked actions of his last three years of life. Their versions reflected their periods' disgust for the man. His DNA showed he was blue-eyed and blond, at least as a young man, and certainly not the Bard's hunchbacked villain. Finally it all made sense. Richard III's career prior to usurping the throne from his nephew in 1483 indicated a capable, courageous military leader and governor of the North, more loyal to his older brother Henry VI than their conniving sibling, the Duke of Clarence. He was the perfect, logical choice as Protector of the twelve-year-old Edward V.

However, we view history through the lens of the ultimate victors. Richard III's death at Bosworth Field in 1485 implied his usurpation of his nephew's position had not found favor with God. Accordingly, his victorious adversary, now King Henry VII and his four royal descendants had every reason to encourage everyone to think that Richard had been a horrible, crippled, vengeful man who deserved to be replaced by his distant Welsh cousin. Not only did it make the Tudors look good for avenging the presumed deaths of Edward V and his younger brother in the Tower of London on orders from Richard III. The propaganda also promoted the stability and godliness of a fresh dynasty in need of every support possible for their shaky claim to the crown.

Even in fifteenth century English politics, participation or holding back mattered immensely. For starters, Henry Tudor brought some troops, English exiles and French mercenaries, when he sailed from Brittany (the duchy not Spears) to make his move. He entered through Pembrokeshire and about tripled his force as he crossed Wales to Shrewsbury. Welshmen were happy to support one of their own win the English crown. That still gave the King a large advantage in troops when the armies encountered each other at Bosworth Field.

The tide turned against Richard III in four steps, any one of which not occurring probably would have saved him. First, the Earl of Northumberland ignored his sovereign's signal to advance to support the troops under the Duke of Norfolk who had engaged Henry's troops under the Earl of Oxford. Second, Richard decided that he had better charge directly at Henry to demonstrate his desire to retain the throne and kill the pretender. Third, Thomas, Lord Stanley, and Sir William Stanley had outright refused Richard's demand that they order their men to join him at the start and equivocated when Henry did the same. They wanted to first see who was most likely to win. Now fourth, the Stanleys decided that Richard's charge looked like an act of desperation. They swooped in and rather quickly unhorsed and assassinated Richard. The ferocity of the attack on the king's person was so great that Richard's mistress had to be brought out to identify the remains.

Coming to or refusing to aid a monarch or his successful challenger had significant implications on a battlefield near Leicester in 1485 for subjects, recruits, and nobles alike. Richard was holding Lord Stanley's son hostage to force him to assist his king. When Richard said he would execute the son if the Stanleys did not engage, Lord Stanley replied, "I have other sons." Loving father that he was, he probably didn't deserve to end up being reunited with his son after the battle; Richard's lords insisted the execution could wait until after the battle. Then again, it would have been, sadly, his son's loss not his.

It is remarkable we have so much information to analyze 531 years later. Of course, everyone at Bosworth Field that day must have known history was going to be made. A king going into battle? Of course. It is so much easier to preserve evidence and get the eyewitnesses' observations recorded if everyone knows people in the future will find an event or person worthy of study. Of course we say that and someone as noteworthy in his time as Shakespeare inspired no known contemporaries to even verify he wrote all those plays. Someone may have but one man's treasure is another man's trash. Just think how many records have been lost in so many different ways.

That is why it is even more remarkable finding Richard III's bones 527 years later. The bones of monarchs usually wind up stowed under a sculpted sepulcher in a cathedral in Roskilde or St. Denis or some other town people forget exists. And then we discover his bones tell us things about him that prove our previous sources were inaccurate. On the other hand, sometimes later discoveries verify what we think we know. The remains of Russian Tsar Nicholas II, his wife, and his children eventually confirmed the reports of how they had been murdered by the Bolsheviks. What is not remarkable is the number of television programs about the past that use the word "mystery" in their titles. We are fortunate that we frequently know what we don't know even though we don't know necessarily how to find what we don't know. At least we can be entertained by shows that show us what we don't know and also show us how we may find what we don't know.

Serious problems arise when our knowledge comes from multiple, somewhat conflicting, apparently incomplete sources like the four Gospels. Jesus of Nazareth remained rather coy about who he was and what his purpose was almost up until the end. As a result, his apostles spent their time listening to him preach and doing what he asked so they could learn from him. If they had a clearer idea of his importance or hadn't been so thick-headed they would have pulled out their iPhones to videotape every move he made and hired stenographers to record every word he said.

Instead the Gospels were written long enough after his ministry and even his appearances after death that nonbelievers understandably wonder how reliable the accounts are. Of course, they have a value apart from believing Jesus to be the Son of God. Muslims consider Jesus to be the last prophet until Mohammed. One does not have to believe that a man named Laozi, which just means "old man" or "old master," wrote the 81 entries that make up the *Daodejing* to recognize the value of those entries as an enlightened philosophy worthy of study and application in our daily lives. The teachings in the Gospels are far more important than the information regarding Jesus' activities and those of his apostles, followers, and others mentioned in the texts. The events described provide a context for the ethics defined.

Even in modern times, four eyewitnesses to one accident or alleged crime are capable of testifying under oath to having seen four distinctly different events. Good cross-examination can lead to even more iterations of what happened. What is in our field of vision and what we register as seeing are two completely different things. Look on YouTube for studies in which a person in a gorilla suit walks around. People stopped will say there was no person in a gorilla suit or swear the person was wearing a bear suit. Physical evidence may not always tell us everything we want to know, but at least it is objective and we only need worry about our own subjectivity in examining it.

Not that subjectivity is always bad. The most immediate and touching reminder of the destruction of the World Trade Center is in the New York State Museum in Albany during a fundraising event called New York in Bloom held each February. Local florists and garden clubs design flower arrangements for all of the museum's exhibits. On the weekend of the event, the area displaying debris and other artefacts from the twin towers includes containers of flowers chosen and placed to echo the materials exhibited and reflect the emotions people have seeing those materials. Given our culture's use of flowers to express condolences and the fact visitors are viewing objects from an historical event that occurred within their lifetimes, the experience is as profound as visiting the memorials in Washington, DC but incredibly more intimate given no more than a handful of people are in that quiet, relatively small space at any given moment.

The United States became a far different place after September 11, 2001. A majority of people insisted that their government take measures to make them feel more secure. Their government responded by enacting laws and taking actions that politicians said were intended to make the country safer from terrorist attack. A great debate has raged since about 2003 whether those laws and actions really did what the politicians claimed they were intended to do and whether they were even designed for the purpose of making the USA safer from terrorist attack.

We are not going to discuss that debate. Discussion is warranted but here we are more concerned about the consequences of the changes that occurred or were made to politics in the wake of those laws and actions. As was mentioned earlier, the implementation of an ideology often results in consequences that were not intended. The people promoting the ideology often do not see how or why the effects are different than was intended. Their intentions are useful in determining whether they violated any laws; they are not relevant to our topic. Those who implemented the policies definitely should be held responsible for the consequences. They have not.

Those negatively affected by the consequences are responsible in a democracy to insist that their government remedy the situation and hold those whose policies caused their problems to be judged and penalized, if guilty, according to the law and equity. These are circumstances in which participation by the usually unengaged is necessary. The unengaged can join the Duke of Norfolk and Earl of Oxford entering the fray immediately to win a decision favorable to their interests and values. They can sit back with the Stanleys and wait until events point to one result or another, although they risk losing something as valuable as a son or choosing coldly that it can be lost.

What the unengaged ought not to do is stand with the Earl of Northumberland refusing to get involved at all. Although he safely managed to gain favor with Henry VII, he ended up being the victim of a different sort of political movement. In 1489, four years after the Battle of Bosworth Field, he was lynched by the citizens of York for his role in collecting new taxes imposed by Henry VII to pay for a war Brittany wanted to wage against France. Indeed, the Earl may well have done better to have intervened on behalf of Richard III when ordered to do so. Richard was well-known for his administrative abilities and indifference to accumulating wealth or entering into foreign wars. Henry VII also preferred to avoid foreign wars but owed Anne of Brittany a debt for sheltering him and the English exiles. He also turned out to be one of England's most rapacious monarchs, raising and collecting taxes in old and innovative ways just for the sake of obtaining more money. Sam Walton probably used him as a model for building a fortune to leave to his children.

Henry's heir, Henry VIII, however, did not sit atop his father's pile of gold like the Walton heirs, who only spend their piles to influence politics. King Harry spent his inheritance to dazzle the country and the ambassadors with tournaments, palaces, tapestries, and battles, started calling Parliaments when he ran out of money, and eventually found a new fortune by dissolving the monasteries and abbeys. Despite his tempestuous reign and legendary six marriages, his energy in asserting that

England was as worthy as any of the continental powers made him popular enough that his revolutionary act of making himself Head of the Church of England in place of the pope was received amazingly well. All he needed to do was adopt Martin Luther's emphasis on observing the Ten Commandments, particularly the Fourth. Henry's subjects readily agreed that their king was like a parent who God expected to be obeyed.

Henry wisely refused to move the Church of England all that far into Reformation territory, maintaining all of the trappings of the Latin Mass and much of the teachings of the Roman Church that he had so eloquently supported only a few years earlier to earn from the pope the title Defender of the Faith. As a result, the opposition only included officials who could not condone replacing their sacred allegiance to the Bishop of Rome in spiritual matters and reformers who wanted to change worship more along the line of the Lutherans and Calvinists in Europe. What this demonstrates is that regardless of the political system, the best governments are those that attend to the interests and wishes of the people even when doing so requires revolutionary change. The current problem in the USA is the government no longer attends to the interests and wishes of the American people as a whole.

Chapter 2—The Evolution of Political Systems

SOME POLITICAL SCIENTISTS and activists have concluded in the last few years that the United States of America is no longer a democracy. The evidence for this transformation has accumulated over the last decade. Elected representatives pay heed to what lobbyists and sources of campaign funding say rather than listening to and attending to the interests of their constituents. They spend inordinate amounts of time on fundraising. When they do look into issues they focus primarily on ones that appeal to the core of voters that participate in party primary elections, issues that do not generate positive legislation due to the extreme views embraced by these voters. Important political decisions such as the bailout of banks in 2009, the failure to hold financial leaders responsible for the actions that led to the bailout, and the friendliness of the Affordable Care Act to the health insurance industry demonstrate that elected officials are primarily looking out for the interests of Wall Street and big business in general at the expense of middle and working class citizens.

Laws and judicial decisions have skewed toward increasing corporate involvement in politics and reducing citizen involvement. A rash of voter identification laws swept through the country requiring voters to have a government issued identity card of some kind in order to vote. The pretext was concern over voter fraud. No one was supplying any substantive evidence of voter fraud that needed to be addressed, let alone addressed in a manner that clearly imposes difficulties on older, poorer, and minority group voters. The fact that it was a pretext to disenfranchise those voters, who tend to vote for Democratic candidates, was even admitted by a few GOP politicians in remarks that became public. Indeed, one of the more interesting phenomena in the last twenty years has been the dulled responses to outrageously partisan comments and hypocritical immoral activities mostly coming from Republicans, as though Ronald Reagan bequeathed his resistance to self-inflicted wounds to his party's politicians.

Some justices of the Supreme Court of the United States have been just as candid about their biases as political party leaders. The Court's conservative majority has gone out of its way to endorse the concept that businesses are persons while publicly and, more dangerous, privately speaking to and engaging with business groups that benefit from their rulings. These self-titled originalists have even extended freedoms previously restricted to human citizens to business entities. Gone is the overriding principle that businesses are fictitious persons with limited rights because they can be created or extinguished at the whim of state governments and regulated by state or federal bureaucracies. The results have been a diminishment in the effective power of voting citizens and a flood of political funding and advertising that promotes candidates and issues preferred by wealthy individuals and corporate interests. The United States has begun to look more and more like a plutocratic oligarchy, i.e. government expressing the will of the economic elite.

The nominating processes conducted by the GOP and Democratic Party in 2016 drew attention to the wide-spread dissatisfaction among voters of all ages and socioeconomic backgrounds to the entrenched establishments of those parties. Disenchanted observers have railed for decades about the duopolistic nature of party politics in the USA. They have pointed out the lack of differences between two parties that have been trading control of the presidency, Congress, and statehouses for over 150 years. They have decried general elections that always seem to demand choosing the lesser of two evils or having no choice at all as a result of gerrymandering. The willingness of individuals to actively express their dissatisfaction is reshaping the political landscape. Most noticeably, they embraced candidates for the parties' presidential nominations who are decidedly not the preferred choices of the parties' establishments, although one of these candidates, Senator Bernie Sanders, did not win the nomination.

Over the years, a handful of individuals have used exceptional circumstances and considerable skill to be elected independently of the two big parties or drawing substantial support away from those parties in failed efforts to be elected. Those instances have been sporadic but stretch back in the country's history to the end of the Era of Good Feelings when the US was awash in remarkable national figures. The boundaries between geological ages in Earth's history are sometimes marked by mass extinctions followed by rapid adaptions among the surviving species that lead to entirely new species, genera, and even families. The boundaries between political eras or, as historians prefer, political systems similarly see some parties die and others branch out. Sometimes the parties continue but with substantially different policy agendas as issues emerge or die. While we will discuss party functions later, we must look at the lineage of political systems and speciation of American political parties now. A central feature of the current campaign cycle (2015-18) is the manifestation of a seventh political system.

The DNA of a party, the views and priorities of its members, does not disappear when a party becomes defunct. A party may die, but the politicians in that party do not retire; they need to find a new host for their ambitions and principles. For example, in the First Political System, although the Federalist Party rapidly lost its electoral vigor after the presidency of John Adams, the idea of a strong national government trying to look out for the interests of the union rather than its component parts still hasn't died even today. When an issue becomes settled, such as the abolition of slavery, the genetic material of the opposition to abolition gets passed down, in this instance through segregation, discrimination, and profiling, and spurred the opposing forces of the Civil Rights Movement and Black Lives Matter.

The first third party of sorts was the Anti-Masonic Party, which, as its name indicates, was a one-issue creation aimed squarely at Andrew Jackson, who vocally promoted his Freemason membership. Founded by supporters of President John Quincy Adams in 1827, the Anti-Masons contended against two nascent organizations within the only functioning political party, the Democratic-Republicans. Jackson led populists prominent in the south and west. Martin Van Buren headed the Albany Regency political machine. Van Buren is remembered by millions from the word that putatively developed from the initials of his political nickname, "Old Kinderhook." The two men formed a partnership in 1832 making Van Buren Jackson's second term vice president and successor as president in 1836.

The Anti-Masons managed to elect two governors and a fair number of members of Congress. Adams ran for governor of Massachusetts and came in a respectable second in a field of four candidates, taking 29 percent of the vote to the leader's 40 percent. After that, he successfully ran for the House of Representatives in 1830, but changed his party affiliation to the growing Whig Party that opposed Jackson. The Anti-Masonic Party lasted only a few more years.

Adams was by far the most successful and experienced diplomat in US history, representing the country in various European courts during the Napoleonic Wars and the Congress of Vienna settlement, avoiding war with Spain as Secretary of

State when then-General Jackson seized Florida on his own initiative, and authoring what is known as the Monroe Doctrine for the president he served under. On top of that, he served in Congress until his death in 1848 as a Whig leading the anti-slavery faction. Adams' dedication to noble principles, unfortunately, is a quality that is rarely seen among those who rise to the top in American politics. Perhaps not too surprisingly it appears in those with a strong and honest faith that demands action to relieve suffering and injustice. Only two other men continued or have continued to live productive lives of service to others instead of their own wallets or full retirement after leaving the White House. Also one-term presidents with low reviews for their tenures in high office, they are Herbert Hoover and Jimmy Carter. Carter, a Nobel Peace Prize winner, is known for his work with Habitat for Humanity and efforts to promote free and fair elections worldwide.

Hoover probably did more than anyone to rationalize the federal bureaucracy as chair of a commission under Harry Truman and Dwight Eisenhower. Before that, he was responsible for insuring that children and others in post-war Europe received decent, dependable food, taking on a role similar to one he had during World War I. Although vilified for his modest response to the Crash of 1929, Hoover energetically promoted the interests and wellbeing of workers and the poor on every continent except Africa from the 1890s to the 1950s as a businessman, politician, and government representative. On top of that, he was a vocal pacifist despite his and his wife's horrifying experiences during the Boxer Rebellion in China when westerners lived under siege conditions in Beijing and Tianjin for several months.

The fulcrum of the Second Political System, Andrew Jackson, and many of its prominent players were anything but pacifists. The change started with the Anti-Masonic Party and the Whigs opposing Jacksonian Democracy. Being a successful Whig presidential candidate was a death sentence. The party's two presidents were war hero generals: William Henry Harrison and Zachary Taylor. The Shawnee led by the great Tecumseh and the Blackfeet, Seminoles, and Mexicans could not kill these men, but moving to the White House did. Harrison famously died a month after his inauguration from a bug he caught at his inauguration while delivering a far too long inaugural address wearing a far too thin coat. Taylor died fifteen months into his term after eating a bowl of cherries with iced milk in the middle of the hot Washington summer; that snack apparently helped spur a deadly intestinal illness that felled a few others.

Their vice presidents did not have much better luck. James Polk had not convincingly renounced his allegiance to the Democratic Party when he joined the Whig ticket in 1840 and quickly showed his true colors. The Whigs threw their president out of their party. Millard Fillmore, who succeeded Taylor in 1850, had only one good idea as president, which was to recommend that the residents of California and New Mexico, newly acquired thanks in part to General Taylor's success in the Mexican War, petition for statehood as non-slave states before Congress organized them into slave territories. Like the threesome mentioned earlier, Fillmore's greatest achievements occurred after he left office. He helped to found the University at Buffalo and the Buffalo Historical Society. While the Whigs did not throw him out of the party, they did refuse to nominate him in 1852 for a full term.

The Free Soil Party, which later allied with the anti-slavery Whigs and morphed into the Republican Party, and the American Party aka the Know Nothing Movement, which competed with the Republicans for former Whigs, influenced national politics from 1844 to 1856. This jockeying led to the formation of the Third Political System. Former President Martin Van Buren was the first third party "spoiler" in presidential politics as the nominee of the Free Soil Party in 1848. The votes he drew away from the Democratic candidate gave the Whigs their second and last significant electoral victory.

Good old Fillmore was nominated for the presidency by the American Party in 1856 while he was visiting Europe; he accepted upon his return. He did not embrace the Know Nothings' anti-Catholic, anti-immigrant ideas but wanted a platform from which to stop the rising abolitionist vitriol he thought (correctly) was rending the country in two. The alternative, the Republican Party, was too radically anti-slavery for him. His running mate was Andrew Jackson's nephew. The Democrat, James Buchanan of Pennsylvania, the Commonwealth's only President surprisingly, won with a plurality of 45.3 percent of the votes and a comfortable 174 electoral votes out of 296. The Republican candidate, unnamed here because that is the plight of also-rans (no one stopped at the end of the preceding paragraph to look up who the Democrat was in 1848, did they?), won one-third of the vote and 11 of the 31 states. Fillmore finished a respectable third with 21.6 percent of the votes and the eight electoral votes of Maryland.

That election and the next saw the definitive rise of the Third Political System and the emergence of the duopoly. Ever since, the Democratic and Republican Parties have worked toward and long ago insured that candidates have little choice but to rely on them for support in order to be placed on ballots. The only alternative is to expend a lot of money and energy building an organization first to get on ballots. That requires a distinctive political philosophy and a distinctive political candidate for a national campaign.

Not long after the transition to the Fourth Political System the nation saw one such effort. The issues of slavery and repairing the country after the Civil War had transitioned by the end of the century to whether the government was going to be business-friendly or progressive and populist. It started out as the former and moved to the latter after Theodore Roosevelt took over upon William McKinley's death. TR attempted a comeback in 1912 much as Fillmore did 56 years earlier. He was trying to steer the country away from the reluctantly progressive wing of the Republican Party led by his handpicked successor as president, William Howard Taft, and the questionably progressive Democrats and their candidate, Woodrow Wilson. TR thought he would be able to pull out a win from what was the first election in which primary elections were prominent before the nominating conventions.

The convention chose the incumbent Taft. That led TR and his supporters to form a Progressive Party to contest the election. At the time, ballot access was relatively easy compared to the present, but a candidate still required am immense structure to support a campaign. As the most recent ex-president, TR still had plenty of connections to make it work. The result was he beat Taft but split the Republican vote to give Wilson the White House. An important fourth candidate, Eugene V. Debs of the Socialist Party, also ran. He received more votes than Fillmore had in 1856 but the population had grown so much his share was only eight percent, not almost twenty-two. We will see Debs again later.

A substantial change to the dominant political system occurred not too much later with the onset of the Great Depression and the militarization of many countries. Franklin Delano Roosevelt exemplified the democratic socialist and internationalist approach favored by the Democrats: active engagement with the problems facing the country. Republicans took a far more conservative view that had been developing while they controlled the White House in the 1920s and in reaction to Wilson's efforts to force the USA into a leadership role in global politics. The Fifth Political System was a tug of war between looking inward and investing in the economy and looking outward and investing in new technologies and the globalization they were offering.

In many areas, these views overlapped. For example, communications, transportation, and energy all saw substantial support from the Eisenhower Administration as a means to make the United States a robust, self-reliant economy with strong middle class, conservative values. However, that support and its consequences proved to be a boon in the 1960s for leaders who wanted to more actively contain communism, place a man on the moon, and provide development support to the scores of newly independent countries emerging from colonialism. Richard Nixon, Gerald Ford, and Jimmy Carter embodied the synthesis of these syncretic and symbiotic views of political issues. Not surprisingly, the first two managed to accomplish an enormous amount of legislative work with Democrat-controlled Congresses. Were it not for Nixon's Mr. Hyde personality and the shocks of terrorism and the oil embargo, the 1970s could have become a second Era of Good Feelings. Perhaps that is nostalgia talking, but it is worth considering given the divisiveness that followed.

Some historians question whether a Sixth Political System emerged with the Reagan Revolution. Others are reluctant to find a boundary for one they think emerged. It is difficult to understand why there are doubts or difficulties. We will discuss this more fully later, but Ronald Reagan was elected on a platform that was revolutionary down to the core. He succeeded in enacting that platform and instilling in the minds of a large part of the population a fixed, harsh, negative view of government as an amorphous, villainous, and gluttonous bogeyman. That insidious calumny resulted in the metamorphosis of the GOP into a hypocritical harridan and the Democratic Party into a corporate shill. Simultaneously, the very idea of expertise became linked to arrogance, getting ahead or staying afloat at any cost became dicta, parents literally fought over outdoing one another in indulging their children, and classroom teachers and ADHD became the scapegoats for the consequent lack of discipline and attention to studies of their pupils.

Once that last part was in place, the revolution was complete. Americans became addicted to violent video games and movies; sound bites, 140 characters or less, and instant everything; isolating technologies, big box stores, and megamalls that destroyed the old local gathering places; celebrity and fashion over substance and depth; and entitlement to opinions derived from ignorance, goods derived from cheap overseas labor, and anger derived from resentments and bigotry. Americans became addicted to more, more, and more while settling for less from their government. The point came when reason and science no longer mattered. Even if they still did, who was going to notice them amid the dissonance of so many outlets for so many voices? People decided the easiest and most reassuring way to obtain information was to identify a few sources all consistent with each other and all poisonously opposed to criticism or debate. While clearly evident on the right, the bubble chambers soon became almost as popular on the left while everyone in between just put on the best noise-cancelling headphones they could afford. The lines were drawn.

Chapter 3—Our Current Circumstances

THE GREAT DIVISIONS within our society today are all that pretty much anyone under fifty years old has ever known. They originated when the oldest of Generation X were hitting their teens and became entrenched just as the first Millennials reached puberty. What is most stunning about the phenomenon of people shutting out all information other than what verifies what they already believe (not know) is that it is cross-generational. Every group of bubbles huddled together contains people of all ages. Instead, we have developed divisions that roughly place less fully-educated people on one side and more fully-educated on the other. Notice fully not well.

The most significant criticism of US schools has been the issue of students who passed through whether they acquired the knowledge and skills they were supposed to or not. Of as much importance has been the reduction of instruction from a professional craft that relied on teachers to enhance the curriculum and provide plenty of opportunities for every child to learn to a mechanical task that required teachers to drill the information needed for tests into every child. Teachers no longer have the authority to decide how students will be assessed because standardized tests were introduced to make it easier for bureaucrats to show politicians the supposed results of teachers doing their jobs.

The problem with that is the teachers are no longer doing the pedagogical tasks that had been their jobs. The most important task of all is to create many varied assessment tools used often enough for the teacher to gauge her own effectiveness and step up her game when needed. The frequency kept students on their toes and the variety meant that students who expressed what they learned in different ways all had the opportunity to demonstrate what they had learned.

No, we have to treat children's education like we treat mass-raised animals for meat. We have to use uniform tests with multiple choice and essay questions to guarantee that every student is assessed the same way. It doesn't matter that students learn in different ways. It doesn't matter that students show what they have learned in different ways. It doesn't matter that teachers teach in different ways. And the people most in favor of assessment-oriented instruction are the very same people who scream about liberty and denounce socialism as forcing everyone to do the same thing. All of this got underway with the Reagan Revolution, the tragedy that segued the nation out of the mostly friendly (if you were pinkish and not a pinko) Fifth Political System.

Richard Nixon laid the groundwork for the Sixth Political System not just with Watergate, the original and should have been only -gate-gate. Nixon's Southern Strategy went after Yellow Dog Democrats, southerners who always voted Democratic no matter what, mostly poorly educated, poorly compensated, pinkish people. He realized that he would have won by a landslide in 1968 if George Wallace hadn't siphoned off 46 Electoral College votes and 13.5 percent of the popular vote. Nixon did win by a landslide in 1972 and certainly would have even without the Watergate shenanigans. The Yellow Dogs finally were no longer attached to a Democratic Party whose president pushed hard for the Civil Rights Act of 1964. The only bumps in the road for GOP success with this strategy ever since have been two Democrats from the South, Jimmy Carter and Bill Clinton.

Ronald Reagan added to this strategy by attracting

Christian evangelicals. The Bible Belt wraps across the South, except the more populated parts of Florida and, more recently, the more populated parts of Virginia. It also stretches up into the southern parts of the Midwest and Plains states. Contrary to what the GOP establishment would like everyone to think, Donald Trump did not expose any new seam of bigots within the GOP base. He went after the same demographics as Reagan and all of the extremist GOP candidates since then like Mike Huckabee and Rick Santorum, who did well in early states like Iowa and South Carolina. In the past, the GOP establishment has stepped in to undercut the people who relied too heavily on the GOP base in order to have an "electable" candidate. Elections are won by appealing to independent voters and these candidates would not appeal to those more centrist voters. Even Reagan switched to the center after locking in the nomination in 1980.

The differences in 2016 were that Trump had the independent resources to fight off the GOP establishment and almost half of all GOP voters and one third of all Democrats did not waver from supporting anti-establishment candidates. There has not been that level of disgust for traditional politicians since 1980, the last election influenced by Watergate. The reasons Hillary Clinton had so much support were the active efforts of the Democratic National Committee to stop people from getting to know the other Democratic candidates coupled with corporate mainstream media not reporting on Bernie Sanders' huge rallies, continuously referring to Clinton as the likely nominee, and misleadingly awarding Clinton all of the superdelegates who greedily endorsed her before Sanders entered the race but did not have to actually decide who to support until the vote at the convention.

Everyone still shaking their heads about Trump's remarks and popularity are looking at this through the lens of politics since 1980. As we have seen, the political landscape changes every thirty plus years or so. Barack Obama's election in 2008 spurred a level of extremism that hasn't been seen since the

1960s. Due to racism being such a taint on anyone, no one wants to too openly acknowledge that the reasons for this extremism are as easily identified as the pigment of the President's skin. The extremists don't want to be labelled racists and most everyone else does not relish the endless arguments about defining the evidence of racism in a post-segregationist, legally non-discriminating society.

The GOP played it safe in 2012 and still wanted to play it safe in 2016 by avoiding extremist candidates without angering the Tea Party elements. Trump, Ben Carson, and even Ted Cruz recognized that irrationality is rational to a huge segment of the US public. For example, more than half of the population does not "believe" in evolution but does believe in angels. That segment does not know and refuses to learn the difference between faith and reason. Bernie Sanders confronted this irrationality head on and was supported by people who are tired of opinions trumping fact-based conclusions (pun intended). Clinton reluctantly followed his lead.

The biggest mistake the Democrats made in 2012 and 2014 and were still making n 2016 was using fear of GOP ascendancy as their marketing strategy despite the fact that Obama was successful in 2008 by using hope and change as his mottoes. Take a look at any fundraising email from House Minority Leader Nancy Pelosi. She still sounds exactly like Chicken Little. Telephone calls from the Senate side are the same: "We can't let the GOP maintain control of the Senate because the Supreme Court is at stake." The same became true of the principal argument asking Sanders' supporters to vote for Clinton; we must do everything to stop Trump and the GOP from choosing any SCOTUS justices. The messages are anti-GOP, not pro-Democrat.

Clinton's campaign symbol of an aitch with a red arrow pointing to the right shows just how inept the establishment is right now. If you want to indicate progress, you don't use GOP red and you don't have the arrow pointing to the right. All that told anyone was she is a "progressive Republican" now that they are extinct in the GOP. Her support of and from Wall Street only reinforces that conclusion. Of course, she finally, quietly started using Carolina blue in place of red toward the end of her campaign.

Trump and Sanders tapped into firm bases that expect change. For Trump, it is the people who cheered when John Boehner resigned as Speaker and believe (that word again) that their extremist agenda can be made law no matter how impossible that is given the way our system of government operates. For Sanders, it was the people who expected change from Obama and got next to nothing, the people who know the positions of the right are ant-scientific, illogical, and unsubstantiated and therefore worthless to a supposedly advanced society.

The only significant change since 2009, ironically, has come from Supreme Court decisions, the branch of government that has been a greater force for change in the last six plus decades than either the executive or legislative branches. Both extremes agree the Supreme Court has overreached, but, reflecting their ideological priorities, differ on what the subjects are. The differences are reflected in the majority opinions and echo the differences in the political world so closely it is difficult not to conclude the independent, nonpartisan judiciary has chosen the dark side. That said, given that the political world has split into belief and reason camps, at least those justices reasoning their way to decisions are substantially more impartial than those rationalizing their way. For example, the late Justice Scalia claimed campaign donations have no impact on how legislators vote, a position that lacks common sense and is exactly opposite of the evidence. Meanwhile, Justice Kennedy justified marriage equality as providing the same legal dignity to homosexual couples as is afforded heterosexual couples, a logical extension of the principle of equal protection.

The battle in 2016 was reason over belief. The real surprise is that anyone was surprised that Trump and Carson received so much sustained support given that they merely echoed the beliefs of a very large segment of the country's population. The real concern is that no one was concerned that Sanders and his supporters were the only Democrats, engorged with non-Democrats, actively trying to promote reason over emotion, positive action over negative reaction. Even Hillary Clinton's noteworthy experience defies logic since an overwhelming majority of the most highly regarded presidents had weak resumes as public officeholders. The best presidents have demonstrated generalized leadership ability or substantial intellect.

Those qualities do seem to be largely MIA. Many American voters in 2016 were fed up with inaction in Congress, actions by the President to circumvent that inaction rather than face it head on, and reactions to Supreme Court decisions that completely missed the point of having an independent judiciary. The American Republic was once again a house divided. However, it has been a very long time since any work has been done on that house other than to shore up its foundations and make cosmetic repairs. We are discovering now that the renovations initiated in the Reagan years created new problems, further efforts have exacerbated the issues, everything is falling apart, and we wasted too much money on other projects. Now the bank is stepping up its efforts to take the house. The Obama administration promised to reverse the damage, restore what could be salvaged, and put in updates. The contractors were stubborn about how to go about the work and where to begin. Worst of all, they became ridiculously angry at President Obama's DIY fixes in the form of executive orders.

Almost everyone accepts the political system in the United States of America has morphed into some form that no longer seems able to function properly. Almost everyone acknowledges wealthy individuals and their companies have embraced the spending = speaking equation and have been using it to influence elections. Almost everyone agrees the current election cycle will define how the USA will address the problems in its political system. Almost everyone admits that political discourse has lost almost all of its utility now that people broadly believe everyone is entitled to his or her own opinion and every opinion has equal value and validity.

That last one is a principal reason for this book. Somehow, voters have adopted a belief that one does not have to know facts and use those facts in a logical analysis before one can reach a tenable conclusion that will form the basis of a rational opinion. The critical thinking skills that college instructors say are missing among the last few decades of students dropped out of sight just as telecommunications and computer networking made voicing an opinion to a lot of people easier than ever. All of those answers that would have been marked wrong on political science, history, economics, legal, and civics exams suddenly have no one marking them wrong. Anyone can be an authority; acquired expertise through education makes people condescending, not accurate, according to the users of social media and denizens of the blogosphere. Opinions based on incorrect or misinterpreted facts and poorly applied reasoning are considered no different than opinions derived from verifiable evidence and logical analysis.

Some people even insist that classification schemes created over decades so specialists could talk with one another and not get confused suddenly can be ignored. Terms are no longer agreed upon. People insist they can agree to disagree over the definition of the subject they are talking about. Anyone who dares to note that fruitful discussion depends on having the knowledge acquired through education and firsthand experience and the mental faculties capable of applying that knowledge to general principles and standards is just being pedantic, overbearing, and egotistical. To top it all off, people who disagree with a statement or position are not starting a debate when voicing that disagreement results in a response. Political discourse apparently now involves two people piling up balls on their respective sides of the tennis court to practice their service rather than using three balls to play a game.

Why Americans think that the freedom to express one's self comes with no responsibility to respond to valid criticism, let alone to be honest, accurate, and rational, is unknown. The house divided got that way principally because citizens believe they have the right to think and say anything without any regard whatsoever for the consequences. However, the exercise of rights has always come with the responsibility to deal with any negative consequences. To say otherwise is to justify someone starting a bar fight between fans of two rival football teams and walking away. It justifies making threats of bodily harm without taking the blame if the other person takes action to defend himself. Yet individuals still assert their rights are undividable, unlimited, and unconditional. The consequences of unsubstantiated opinions demanding to be treated as an entitlement have been acrimony and prejudice. It is time to draw the line.

Experts among themselves may quibble and nitpick about the details of each other's definitions for things like democracy, revolution, and such; they can all quite easily produce a uniform definition for non-experts to which they can all agree. Everyone engaged in political discussions must use the same set of terms as defined by experts, rely solely on verifiable facts and evidence, and apply logic and critical analysis to the data to draw their conclusions and formulate solutions to problems in the public sphere. Otherwise, political discourse will remain as lawless and fruitless as it has been for about twenty years. We the people built a tower aimed at the heaven of peace and prosperity only to be stopped partway through as babbling became contagious.

The clarity of the contending positions in 2016 could not be sharper. They did not manifest themselves as the usual choice between Democrat and Republican. Party designations are among the terms that no longer have secure definitions. As we shall see, they never really have been all that useful in American politics since both parties have always had large factions within that would likely be separate parties in parliamentary proportional representation systems. Instead, we must take the long way around and describe the positions and then consider whether it is worthwhile to label them.

• There are those candidates and their supporters who do not want the establishment to lose ground. They will say and do almost anything to convince voters that they have the plans and resources to help the USA become stronger than it is already as the world's only superpower. They claim everyone else is delusional. The system can be fixed using existing methods. They deny plutocrats direct policy but rely on plutocrats for support because plutocrats are the fountain of eternal money for the political establishment. They are fighting for the status quo that allows entrenched economic, political, and social interests to maintain or increase their grip on personal and government activities.

• There are those candidates and their supporters who embrace the notion that the political system can be fixed with blunt honesty and decisive action. They claim they can take control of the establishment and use its resources to help the USA become strong again and reverse what they perceive as a decline in power. They blame everyone else for the country's problems and just need to be put in charge for the system to function properly. They openly accept and rely on the support of plutocrats because everyone is supposed to know wealthy people must make the right decisions to have become wealthy. They are fighting for personal liberty and limited government.

• There are candidates and their supporters who see that the establishment and the political system are the same things. They recognize that using the resources of others makes one beholden to those suppliers. Their goal is not to make the USA stronger or strong again, but rather to make the USA better, which implies different. They see a system that no longer functions effectively and needs a complete overhaul. They want to restore a republic founded on the principle that everyone is equal, has an equal say, and deserves an equal share of the benefits of a peaceful, prosperous society. They are fighting for personal freedom from the impediments to truly equal opportunity and responsive government.

If we had to label these three forces they might be called Establishmentarians, Libertarians, and Egalitarians. Unfortunately, labels like liberal, progressive, socialist, conservative, extremist, etc. compose the least well defined terms bandied about in political discussions anymore. They are used as signals to mark opponents who may or may not agree with the designation. They are used as identities that, like opinions, may be more or less solid. At least with these three forces in the political system we can say any labels we give them are based on a definition of the principles and goals of the group, not the perceived echoes of what others with those labels have done before.

Here lies the importance of attempting to assess and sort based not on lineage and the past but rather on present actions and aspirations. Women will agree they support a whole list of policies individually, state they are not feminists, and become baffled when they are told that all of the policies they endorsed are the planks of the feminist platform. Some will become angry and insist agreeing with those policies does not make them feminists.

Similarly, surveys asking for sexual orientation regularly find very few people who self-identify as bisexual. A stigma attaches to bisexuality. Everyone is conditioned to approve of monogamy which can leave bisexuals not wholly satisfied in any relationship or at least lead others to believe so. Identifying as bisexual even among homosexuals is considered improper

However, if people are asked whether they engage in sexual activities exclusively with members of the opposite sex, preferably with members of the opposite sex, doesn't much matter, preferably with members of the same sex, or exclusively with members of the same sex, the percentages between the extremes start to grow. Men in particular are conditioned to consider themselves straight even if they regularly or periodically have sex with other men. Make note we are talking about sexual activities, which are facts, not sexual attraction, which is not.

If we are going to get anywhere in political discourse, it is essential to put aside that kind of baggage that automatically makes some terms weighed down with connotations and misinterpretations. The accretion of subjective aspersions can become so damaging that even a relatively harmless word like liberal can become unrecognizable. Most of the world still uses liberal in its original sense. It has the same root as liberty. It is a political philosophy grounded in the idea of liberating individuals from old obligations, class traditions, and sclerotic institutions. One of the great results of the Age of Enlightenment was the development of liberal thinking, casting aside religion and custom to freely approach political issues. It involves opening up the political system to new voices and new views.

The USA was founded on such liberal principles. However, liberal long ago lost this meaning and took on the definition of generous and accommodating. More precisely, it has been painted as generosity in taking money from some people and giving it to others, the "free stuff" meme. Liberal became such a slanderous term in politics, associated with spending tax revenues to benefit as many people as possible (*quelle horreure!*), the Democratic Party after 1988 consciously put in a great effort to establish itself as centrist or moderate, which really only moved it into the position that Rockefeller Republicans had held before neo-conservatives began their RINO hunt (Republican In Name Only). A quarter century later, the Democratic establishment has long been best friends with Wall Street and the US Chamber of Commerce and smiles approvingly on President Bill Clinton's policies that put more African-Americans in prisons, sent more jobs overseas, and put more restrictions on welfare recipients then the GOP could have ever done. Perhaps not too surprisingly, Democrats never mounted a DINO hunt because the party itself went Jurassic.

The oddest thing of all is that the people primarily behind this change in the definition of liberal are neo-conservatives. Aside from supposedly being averse to change, neo-cons always confidently claim they have the best understanding of the intentions of the Founders. The paradox of American politics is the extent to which neo-cons have transformed the roots of liberal democracy in the USA while the people they taunt as bleeding-heart liberals always embraced the principles that established the nation. For all of their allegedly steadfast love of country, veterans, and freedom, neo-con policies look remarkably like the government the original patriots fought to throw off. That is not as odd as it sounds. Russia and China are governed through radically different political structures using the same philosophies used by their predecessor political structures. Keep in mind though that the War for Independence was a civil war fought over who had the authority to govern, just like the revolutions in Russia and China.

Chapter 4—What Is to Be Done?

IN 1776, REPRESENTATIVES of the residents in thirteen North American colonies adopted a Declaration of Independence that set forth the philosophical principles behind their recent and future actions, their grievances against King George III of Great Britain, and the redress they sought. Among other things, that Declaration made note of the unalienable rights of life, liberty, and the pursuit of happiness. Thomas Jefferson, the principal writer of the Declaration substituted "pursuit of happiness" for "property" found in earlier formulations of those three inherent rights. He did so deliberately despite being a member of the landowning class to whom the right to own property and do with it as one chose was as sacred as any other.

After struggle, victory, and peace, representatives of the citizens of the thirteen sovereign, independent states established from initial trial and error, through debate and consensus a new form of government of, by, and for the people. That government has withstood invasion, wars of expansion, defense, principle, ideology and questionable motive, economic transformations, immigration of individuals from every part of the world, cultural awakenings, social unrest and political corruption, assassinations, and a great conflagration that soaked this country's fields with blood from self-inflicted wounds and tore the fabric of a shared civic culture. That government has evolved as its creators intended to meet new challenges and provided infrastructure, regulations, and services as the need arose. That government, despite its faults, remains a beacon of hope for all human beings seeking democratic, representative, responsible, humane, and limited rule over their affairs.

Today, many citizens of the United States of America fear their government has become a creature of the wealthy, the corporations from which the wealthy derive their resources, and the politicians driven to act in the interests of those corporations due to their need for funds to fuel their electoral campaigns. They claim that right to property now overshadows all others in importance and that one cannot live or be free or pursue happiness without the principle of ownership secured tightly against intrusions.

Some of those citizens made their concerns known by occupying parks, streets, and public areas in the cities and other localities of this country. They called upon the one percent that wields power through accumulated wealth and elected office to return the government, its policies, laws, regulations, and justice to the ninety-nine percent that have the capacity to fuel the economy, generate jobs, mobilize society, and move forward but are starved of the resources to do so. Others have clamored for and got individuals to contend for one of the two dominant parties' nominations for the presidential election, individuals who defy the establishment with blunt, honest views on how the nation must act in order to save itself from ruin. These candidates have had an air of demagoguery about them due to the large, raucous rallies they produced. Both the occupiers and the crowds seek change.

As the colonial representatives knew two hundred forty-two years ago, great change must be founded on rational principles soundly developed from evidence, facts, and natural law. Such are the times now that some choose to twist, dissect, or profane the principles supporting change out of fear, ignorance, or self-interest. Nonetheless, the foundations for change are present for all to see. The evidence is clear.

We truly are created equal, endowed with certain rights, among which are life, liberty, and the pursuit of happiness. We all require and are entitled to consistent shelter, social and familial companionship, wellness and good health, education to our potential, full and complete nourishment, adequate clothing, employment of our skills and knowledge, and safety from harm. We build communities, support our brothers and sisters regardless of appearance, physical features, religion, ability, condition, sex, attribute, or characteristic, and treat one another with respect and dignity. We are a diverse nation. Embracing these principles reduces the risk of conflict yet many refuse to embrace them.

The citizens of the United States of America have found their government and political discourse in their country at an impasse. They have reacted in frustration, fear, apprehension, and sadness to the growing sense that their great nation has taken an unproductive and dangerous path. That path now stands clearly marked behind them and stops where they now stand. Witness the facts:

- The wealthy have steadily increased their share of the nation's wealth at the expense of the poor and middle classes;
- Politicians have pledged to enact no taxes despite the necessity for revenues to meet the needs of the people and revitalize our nation's infrastructure;
- Corporations have been deemed persons with political rights, allowing these corporations to support candidates and political causes financially, thereby drowning out the voices of voters;
- Elected officials have engaged the nation in lengthy, unwarranted wars that have sapped the economy, killed and harmed tens of thousands of people, invoked ill feelings toward the USA and its people, and further destabilized

regions of the world causing new forces to arise that terrorize, kill, and displace innocent people;

• Legislators and governors have used the narrow tenets of religious minorities as the basis for laws that restrict the exercise of fundamental human rights in order to maintain political support;

• Politicians have set out arbitrary and selfish requirements prior to debates on issues that require negotiation and consensus;

• Companies, business groups, and single-issue interests have used their resources to influence and shape legislation and regulations for their benefit, squeezing out the common good from being the priority;

• Representatives have conducted inquiries and provided earmarked funds whose primary purposes have been their own self-promotion or political vengeance;

• Laws have been passed to address issues that do not actually exist and other laws have not been taken up that would address pressing concerns, all in the name of partisanship;

• The judiciary has become suspect of issuing opinions based on ideology and party affiliation rather than the law and common sense;

• Financiers and investors have used the markets and banks with little oversight and adjustable scruples to speculate, profit, and gain without adding any real value to the economy;

• Many news media businesses have adopted clear ideological perspectives and even defamed individuals and ignored events inconsistent with those perspectives while continuing to claim the mantle of unbiased journalism;

• The United States Senate has adopted rules that require almost all legislation to find support from many more than half plus one members of the chamber, making a mockery of the idea of unlimited debate established by the nation's Founders;

- Candidates for public office have created the endless election cycle in their quest to hold onto their offices once acquired.

These are reasons for deep concern regarding the future of the United States of America. Their mitigation and elimination require substantial action. Now that the problems have been identified so manifestly, the nation can move forward. Resources must be identified to correct the deficiencies that have arisen. There is hope. The Republic can be restored.

The remedies are within our grasp. In order to see them take effect, the people of this country must first align themselves with the proposition that the time for great change has arrived. We, as a nation, must stand together, on the same page, united in our desire to address the problems we face. We have lost hope in a future that relies on the political system now in place. We have struggled with our household finances, our ability to educate ourselves, the care of our health, and our desire to improve our condition. Our essential needs are not met. Meanwhile, the wealthiest citizens have grown wealthier with each passing year, creating an income and lifestyle gap unimaginable short decades ago. But the change that must take place is not about money per se, it is about resources.

Since 1981, the American people have withstood a monumental shift in the control of the resources available to drive the economy, correct political policies, and guard against oligarchy. Not only have those resources shifted, they also have been corrupted and twisted. They are not the same animated materials and effects they once were in the hands of the country's working families and aspiring individuals. Rather, the resources of the nation have become dull objects to be held and counted. These resources are the ballast of the ship of state, most useful to their owners when not in active use. Unsurprisingly, the United States of America has foundered as the ballast grew much greater than was helpful.

In these times of distress and weariness, it is incumbent upon us not to cast about searching for those at fault. Indeed, we are each to blame, having freely given away what has been fought for and defended countless times on distant shores and within our borders. While some cried out in protest or foresaw the consequences of our inaction, many thoughtlessly allowed the resources that sustained us to seep away. Now, we must make amends. We must reclaim that which we know makes our country an example to the world. We must take action to correct our previous negligence.

The remedies depend upon the return of the resources held by the few to the people best able to correct our course through diligence, engagement, and innovation: the citizens of this nation. How can we make this transfer? The resources involved are as numerous as the troubles caused by their accumulation in the hands of the few. Accordingly, each issue depends on resources unique to the remedy required to correct it. And each set of resources has its own path for being returned to the many. The point now is not to decide those paths but to establish a government capable of choosing the best paths and seeing to their construction and use. Essential to the resolution of every issue is the agreement of the American people that the time for change has arrived. All Americans can use their individual strength together to move the civic culture and political system to the position where everyone is treated with respect and discourse is amicable. Only then can we move forward to resolve the concerns that have created our difficulties.

This process of restoring the Republic reminds us that we consent to be governed. We establish governmental bodies and elected positions solely from necessity to be the instruments of our will and our conscience. Ours is a government limited by its people. That government acts within structures designed to balance interests and check power. Nonetheless, it is a human design. It requires correction from time to time. Recent history explains. Bodies become choked; positions become entrenched; instruments become corrupted. The whole becomes unworkable. The day has come to inspect, repair, and recalibrate the structures that have served so well. The need arises to unclog, loosen, and clean the paths by which good ideas become good law and policy. Yes, we are reminded. A government of, by, and for the people is as engaged and responsive as its citizens. It can be no more or less.

Despite what constitutional originalists want to believe, history demonstrates that political institutions evolve over time even when they have been established by a written document. Maps gradually become less and less accurate within a human lifetime even when natural processes generally are not changing the features of the area depicted. Some of the Founders expected the states or citizens of the USA to regularly hold conventions to discuss how the Constitution needed to be updated. Thomas Jefferson thought the country could do with a revolution every few decades. Those things not having been done, the country engaged in an internecine war that resulted in addressing the abomination of slavery, the power dynamic between the states and the national government, and the necessity of equal protection for all citizens under the law. In the century and a half since that substantial re-engineering of the relationship between state and national governments demographic, technical, scientific, economic, and cultural changes have created a radically different environment for the political system.

Such a dramatic transformation of an ecosystem naturally would prompt species to acquire new characteristics if they were to remain there and survive. Unfortunately, nature has no hand in political systems. The citizens within a political system must consciously modify its characteristics to keep up with change, a responsibility of even greater importance when the system is a democracy.

Democracy has had many manifestations in various times,

cultures, and places. The structure of government, the method of organizing partisan politics, and the definition of citizenship all have taken many forms. No two democracies are so alike as to be twins, but the resemblances make clear they are all related. Like living organisms, democracies are born. Examples of democracy being imposed are rare. The two clearest instances, Japan and Iraq, provide contrasting evidence, but the latter's troubles stem more from how the country was created after World War I rather than the propriety of founding a government on democratic principles. Factional resentments test democracy. This form of government must be attractive to the populace as a whole if it is to survive. Even then, democracies develop, flourish, waiver, and die. Some arise from the ashes of autocracies and totalitarian regimes, while others become submerged by the anxieties of a leader.

Currently, all but four countries (Brunei, Burma, Saudi Arabia, and Vatican City) claim to be democratic. Approximately 118 of the 195 countries of the world actively embrace democratic institutions according to Freedom House. It would seem that democracy has an evolutionary edge. The same could have been said about dinosaurs just before the end of the Cretaceous period. Before we dismiss the analogy, let us remember the perceived vigor of monarchies and one-party dictatorships before calamitous events brought them to the brink of extinction. Constitutional monarchies salvaged some DNA of a formerly robust species of government just as surely as chickens preserve so much of what made tetanurans (stiff-tailed dinosaurs) so plentiful.

Is democracy on the rise? Are some nations always going to flirt with democracy while depending on oligarchic structures and practices? Do citizens become less involved as democracies age? Why do citizens in some democracies use the ballot box to achieve undemocratic goals? Must we insist on using liberal democracy, as it developed in the United States and parts of Europe, as our sole benchmark for determining whether the popular will is being realized? All but the last are unanswerable questions yet the last is seldom posed. We pose the others because exploring them helps us understand the limitations of democracy. The last question, however, helps us understand the limitlessness of democracy. That understanding provides us with a foundation for restoring the Republic.

Chapter 5—Sovereign Will Expressed

DEMOCRACY IS GOVERNMENT expressed through the will of the citizens of a polity in which those citizens are all equal before the law. That expression of will may be direct, in assemblies, or other means of polling the citizens, or filtered, through the election of representatives. Due to the difficulties of gathering large numbers of citizens in one place, direct democracy is rare or paired with representative democracy through the use of referenda and ballot measures. Representative democracy has taken many forms depending on how representatives are elected, how the three powers of government (executive, legislative, and judicial) are structured and interact, and how many layers of government have been created. All of these attributes of government are set out in a constitution usually written by a specially chosen set of representatives of the citizenry. A democratic constitution also contains protections for the liberties of the citizens, positing freedoms citizens can enjoy and proscribing actions government can take. These safeguards are essential to the continuing success of a democracy; they forever remind the government that the citizens remain free to exercise their unalienable rights as individuals in a well-ordered society.

Democracy has been adopted or revived by scores of countries since the 1970s. In some cases, these states have demonstrated how unleashing the will of the people can lead to very undemocratic outcomes. The evolution in government and politics of the Russian Federation since 1991 is a prime example. The other former republics of the Soviet Union, save for the three Baltic countries, have failed to transition fully to democracy. Ukraine has come closest. Democracy has stuttered in Ukraine due to the existence of a large Russian-speaking population that desires closer ties to a Russia actively promoting closer ties. The Ukrainian-speaking population largely desires closer ties to the European Union. This tug of war over the future of a state has resulted from the way Ukraine acquired its territories; the country was pieced together when popular will did not decide policy.

Ukraine's difficulties are just a new occurrence of an old problem, a fall back to the same issues faced by British, French, and other colonies of European states in Africa and Asia that became independent nations and attempted democracy in 1945-75. These instances raise questions as to whether some societies are prepared for democracy or value democracy. Russia presents the perplexing issue of citizens relinquishing their voice through the ballot box. The Germans, in essence, did the same thing in 1932 when they made the Nazi Party the largest in the Reichstag in two elections. Voters in Egypt, Serbia, Palestine and other states have done likewise. These were largely free and fair elections unlike the referendum for Crimea to be transferred from Ukraine to Russia in which some districts reported more votes "yes" than there were eligible voters in the district. Voters truly do sometimes use democracy as a means to dispense with or limit it. Democracy is hoisted with its own petar.

At the same time, democracy remains strong and stable in most of Europe and elsewhere. The socialist democracies of Scandinavia appear to have created the healthiest communities in the world no matter what measure is used. Most of the former Warsaw Pact countries of Eastern Europe and the Baltic republics have become stable democracies since 1990 after decades of single party rule. Many other countries can lay claim to continuing success in having robust democratic governments that change hands seamlessly and remain committed to realizing the wishes of the electorate. The demonstrations that made up the Arab Spring brought new democracies to North Africa. Those societies are still finding their feet and the future for democracy in the region is uncertain. Nonetheless, it is remarkable that the popular will aggregated and became vocalized. Expressions of popular sovereignty are rare. When they are expressed, they are rendered most often in the language of democracy.

This is not to say that democracy is the most sublime, attractive, or best form of government. As noted before, people turn to other political systems willingly. Circumstances, culture, and needs can make alternatives desirable and effective. As Winston Churchill famously remarked, "Indeed, it has been said that democracy is the worst form of government except all the others that have been tried from time to time."

Less frequently quoted is his statement, "The best argument against democracy is a five-minute conversation with the average voter." Herein lays the crux of the problem. Rarely will any politician acknowledge it, but citizens are limited by their intelligence, range of information and experiences, education, socioeconomic status, prejudices, and interest in the public sphere. This is not to say voters are dumb or incapable of determining their own best interests. It is saying that voters sometimes make choices just as everyone sometimes make choices based on insufficient or inaccurate data using reasoning colored by subjective and dubious logic.

Donald Trump is not insulting his supporters when he says some are poorly educated. He is acknowledging a fact career politicians shrink from. Facts relating to negative characteristics are generally considered to be rude to point out, but a fact can only be an insult if communicated with contempt or disdain. Trump is quite capable of insulting people just as others are quite happy to insult him. He knows that the GOP has pursued undereducated and poorly educated people for decades. Unlike what the GOP has been doing, he is not using them so much as he is endorsing their ability to still participate in civic matters. In fact, one of their complaints is that schools are doing a lousy job of teaching children. Trump is saying there is no shame in being poorly educated because that only means the system failed them, not that they failed or lacked the intelligence to succeed. The interesting part is that the people who pile up on Trump for openly noticing poorly educated voters assume he is denigrating them because that is exactly what they have been doing by not even acknowledging them.

Regardless of the adequacy of anyone's education, people are not helped in making better decisions by politicians and media sources who know they will get a better response appealing to emotions rather than reason. People on the right particularly will go on about how all politicians are snake oil salesmen and never to be trusted. Next chance they jump at the opportunity to support Donald Trump who has spent his life trying to increase his profits through branding, the most refined snake oil pitch around, because he is voicing their opinions. Mr. Trump excels as the Pied Piper of the GOP; he is fully and completely saying the things other GOP politicians only hint at for fear of appearing too extreme for a general election.

Mr. Trump could be using his personal wealth and flame retardant ego to seriously lead a Tea Party-like rebellion against the GOP establishment or to identify the nation's diehard bigots and haters so they can be placed on a federal database. He could even have been conspiring with Bill and Hillary Clinton to pave the way for them to reside once again at 1600 Pennsylvania Avenue. Whatever his true purpose, he demonstrated how easily voters can be drawn out by appealing to their emotions. Conversely, Senator Bernie Sanders demonstrated the difficulty in getting past emotions to appeal to rational decision making. He was faced with supporters of Hillary Clinton who were emotionally invested in electing a female president and maintaining the political status quo. Not surprisingly the response to Sanders' effort was primarily emotional, disregarding facts and contending his policies are thoroughly unfeasible.

The good thing about this hubbub is that it draws attention to politics and the role of the people in shaping their government. Governments in all countries with public primary and secondary education try to instill civic mindedness and socialize children to understand and support their constitutions and basic forms of political activity. They want their citizens to be aware of their duties and responsibilities, as well as to pledge their allegiance to the state. Generally, this works well enough in democracies that usually more than half of the citizens participate by voting in elections. Scotland's referendum in 2014 on the question of independence from the United Kingdom roused intense interest. In the end, an astounding 84.6 percent of the citizens voted. Not every election can be so invigorating. Around two dozen countries go so far as to mandate going to the polls, although more than half of these do not enforce the law.

Those laws respond to the fact that participation in democracy is a chore. Doing the responsible, mature thing usually is. Those encumbered to complete this chore do not always put their whole heart into it. Such is the nature of man that he wears his duty to society lightly. He may have great expectations of his government or he may support severe limitations to government. Regardless, community, legislation, and infrastructure rarely rise to the top of anyone's priorities. People have other things on their minds, other things to do. The significance of this lack of urgency appears in the ways democracies end up working. Even in the best of times, the voices of a small pool of active citizens keep things going. Everyone else just seems to be along for the ride. And yet, the people in democracies treasure their role even when they do not lift a finger to be active and even when their choices lead to undemocratic ends. Participation runs the gamut from full engagement to vacant indifference, but almost all citizens act as though they have skin in the game. The fact that they are sovereign individuals justifies that view.

In order for democracy to work, the instigators must assume that all citizens initially possess sovereignty, are all equal because no one possesses more sovereignty than the next person, and are all willing to give up the same amount of sovereignty in order to form a democratic society. Other forms of government modify one or more of these precepts. For the moment, we will put aside the distraction of what a citizen is and the problems accompanying the fact that non-citizens within a community are neither sovereign nor equal. That discussion requires a chapter in itself. Instead, we will look at sovereignty, theories that explain the circumstances in which individuals relinquish their sovereignty, and the parameters of the keystone idea upon which all democracies depend, which was set forth in Thomas Jefferson's immortal statement, "all men are created equal."

Sovereignty is the condition of independence and free will. It signifies the endowment of the power to do things without reference to any superior authority. Monarchs are sovereigns because they have been given the right to rule. How they came to be given that right depends on force, fame, wits, and wealth used in a way to assert some amount of control over people and place that supports a claim to the role of leader. Absolute monarchy implies that there are no bounds to the king's sovereignty. The idea was captured succinctly in Louis XIV's reputed declaration, "*L'état c'est moi*," whereby he conflated his person with the sovereign state he led.

There have been many rulers who have claimed to rule absolutely. Reality has taken its toll on such claims. Sovereignty may mean that there is no superior authority, but that does not preclude the existence of equal or lesser reservoirs of power that impinge upon it. An atheist living an autarkic hermit's life could claim the purist form of sovereignty, but this only demonstrates the lengths one would need to go to realize this ideal as purely as humanly possible. Sovereigns always border other sovereigns or sources of power. Those bordering each other have an effect on the exercise of independence and free will by the other.

A monarch is sovereign hence the words can be synonyms. Alternate sources of power become most apparent when monarchs die. Although we think of kings and queens inheriting their titles in direct line as some natural process, unchallenged succession from crowned head to closest (often male) kin is far from the norm. Even the most seamless handover at the very least rests upon the consent of those near the throne. Laws are enacted setting up the rules of even the most straightforward succession, thereby giving the imprimatur of forward-thinking, reasoned debate.

A genetic relationship to the last monarch is hardly mandatory. Eurasian tribal societies held elections to install new rulers, a tradition maintained when some got to Ireland and others settled in Poland. After Nero managed to kill off his Julio-Claudian family, most Roman emperors were chosen by one segment of the army or another who retained the cognomen Caesar as a title. But even in cases of hereditary succession, the activities surrounding the transfer of sovereignty to a new monarch demonstrate that monarchs are truly chosen. The selection is made by those who wield influence by dint of title, relationship, wealth, or office. In some cases, those making the selection are stymied by popular will. This brings to the surface the role popular acquiescence in government plays even in the most undemocratic situations.

Such was the case in England in 1553 upon the death of the third Tudor monarch. The Tudor dynasty has been the source of scores of books, films, plays, television series, and other forms of entertainment going all the way back to 1613 and William Shakespeare's next to last play, *Henry VIII*. Much is made of the personalities and relationships of the five monarchs who reigned from 1485 to 1603, particularly the politics of succession and especially King Henry VIII's obsession about producing a male heir.

His anxiety derived not only from concern about his masculinity, despite having been an athletic and handsome young man. He had succeeded a father who had usurped the throne by defeating and killing in battle Richard III who, as explained earlier, himself had usurped the throne from Edward V. Richard had persuaded Parliament his nephew was illegitimate because the boy's parents' marriage was supposedly invalid. The real legitimacy question was the Tudor claim to rule England, which rested precariously on clear right by battle, tenuous right by blood, and questionable right by acclaim. Henry VIII thought that a third king in a row would strengthen the right by blood since he would be the grandson and son of anointed kings. And it would positively affect right by acclaim since the people would be quite happy to see a male heir who could almost guarantee a stable transfer of power.

As almost everyone knows Henry VIII had six wives. He annulled his first marriage by making himself Supreme Head of the Church of England after his wife produced one healthy daughter and several sons and daughters who were stillborn or died within two months of birth. He ended his second marriage by finding his wife guilty of treason after she produced one healthy daughter. His third marriage ended when his wife died after having given birth to a son healthy enough to be expected to outlive his father. He annulled his fourth marriage after discovering his bride had too great a personality for him to consummate their union, although he was decent enough to legally make her his sister and provide sufficiently for a household befitting that royal rank. His fifth marriage may have been an effort to produce a spare heir, but this wife actually was guilty of treason and beheaded. His sixth marriage ended when his wife became a widow in 1547.

King Henry had determined through his will and with the consent of Parliament that the line of succession would start with his son followed by his daughters and then the descendants of his younger sister, Mary. Henry ignored the descendants of his older sister, Margaret, who had become Queen of Scots by marriage. Either Henry did not want a King of Scots on the English throne or he thought the common law prohibition of foreigners owning land would apply and prevent her Scots children from owning the royal estates in England.

King Edward VI, a sickly youth who succeeded his father as set forth in his will, named his cousin, Lady Jane Grey, the oldest grandchild of Henry's sister Mary, as his successor, bypassing his two half-sisters and Jane's mother, not to mention Auntie Margaret's brood north of the border. He did so at the instigation of his chief councilor, the Duke of Northumberland, who happened to have his son married to Lady Jane after she was named heir to the throne, making her Lady Jane Dudley. However, Edward also was intelligent and a fierce Protestant. He was none too keen on having his Catholic half-sister, Mary, follow him. Besides, Mary and Edward's other, Protestant half-sister, Elizabeth, had been ruled illegitimate by act of Parliament.

Bastards in the legal sense do not become monarchs even though they usually have as much royal blood as their legitimate half-siblings. That was the loophole Richard III had used to depose his nephew, the never crowned Edward V. On the word of the Bishop of Bath and Wells Parliament happily agreed that King Edward IV's marriage precontract to Lady Eleanor Butler, entered into as the quid pro quo for Lady Eleanor's agreement to sleep with the king, invalidated his subsequent marriage to the nepotistic Queen Consort Elizabeth Woodville.

Had none of Henry VIII's wives produced a son an exception to the no bastards rule might have been made. The king publicly acknowledged paternity of Henry Fitzroy, Duke of Richmond and Somerset. Even before Henry honored his illegitimate son with two dukedoms he made him Earl of Nottingham at the age of six. The king just wanted to make clear that he was not the reason his first wife, Queen Catherine of Aragon, had not produced a healthy son as was her only duty. Unfortunately, Lord Richmond was 17 years old when he died in 1536 most likely from tuberculosis.

In 1553, Richmond's half-brother Edward VI also died from tuberculosis at the age of 15. His council, led by Northumberland, declared Lady Jane Dudley queen as per Edward's wishes and moved her to the apartments in the Tower of London where English monarchs stay until being enthroned. Edward's half-sister Mary was informed by a letter from the council that Edward was ill, a ruse intended to buy time. Mary began to make her way to London, discovering two days into her journey that Edward was dead. She sent a letter to the council, declaring herself queen. Mary gathered an army of supporters, including, by the eighth day, all of the council that had put Jane forward save Northumberland. Meanwhile, the people of London began to revolt against the declaration of Jane as queen. They expected Mary to be their new queen. By the ninth day, Mary reached London and was proclaimed queen. Even Jane's father, the Duke of Suffolk, changed allegiance.

Lady Jane Dudley, the de facto Nine Days Queen, never set out to rule England. By all accounts, she believed Mary was rightfully queen after Edward. The council agreed with Edward that England should not have to face having a Catholic queen given that the Church of England was doing quite well, having produced the Book of Common Prayer under Edward and banned masses. Then there was the problem of all the monasteries and abbeys dissolved under Henry. The priests, monks, and nuns might want their church's property back under a Catholic sovereign. The fact that the chief councilor would be the queen's father-in-law if Jane reigned might be excused as a happy coincidence. Interestingly, the sole act of sovereignty made by Jane was her sincere and repeated refusal to recognize her husband as a co-ruling king. She gladly would make him a duke but had no intention of him being anything but a nonsovereign consort.

None of that mattered. Mary had gained the public support she needed to ignore Edward's wishes and use Henry's will to establish she was the rightful heir to the throne. For unknown reasons, Jane did not leave the Tower when Mary entered London. There is no record that the guards refused to let her go or were ordered to keep her locked up. It was most likely inertia that kept her there. She was moved to other apartments and eventually tried and found guilty of treason.

Mary was not inclined to sign Jane's death warrant. Jane was her first cousin once removed, obviously a pawn in her father's ambitions, and technically a deposed queen since the council had recognized her under the authority of the late king's will. Mary's half-sister Elizabeth would face the same problem but with higher stakes thirty-some years later with a first cousin twice removed. Later Mary felt she had no choice. Jane's father joined Wyatt's Rebellion, a rising early in 1554 in opposition to Mary's intended marriage to Prince Phillip Hapsburg, heir to the throne of Spain. That was the first sputter of popular and noble regret for backing Mary over Jane and the trigger for Mary to sign the warrant. Mary lost further support when she began enforcing her new heresy law against leaders of the Church of England in 1555. Nonetheless, she held onto the throne until her untimely death in 1558.

Despite Mary's short reign, she did enough damage to be known in history as "Bloody" Mary. However, without her successful claim to the crown with the crowd behind her, the Dudleys may well have held on, Henry's will discarded, and Elizabeth would not have had the opportunity to make her mark as monarch of a golden age in English history. Mary cobbled together a legal right under Henry's will and an Act of Parliament, popular support in the Home Counties as she traveled to London, elite endorsement once the Council saw that popular support, and finally approval by the citizens of the capital city to solidly become England's first acknowledged

Queen Regnant.

More than anything, this established that the people expected the crown to go to an heir apparent, the next male in the line of inheritance, or to an heir presumptive, the next female if there were no males before her in the line of inheritance. The presumption was that the stork might deliver a male baby before the female ascended the throne. The appearance was that the next male was legitimate. Seventy years earlier Richard III had successfully taken the throne from his nephew on the legal grounds that the fourteen year old heir apparent, Edward V, was a bastard and therefore not in the line of succession. On that basis, he was not a usurper but the legitimate monarch. Of course the more pressing concern was the possibility of Edward V's grasping mother and her family ruling England through her young son. Parliament and London thought it best to go with a seasoned military leader and experienced administrator over a boy fronting for a greedy family of the middling sort.

Like Mary, Richard III wore through that goodwill quickly and was deposed in battle by Henry Tudor in 1485 who became Henry VII. Henry VII determined that the Bishop of Bath and Wells had lied. He ordered all copies of the Act of Parliament choosing Richard III as rightful king destroyed. One copy escaped destruction and has formed the basis of many arguments over whether Richard III was or was not a usurper. He certainly had more legal right to the throne than Henry Tudor who won the throne through right of conquest. More importantly, he had the backing of the nation's representatives in Parliament and the residents of London.

Similarly, the citizens of London, the nobles on the council, and the people in the communities through which Mary passed on her way to London agreed with Henry VIII's logic in his will. They decided the line of succession, not the political elites who had put forward Jane. The immediate consequence was the widespread understanding that the descendants of Henry

VIII's sister Margaret were next in line after Elizabeth should she have no children. That created a great deal of drama in the second half of the sixteenth century as Elizabeth toyed with suitors while clinging to her image as the Virgin Queen and Catholics schemed to place Margaret's granddaughter, Mary, Queen of Scots, on the throne of England. This Mary wound up beheaded as a result of being caught out in these schemes, but her son was the only heir Elizabeth's councilors even considered when the Virgin Queen died without directly naming a successor.

Much later, in 1688, the popular decision to recognize Bloody Mary in 1553 provided Parliament with a way to rid the country of Mary, Queen of Scots' Catholic great-grandson, James II yet still maintain the succession. Parliament determined that no Catholic could rule England since the monarch was Supreme Head of the Church of England. That barred James and his infant son by his second wife but recognized James' older daughter Mary by his first wife and her husband William of Orange, Stadholder of the Netherlands, as his replacements. James abandoned the throne when William and Mary landed in England with Dutch troops. William's insistence on being named co-monarch was not much of a stretch because he was, like his wife, a grandchild of Charles I. We probably should not overanalyze why the female Tudors executed their first cousins and this female Stuart married one of hers. Both strategies only served to give Henry VII's descendants fewer opportunities to carry on the line.

William's intervention permitted Parliament to firmly establish through a Bill of Rights in 1689 that Parliament henceforth was England's sovereign. Popular will expressed in supporting Mary I as Edward VI's rightful heir as sovereign set the precedent for Parliament to assert itself as sovereign by inviting William III and Mary II to become King and Queen of England. The representatives of the people had seized power in a Glorious Revolution.

Legal claim supported by some form of popular support in warrior societies is established by success in battle. That defines how Henry VII was able to secure the throne of England against Richard III. To a lesser extent, William III also had to prove his claim, or rather his wife's claim, to the crown of Ireland in battle after having been more or less elected to the crowns of England and Scotland by the nation's representatives.

The very long history throughout the great breadth of Eurasia of obtaining legitimate sovereignty over a people in any realm after victory in the field followed by acclamation pretty much ended with Napoleon's ascension to the wholly new title of Emperor of the French in 1804. By then, succession through primogeniture had taken root in all monarchies. As a result, European states along with some Asian ones had settled into a peaceful, predictable habit of transferring sovereignty from one ruler to the next just in time for some elements to start wondering why sovereignty could not be passed from one set of elected representatives of the people to another just as smoothly.

The only other justification for wielding lawful power over a society is divine will. Most Mesopotamian and Mesoamerican kings segued from being religious leaders early in their cultures' histories and retained priestly communication with the gods, thereby explaining their right to govern. The autocratic tsars of the Russian Empire claimed to be temporal and spiritual leaders as well. Similarly, Muslim rulers have tried to highlight links to the Prophet Muhammad or assert special favor from Allah. The Egyptian pharaohs, some Mesopotamian kings, and Aztec and Inca leaders claimed to be gods themselves. A handful of English, Scottish, and French kings and queens in the sixteenth and seventeenth centuries (most notably, Elizabeth's successor James I of England, while he was still James VI of Scotland, and Louis XIV of France) argued that they received their authority from God. Revolution put that fire out temporarily in 1649 and permanently in 1688 in Great Britain and in 1789 in France.

Chinese emperors were empowered by divine will called the Mandate of Heaven, which could be withdrawn if the emperor acted unjustly. Success and good fortune meant the emperor had it, while failure and disaster meant he had lost it. Of course, popular support of the emperor waxed and waned in unison with how well things were going for China. One could only really tell if the Mandate of Heaven had changed if rebellion proved successful. That, in itself, tells us that divine will still depends on the consent of the governed. Even the Bishop of Rome, head of state of Vatican City, who has the best claim to sovereign leadership by divine right, is prayerfully elected by the College of Cardinals.

In political theory, sovereignty mostly has been relegated to discussions about nation-states, not monarchs. Ever since the Peace of Westphalia in 1648, polities large and small have clung to their sovereignty and the idea that others should back off from interfering in their affairs. In recent decades, China has used sovereignty as a Great Wall to reject foreign protests regarding its human rights and civil liberties policies. But who gets to be a sovereign state?

China's former province, Taiwan, is officially considered by both the Chinese and Taiwanese governments as an integral part of the sovereign state of China. Taiwan became separated from China when the US Navy intervened late in the day to preserve the losing side of the Chinese civil war despite earlier diplomatic efforts by the US to broker an agreement between the two political parties that were fighting. Neither government on either side of the Strait of Formosa considers its rival to be the legitimate government of the sovereign state of China and neither will accept official relations by other states with its rival, giving the world two Chinas to choose from. The rest of the world may be able to live with two Chinas, but the two Chinas cannot. Unfortunately, this kind of stalemate tends to heat up, create friction, and release energy unexpectedly like tectonic plates causing an earthquake. The two Chinas are separated by a fairly active fault.

Further US support, particularly in the United Nations Organization, gave the nod mostly to Taiwan until US policy began to change in the early 1970s. Mainland China started to turn the tide of recognition in its favor in the 1960s by assisting newly independent former European colonies with infrastructure projects. Richard Nixon's pragmatism trumped his anti-communism when he acquiesced to seating the People's Republic of China (PRC) in the U.N., thus removing the Republic of China, Taiwan's official name, from that organization. This policy culminated in the US officially recognizing the PRC as the legitimate government of China in 1979. Taiwan is still recognized officially as representing the sovereign state of China by just more than a score of other states, most of whom receive generous development funds as part of the deal, including a few that recognized mainland China and changed their minds. It is not the first time in history that a government essentially bribed other states to respect its sovereignty, but it is one of the most transparent.

The economic angle is so strong that even Mainland China acts as though Taiwan is a sovereign polity when it comes to commerce despite the hawkish rhetoric claiming the island is an integral part of the Chinese nation. One wonders whether the PRC believes it can establish so many commercial ties with its wayward island province that it becomes a de facto part of China without resort to violent invasion. If so, they are swimming upstream against a tide of insular sentiment that, 65 years on, gives the citizens of Taiwan reason to hope their society may, instead, drop its claims to represent all of China and become an independent, sovereign state.

De jure secession, legally breaking away from the parent sovereign society and polity, normally does not take place in slow motion like this. A century and a half ago, the United States of America fell into civil war over differences of opinion regarding the sovereignty of the sub-national states that form the union in its federal system of government. We will deal with the peculiarities of federal systems later. For now, it is interesting to note that the seceding US states formed a new federative national government, the Confederate States of America (CSA). They even toyed with the idea of becoming a constitutional monarchy with Queen Victoria of the United Kingdom as monarch to gain the support of her realm.

The South had other choices. The seceding states did not claim the Confederacy was the rightful government of the United States of America despite their belief that they were interpreting the US Constitution correctly. Nor did they remain separate and sovereign, which would have bolstered their argument that the constituent states of the United States had enough autonomy to reject federal laws. In other words, the rebels took steps that indicated they knew full well their sub-national states did not have sufficient sovereignty to challenge the federal government's superior sovereignty. By establishing the CSA, the South clearly indicated it did not secede over states' rights. The War Between the States was certainly not part of any political revolution given the South's adherence to the same kinds of federal relationships as the Union.

Secession is a tricky means of establishing a sovereign state and not just because it often involves violence. In most situations, the declarative theory of sovereignty officially holds sway. Arising from the principles established by the Treaty of Westphalia, a government providing laws for an established population, controlling a defined territory, and able to conduct affairs with other states can declare it represents a sovereign state. Sounds simple enough, right? That would make the Confederacy a sovereign state for its brief life. And technically, it was, even though the declarative theory wasn't written down until the Montevideo Convention in 1933. However, the Confederacy was never officially recognized as a sovereign state by any other state. Rather than risk war with the US over an internal matter, foreign states did not recognize the

Confederacy, although a few sent military advisors to both sides during the Civil War.

In some circles, and to be subject to international law, recognition by another sovereign state, preferably a "great power," is essential. Called the constitutive theory of sovereignty, no one will play with you unless one of the big boys takes notice of you first. This idea was put forward under the Congress of Vienna in 1815, which recognized thirty-nine sovereign states in Europe at the end of the Napoleonic period, five of which were great powers: Austria, France, Great Britain, Prussia, and Russia. The principle was put to the test fairly quickly. Greek nationalists declared independence from the Ottoman Empire in 1922. Five years later, three of the great powers intervened by destroying the Egyptian navy sent to protect Ottoman interests. In 1830, the great powers got around to imposing Greek independence on the Turks and, for good measure, noticed the Catholic population of the Netherlands wanted independence, too, and so created Belgium.

This set up two domino effects, one released within decades and another almost a century later. Greece was the first of several nation-states hived off from the European side of the Ottoman Empire in the 1800s, providing opportunities for some of the least objectionable Germanic princes to acquire kingdoms of their own when the newly independent countries decided to form monarchies but didn't trust elevating one of their own citizens to the position. More catastrophically, the United Kingdom of Great Britain and Ireland set in stone a guarantee of neutrality for Belgium that was optioned when Germany ignored Belgian sovereignty to get at France around the Maginot Line in 1914. By that point the British Empire had substantial global interests, which brought even more players into what became a world war in short order.

A corollary to the constituent theory of sovereignty is that no one will notice you if you exist as a result of an illegal aggression. The Turkish Republic of Northern Cyprus is recognized only by Turkey, the aggressor that carved the territory out of the island Republic of Cyprus. The world is still sorting out the legality and timeline of Russia's annexation of Crimea from Ukraine, so it is not hustling to recognize the act of popular sovereignty that Russia arranged to justify its invasion. While not a declaration of independence, the Crimean situation fits the category. There has been even less interest in being polite to the Federal State of Novorossiya (declared independent in 2014), which consists of the easternmost provinces of Ukraine where Russian troops and agents have been milling about.

South Ossetia and Abkhazia declared independence from Georgia in the 1990s, but only a handful of nations have accepted their sovereignty. Even though, or perhaps because, one of those nations is Russia, neither territory has received a warm welcome into the international community. Substantial populations of ethnic Georgians resided in these areas, although military activity has scared these people from their homes. Further back in terms of acquiring recognition are the Pridnestrovian Moldavian Republic aka Transnistria (declared independent from Moldova in 1990) and the Nagorno-Karabakh Republic (declared independent from Azerbaijan in 1992). These territories have the distinction of being recognized by one or two of the other non-recognized "states" only. Even Russia has kept away. On the other hand, Timor-Leste, Kosovo, and South Sudan declared their sovereignty from Indonesia, Serbia, and Sudan, respectively, and were recognized by a majority of countries and the United Nations. What sets them apart from the others is a clear history of oppression by the sovereign state from which they seceded rather than the simple self-determination of a minority ethnic group asserting its independence.

Self-determination, promoted most strongly by Woodrow Wilson, the only US president with a PhD in political science, was a concept inspired by two factors. First was the need to restore sovereignty to the people of Poland at the end of World

War I. The Polish-Lithuanian Commonwealth, once the largest state in Europe, vanished in 1795 after the third cannibalizing action by its three greedy neighbors (Austria, Prussia, and Russia), following partitions in 1772 and 1790. Second was the need to decide what to do with the territories of the multinational Dual Monarchy of Austria-Hungary, which, of course, included Austria's bit of Poland, the Kingdom of Galicia and Lodomeria. The Austro-Hungarian Empire's internal nationality issues, after all, sparked the war when a Bosnian Serb activist who thought the population of Bosnia-Hercegovina should be under the authority of the Kingdom of Serbia as part of a larger kingdom of south Slavs (Yugoslavia) assassinated the heir to the Austro-Hungarian throne and his wife in 1914.

Wilson thought the peace talks at Versailles would be a good place to give every major European ethnic group its own nation-state. Indeed, as a result of the negotiations, Poland was recreated, Austria and Hungary were sized down and made into two independent states, and six new sovereign states were formed: Czechoslovakia, Estonia, Finland, Latvia, Lithuania, and Yugoslavia. Sure, the first and last on this list were amalgams of smaller nationalities, but it was better than before. Who knew they would be so eager to end these arranged marriages 70 years later?

The idea of national self-determination leading to a sovereign state sounds ideal, with every atomized ethno-historical, lingua-cultural group getting its own government. The vibrancy, color, and diversity of governments created by indigenous peoples in Africa, the Americas, Asia, Australia, and Oceania before colonialism and internationalization demonstrate that human beings are quite creative when expected to bring order to an over-extended family. However, the cold, hard fact is that most nationalities are too small to sustain a workable sovereign state now that internationalization has been succeeded by globalization. And the territories in which nationalities are found are, more often than not, mixed with the territories of other nationalities, representative of a nomadism that suddenly was untenable.

The smallest sovereign states depend for survival on mountains of good will and financial aid from the international community. They are quirks of history or island states. Quite a few have made a name for themselves as tax havens and playgrounds for wealthy travelers. If they proliferated, international law might have to add "economically sustainable" to the list of qualities that make a state sovereign. At its base, that seems to be the issue with Abkhazia, Nagorno-Karabakh, South Ossetia, Transnistria, and the Turkish Cypriot Republic. Each depends on outside economic and military assistance. Who wants more sovereign states if they can't pay their bills or protect themselves? They are adult children who don't move out of the house. As we shall see, the citizens of these polities aren't even getting a good bargain.

Other, larger self-determining hopefuls wait in the wings, like the Basque Country, Catalonia, Kurdistan, Scotland, and Western Sahara. They have a better shot at providing a well-rounded foundation for their citizens without assistance from foreigners. The Basques, Catalans, and Scots all have long histories of independence under dukes, counts, and kings into the early modern period, as well as considerable autonomy in various forms since their absorption into larger states in subsequent centuries. They did not quite make it to the finish line when national sovereignty became the rage in 1648.

Scotland was technically its own, independent kingdom until the Act of Union in 1707. However, when James VI of Scotland became James I of England in 1603, he almost immediately began to refer to himself as King of Great Britain, which was acceptable to everyone but the English Parliament. Even the Welsh were agreeable. They could live with being a constituent part of Great Britain, but had a hard time stomaching the thought of being part of England much longer. The Stuarts' absolutist theory of kingly rule, set forth by James to his son in a book of instructions, *Basilikon Doron*, coupled with their need for money from the wealthier, southern end of the island of Great Britain to pay for a lavish court and foreign adventures, kept them securely as English monarchs first and masters of Scotland as an afterthought. After more than four centuries of playing second fiddle, the Scots voted against independence in 2014. Meanwhile, the Catalans also want a referendum and one for the Basques has been placed on hold.

The Kurds can claim to have stayed in the same mountainous regions equidistant from the Black, Caspian, and Mediterranean Seas as long as the Greeks have lived in Greece, despite centuries of being the hinge between great empires like Rome and Persia. More recently, it has been discovered that they are genetically related to European Jews. The size of their population conforms to that of many smaller countries. The facts cry out for a homeland. Indeed, Kurdistan was conceived at the end of World War I when Kurds latched on to Wilson's idea of national self-determination. However, when Britain (for Iraq), France (for Syria), Iran, and Turkey made out the maps a few years later, the nation was forgotten, most likely because the Kurds had no representatives to speak up for them that time. After almost a century of being treated poorly by the four stepparent countries into which they were fostered, some hope arose when Iraqi Kurds were given autonomy in the aftermath of the 2003 US invasion of Iraq. That promise became doubtful with the rise of the Islamic State in 2014, a Sunni Muslim concoction born from opposition to Shi'ite dominance in Syria and Iraq, the mess made by American arrogance, and the reverberations of the Arab Spring. The concept of autonomy, which has been touched on lightly so far, will have its moment in the sun a few chapters down.

The smallest and poorest of these nascent nations, Western Sahara, has half a million people, would be no worse off independent than it is as an underdeveloped province of Morocco, and is the only former European colony in Africa that was not immediately welcomed into the family of nation-states after its imperial power freely ended its rule. The fact that the Sahrawi, the people of Western Sahara, have been waiting to make a choice since 1976 is testament to the reality that superior, usable force trumps sovereignty in the international arena. Unlike a decision in family court, where the interests of the child take precedence, the Sahrawi have been told that Morocco's interests must be satisfied in their battle for self-determination, which doesn't sound anything like true self-determination. While the Sahrawi have waited to vote on the direction they should take, Morocco has sent Moroccans down to the territory to take up residence and be counted among the indigenous population. Nomadism indeed.

The naturally plaid distribution of nationalities in many areas of the world is the result of centuries of activity. It is not easy to decide who lives where, let alone deciding how to map out a country that gives a nationality a home. Two examples in the 1940s serve to remind us that people do not like to be uprooted or become a minority in their place of birth.

The lines for Israel and Palestine were all drawn by the United Nations. The problem was that there were far too many Palestinians left in lands that were set to become Israel. The queue to check out stuttered and the Israelis sprang ahead declaring independence. The result was war, standstill, more war, negotiation, terrorism, still more war, embargoes, standstill, serious negotiation, a few hopeful Nobel Peace Prizes, frustration, illegal actions, and generations of Palestinian refugees living out their lives somewhere other than where their families originated.

In the other example, the British Empire decided to create a Muslim state out of parts of India to accommodate this substantial minority and give the majority Hindus the remainder. Mohandas K. Gandhi called for India to remain united, but the politicians, particularly in the Muslim League, convinced the Viceroy otherwise. Two provinces needed to be split in half,

Bengal and Punjab, and even then millions of people ended up in the “wrong” state. The result was massive communal violence and forced removal by mobs, leaving about half a million people dead and another twelve million refugees. Muslim Bengal was denied separate independence and became East Pakistan for 24 years before getting its wish as Bangladesh. Even after all that, India has the third largest Muslim population of any country, after Indonesia and Pakistan, and may well surpass Pakistan before 2020.

Nationalities seek sovereign states like water seeks its own level. All sovereign states, great and small, are legally equal. They possess the authority to do as they please within their borders without reference to any other power. The point is to provide order and security for the people and territory under the state’s watch. Sometimes, we forget that. Stark reminders come when that sovereign authority disappears. During wars of occupation, like World War II, the sovereign authority may be displaced, becoming a refugee just like its citizens. The occupying power carries on while the legitimate government does what it can from a distance in the propaganda sphere, sometimes aided by the adventures of the occupied country’s escaped armed forces working with an allied command.

The more difficult case occurs when central authority crumbles and no one has the resources to fill the vacuum. China faced this situation in the late 1910s through much of the 1920s. Lebanon had the same experience during its civil war. Somalia lost its sovereignty when rebellion overwhelmed the national government and left nothing to replace it. China and Lebanon eventually restored national government with strange bedmate coalitions and quite a bit of coercion, but were hampered in achieving stability by invading neighbors intruding over decades. Somalia remains a ship adrift.

China is a remarkable case with regard to sovereignty, democracy, and the social contract. We will dig deeper later. For now, it is worthwhile to note that China is incredibly feisty about shielding its internal affairs and human rights record from criticism. This attitude is, in part, a reflex response to the trauma the country suffered from 1838 to 1949 when Britain, France, Germany, Japan, Russia, and the United States freely and frequently ignored Chinese sovereignty to the point where whole city districts in some ports were "extraterritorial," meaning foreign, not Chinese law applied.

The practical use of superior military force often proves sovereignty to be a paper tiger, something China learned from Great Britain in the First Opium War and time after time for eleven decades until the country had a strong enough government to fight back when United Nations troops under General MacArthur threatened China again during the Korean conflict. As long as the target is significantly weaker than the aggressor and has no other countries responsible to protect it under a treaty, the international community may grumble but does nothing. Last decade, the US brushed aside sovereignty concerns, if the idea even came up, to destroy governments in Afghanistan and Iraq. More recently, Russia invaded two of its neighbors, Georgia and Ukraine, in support of secessionist sentiment. Clearly, sovereignty is dependent upon other sovereigns playing along.

States obtain their sovereignty somewhere. That somewhere is the clear enunciation of a group of people in a particular territory that they wish to band together in a society and form a government that will defend them against aggression and order their interactions with one another. Although the particulars of this popular action to create a sovereign entity have been debated since Ancient Greece, the terms we use today surfaced in the seventeenth century, around the same time as the Peace of Westphalia. The name given to this action is the social contract.

Chapter 6—The Social Contract

A CONTRACT IS an enforceable, mutual exchange of promises between competent persons that requires the promises to be fulfilled. The three philosophers primarily associated with the development of social contract theory are Thomas Hobbes, John Locke, and Jean-Jacques Rousseau. Each in his way explained the terms of the agreement and nature of the promises. All agreed that the participants in the contract were human beings endowed with natural rights who sought safety, order, and prosperity. Yet these men fell short. Luckily, all they need was an assist from a fourth philosopher who actually came before them.

Thomas Hobbes argued that individuals hand over all of their natural rights except the right of self-defense to a sovereign in exchange for protection from aggression and the benefits of living in society. The social contract arises from the proposition that reasonable human beings prefer a communal life subject to rules imposed by a government over a solitary life in which one can do as one pleases yet is constrained by the need to do everything for oneself. Without rules, everything is chaotic, violent, and transient. According to Hobbes, the sovereign can be an absolute ruler or an all-powerful parliament. This leaves everyone but the governor as subjects, not citizens. Nonetheless, logic and self-preservation lead men and women to bow to a higher authority rather than endure a life that is "nasty, brutish, and short."

John Locke wondered whether individuals really had to give up all save one of their natural rights to create a government with authority over them. He saw a need for order flow from the desire of individuals to protect the property they possessed, used, or created to fulfill their basic needs and satisfy their personal wants. Locke argued that the social contract was a unanimous agreement to endow political structures with sufficient sovereignty to adopt rules by majority consent that would allow members of society a stable environment in which to safeguard their property and pursue their individual lives and liberties. Life, liberty, and property were natural rights that could not be surrendered. He therefore rejected the notion of an absolute sovereign, whether monarchical or parliamentary. Indeed, Locke believed popular will had a continuing role to play regardless of the form of government used to exercise sovereignty. Members of society had an obligation to overthrow a government that no longer looked out for their interests and substitute a more responsive one.

Jean-Jacques Rousseau went back a step and then some to argue that individuals tender all of their natural rights upon entering the social contract to create the sovereign. However, he argued that individuals receive civil liberties in exchange for the bargain. Thus, the members of society subject themselves to the will of the community but retain their freedom as citizens. Lest one think that frictions may develop between the exercise of sovereignty and liberty, Rousseau posits rather optimistically that the sovereign can only act in the interests of the common good and citizens must always fulfill the obligations placed on them by the sovereign. Reality steps in where Rousseau introduces government as a mediator between the sovereign and citizens that establishes the laws and organization necessary to fulfill the terms of the social contract. Government may attempt to act according to its own needs to the detriment of the citizens, but this dissolves the bonds of social union and destroys the body politic. Similarly, the state deteriorates and laws cease to be valid if citizens withhold their participation in the affairs of the community. That last bit holds particular resonance in present times.

Missing from these conceptions is the notion put forward by Hugo Grotius that individuals, on their own, are sovereigns. Grotius argued a few years before Hobbes that individuals cede some of their sovereignty to the state, thus endowing the state with the right to make war and keep peace. Individuals maintain the rest of their sovereignty to make decisions in their personal lives. Grotius focused on defining just war in the time of the great conflagration known as the Thirty Years War, which was concluded by the Peace of Westphalia. As a result of centering his attentions on the exercise of sovereign state power against another sovereign state, he was sensitive to how war should not be seen as a breakdown of the rules of conduct. War is not a tantrum or emotional outburst. Rather, war must have its own rules, norms to be observed even in the heat of battle.

While Grotius' idea only further developed the chivalric and Christian conventions that had developed since the end of the Western Roman Empire, such as trying to capture for ransom rather than kill nobles in battle or refraining from massacring the inhabitants of a city who defended against a siege, putting it in writing was a big step. Inherent in this idea is the supposition that states have created their own form of society, the members of which generally keep to themselves but out of necessity must order their relations with others. He thereby set the stage for the remarkable assemblage of diplomats representing more than 100 kingdoms, principalities, duchies, counties, and imperial cities, as well as the Dutch Republic and the Swiss Confederation, that forged the Peace of Westphalia.

More importantly, Grotius laid the groundwork for the entire field of international law. Some of the most important laws among nations were the codification of wartime practices and the consequences of war. The Geneva Conventions, four treaties and three protocols starting in 1864 and concluding with one in 1949, establish the standards for the humanitarian treatment of combatants in war. These agreements detail the rights of enemy military personnel and civilians captured and of non-combatants and the protections to be afforded the wounded and civilian populations living in or near war zones. The Hague Conventions of 1899 and 1907 define acceptable uses of weapons and the Geneva Protocol of 1925 governs the use of chemical agents in hostilities. A separate convention in 1951 defined and set out the rules for dealing with refugees. It is a testament to Grotius that so much effort has been put into regularizing how states at war are going to treat the sovereign citizens of their enemies or neutrals.

The social contract theorists who followed Grotius did not use his concept of individuals as sovereigns when they set out their positions. Hobbes almost described individuals as sovereigns by arguing that in the state of nature humans may do as they please. Locke and Rousseau did not view individuals as sovereigns because they held that natural law, given by God, constrains humans to act morally. The fact that humans break this natural law on a regular basis pushed Locke and Rousseau to formulate their conceptions of the social contract to create a mechanism to enforce the law. All three men described a process whereby the natural rights of human beings were tendered as consideration for the rewards of community, which include rules designed to identify, apprehend, and punish people for transgressing the principles of natural law.

Hobbes, Locke, and Rousseau used philosophical alchemy to transform the natural rights of individuals into the sovereignty of states. The problem is that natural rights and sovereignty are two related but distinct things. How can one become the other? It is a logical leap to say that people give up something and, when compounded, their collective somethings become something else entirely. That leap is unnecessary. If we view individuals as sovereigns, we recognize that they have all the natural rights credited to them by the social contract theorists, we understand that they have the capacity to violate natural law, and we establish that they must part with some of their sovereignty to create a separate, communal sovereign able to intercede when natural law is violated by individuals.

Working from this viewpoint enables us to conceive the idea that individuals retain all of their natural rights when entering the social contract. There is no need to have natural rights exchanged for civil liberties. Civil liberties can stand on their own as freedoms agreed upon to enhance everyone's contributions to society. As we shall see when we address civil liberties, it is important to leave civil liberties as a distinct product of the social contract rather than part of the consideration received for entering the social contract. Unlike natural rights, civil liberties are not absolute; there must be exceptions whereby some actions are not protected by an agreed upon freedom. Natural rights are unalienable and absolute because they are part of what makes us human.

Sovereign individuals hand over some of their sovereignty and retain the rest. This preserves the notion that everyone can do as one pleases, but now it will be limited. Given the purpose of pooling a bit of everyone's sovereignty, which is to reduce conflict, it is necessary that the limit be the point where those actions violate the rules established by the new, communal sovereign or interfere with the exercise of sovereignty by other individuals. We are ordering our relationships by entering the social contract and in so doing recognize we can no longer give self-interest unfettered freedom. We become cognizant of and take into account the interest of others and the interest of the group as a whole. Power is no long wielded absolutely and in isolation, but rather exercised in concert with the power of others. We are expected to and, in a perfect world, always required to take responsibility for how our individual exercise of our sovereign, unalienable rights affects others.

This mirrors what Grotius had in mind and the diplomats in 1648 created in the international order of sovereign states.

Sovereign states, like sovereign individuals, generally mind their own business, recognize the limits of what they can do when dealing with others, have laws (known as treaties, conventions, and protocols) that order their relations, allow the weak to be dominated by the strong despite a universal concept of equality among all, and sometimes resort to violence against one another that is often founded on unjust grounds in contravention of the law. When they do so, they are subject to discipline by the other sovereign states if those other sovereign states choose to enforce the rules.

How much sovereignty do individuals part with to create the social contract? That depends to some extent on how much sovereignty individuals have to begin with. Are human beings naturally invested with complete sovereignty? Grotius and Hobbes thought so. That is why mankind fights. Everyone is a sovereign and can do as he or she pleases. Doing as one pleases results in conflict when what Johnny wants to do infringes on Suzie's ability to do what she wants.

This occurs every day on highways throughout the world where drivers stay in the passing lane when they are no longer passing anyone and obstruct drivers who want to pass them. The driver unable to pass often tailgates the miscreant because passing in the traveling lane is improper (and sometimes illegal) and aggression seems to be the appropriate response when one does not get one's way. This is a sign of conflict. The conflict can be resolved if the first driver puts on a directional and edges into the traveling lane. The conflict can remain at a standstill for miles. The conflict can escalate with the first driver slowing or braking, saying, in effect, "Hey! Get off my back!" The second driver may back off, drive even closer to the offending vehicle, put on a directional and pass in the traveling lane, zoom around the offending vehicle in frustration, or clip by glaring, screaming words that no one will hear, and giving the bugger the finger. No wonder Hobbes thought life before the social contract was "nasty, brutish, and short."

We cannot agree with Locke and Rousseau that human sovereignty is limited by natural law. Aside from the fact that it usually requires a belief in God, who we should only rely on as a last resort if we agree that humans have free will, natural law's ability to restrict human sovereignty would mean everyone should have deeply ingrained positive moral standards, those standards should be universal, and they should be applied consistently.

The first of the three requirements is met. We are well aware of individuals in the course of history that have shown few if any signs of positive moral standards affecting their actions. We may know such individuals personally. However, they do not lack those standards. They possess those standards and choose not to apply them, just as someone with a fine voice may not sing. Similarly, we can list standards that appear to be universal, such as avoiding harm to others, treating others well, respecting autonomy and privacy, or being honest or faithful. That takes care of the second requirement. Unfortunately, individuals may violate these standards purposefully. These standards also may be violated mistakenly, given that humans are prone to err. Either way, the third requirement is not met. The vast majority of American situation comedy television shows rely on humans' serendipitous fallibility when it comes to natural law. The bottom line is what good are universal moral standards as a limit on sovereignty if they can be broken? They are no limit at all. Sovereignty must be complete.

If sovereignty is complete and individuals have free will, we cannot avoid the conclusion that all individuals are equal to one another. They are not equal in terms of aptitude, intellect, or physical characteristics. However, human beings are all equally invested with the power to act as they see fit. No person has any more or less independence than any other person. Everyone is equally sovereign. We can discuss skin, eye, or hair color, height and metabolism, sex or sexual orientation, abilities, beliefs, and ancestry. Those are descriptors. They do not make us human.

We are created equal.

Three formulations of this concept are enshrined in documents of lasting importance. The United States Declaration of Independence of 1776 states, "We hold these truths to be self-evident, that all men are created equal, that they are endowed by their Creator with certain unalienable Rights, that among these are Life, Liberty, and the Pursuit of Happiness." The French Declaration of the Rights of Man and of the Citizen from 1789 proclaims, "Men are born and remain free and equal in rights." The Universal Declaration of Human Rights adopted by the United Nations in 1948 says, "All human beings are born free and equal in dignity and rights." All tie the equality of humans to the rights with which they are naturally endowed, rights they cannot give away because they are integral to their being.

While natural rights are unalienable, sovereignty is alienable. We give away some of our sovereignty in the social contract to establish the sovereign state. In order to create a democracy, every individual must hand over the same quantity and quality of sovereignty as everyone else. No one would agree to a social contract establishing a democracy if members of society retained varying levels of authority to act. The exchange must keep everyone equal to everyone else. Otherwise, stratification sets in, which is the hallmark of most other types of government. This makes sense. The power to order society must come first, and that power comes from the constituents of society as it is formed. If they decide that all but one person will relinquish some of their sovereignty, the participants will form a dictatorship. If a group of participants retains more sovereignty than the rest, an oligarchy is being formed.

Social contracts, like everything else, change over time. As a result, individuals in a democracy can gradually hand over more of their sovereignty to elites through apathy, frustration, ignorance, or sloth. They can get it back, but doing so will be far more disruptive and difficult than giving it. It is the political equivalent of trying to lose weight after one has spent even a short time forgetting to eat sensibly and exercise regularly. Gaining weight is giving sovereignty away; losing weight is repossessing sovereignty.

For democracy to work, we must retain enough sovereignty to support free will and exercise our natural rights. It would be preposterous for the level of sovereignty needed to be withheld differed from one person to the next if the equitable distribution of free will and natural rights remains intact. Most importantly, participants will have the same goals in parting with their pieces of sovereignty to establish the state. They will want to continue to do as they please without interference unless doing as they please results in others not being able to do as they please. They will want to establish rules to decide who gets to do what when one person's pleasure becomes another person's pain. They will want things done for them that they cannot do for themselves. After all, it is a contract, and all of the parties to the contract must agree to the same terms.

Some people claim they have never agreed to any contract and believe individuals retain absolute liberty and sovereignty and have formed a government designed to protect that liberty and sovereignty. They reject the idea of a social contract because they personally did not agree to any such thing, cannot wrap their heads around the idea of implied consent through positive action, and believe everyone is entitled to the *liberum veto* whereby the voice of one dissenter can block a law. This permits them to equate taxes with theft, to claim that all laws are obeyed due to the coercive power monopolized by the government, and to object to public programs that promote the common good. The most polite term for these people is "pure libertarian."

Individuals like this view the least government intrusion and maximum freedom of action by individuals as the indispensable formula for economic prosperity regardless of the information and opportunity deficiencies that individuals face. The Constitution is seen as a blueprint for limited government and nothing more. They believe that document has been massaged and stretched completely out of shape in the 241 years since it was written. While the principle of limited government is a sacred element of the United States' political system, supporters of this conclusion do not recognize that circumstances and issues have arisen in that time period thanks to a growing and prospering nation that require full use of those enumerated powers in ways unforeseeable to the Founders but consistent with their intentions. They want an eighteenth century government suitable for a relatively small, coastal, preindustrial nation.

The premise that American citizens retain absolute freedom and sovereignty can be shown to be false simply by going back to the analogy of driving a car. The road was built by the government for everyone to use paid for with everyone's taxes. Drivers generally obey the traffic rules set down by that government they were taught in driving school and of which there are reminders by way of signage and signals. Obedience arises not so much from the threat of punishment if they do not observe them but the fact those rules make sense. Experience has shown people will get where they are going without accidents or road rage if they follow them.

People are free to operate a vehicle because they have been licensed by the government after following the instructions to obtain a license and, in most states, have insured the vehicle at the direction of the government to cover the damages if an accident occurs. Drivers pay attention to the other sovereign individuals in their vehicles in order that they do not slam into them. All of those things are limitations on liberty and sovereignty that we agree upon with the help of our government in order to go to other places in our private vehicles. No one has either complete liberty or complete sovereignty in this context.

What is striking about advocates of pure libertarianism is that their positions cannot meld with the positions of others to form a consensus to make decisions on what laws need to be passed. By rejecting the social contract they inhibit any form of cooperation or negotiation with others in the political arena. They do not have to play by the rules because, according to them, they did not agree to the rules. They are playing Calvin ball from the comic "Calvin and Hobbes," in which the rules are made up by a rather self-centered kid as the game is played. What is missing from their conduct is any sense that people hold differing views from theirs for logical, rational reasons. They are the voters Winston Churchill warned us about. No amount of suasion based on facts, data, evidence, science, or law will dissuade their ilk that they are wrong to ignore the social contract and all that flows from it. It is the civics example of the debate between evolution and creationism.

These citizens of the USA believe they are free to do as they please as human beings without the shackles of conformity to the agreed upon principles that society offers us. It is a matter of faith. Live free or die. The only problem with that is there is no basis for avoiding the social contract. Indeed, their zealous defense of the United States Constitution warrants they should be exulting in the social contract given that document is the granddaddy of defined, written social contracts. Instead, they deny it in favor of an anguished grip on liberty. They cannot see the freedom wrought by well-turned order, the paradox that by relinquishing complete sovereignty we create a sturdy foundation on which to build prosperous, creative, unlimited lives with what sovereignty remains. Perhaps if they read a bit more Shakespeare, they would see how wondrously inventive one can be within a self-imposed structure.

Chapter 7—Respect for the Law and Civil Liberties

SOMETIMES, WHAT HOLDS us together is the intuitive knowledge of right from wrong. Just as a person acts in a manner that comports with a long list of principles, feelings, traditions, and characteristics singular to that individual, societies order themselves in ways that reflect the long list of beliefs, perspectives, experiences, and mores specific to their communities. We have as much trouble unravelling the psychology of human beings as we do the sociology of nation-states. There are just too many variables. Time is another enemy, for as time passes, circumstances change. On the other hand, humans have not lived in communities long enough to have evolved adaptations to living communally. We have the same genes Homo sapiens had when social units were no larger than extended families.

What we have done is gradually built a knowledge base of what does and does not work as we have established societies, chosen leaders, designed governments, written laws, divided labors, and created cultures. No matter how complex things get, the component parts remain the same. Ideas are tried repeatedly with slight variations due to time having passed from the first go or manifestly revised when they thoroughly fail. Some avenues explored are forgotten while others become grand boulevards with clear records of how we got here from there. At bottom, we remain human beings interacting with other human beings. And as human beings, we know right from wrong.

It takes a clear head and heroic character to act properly as close to all the time as possible. Trivialities impinge on decisions. Needs must be weighed. The seven deadly sins and many less lethal failings must be avoided. We are doomed trying to do all right and no wrong. One of the greatest resources for learning how to live life are fairy tales and other stories told to children. There will always be a positive moral at the end and evil will be put in its place. Pure hearts and purposes succeed.

Nonetheless, the winners cut corners. The protagonists are frequently devious. Attentive readers are left with the impression that good goals proceed from good intentions but the ends justify the means. Cinderella may be the loveliest, hardest working, and most dutiful step-wench in the land, but how she lands a prince relies on the equivalent of hitting the lottery. Who needs magic Jesus when one has a miracle worker fairy godmother? The miller's daughter in Rumpelstiltskin uses tears to beg off from her bargain with the dwarf who saved her life and made her queen. The dwarf relents and changes the terms of their agreement, whereupon the newly made queen sends the castle staff out for two days to search for clues to the title character's name. Having been given the answer by a hardworking, dedicated servant, the now royal daughter of the miller publicly humiliates Rumpelstiltskin when she gets his name right. No mention is made of rewarding the servant either. These are the lessons children learn: guile, beauty, and charm work miracles, fantastic beings will help you when you are in dire straits, and merit without magic will not move you up the socioeconomic ladder. So much for right and wrong.

Somewhere between innate sense and confusing fiction, our world requires some order. Children learn rules from their parents and other adults as they grow up. They are introduced to expectations of good behavior by family and teachers. Then they are given opportunities to test the rules and enough space to demonstrate their behavior, preferably in groups of their peers under some supervision. Instances of breaking the rules or misbehaving provide children with the experience that their actions have consequences. The process continues, repeating itself, for years. Conforming eventually becomes second nature for almost everyone. Happiness lies in getting along. Who doesn't want to be happy? But as children mature into adulthood, the rules of parents become the rules of law and the standards of good behavior become the standards of social etiquette. If all goes well, we continue to conform and seek happiness, learning along the way that the consequences for misconduct or transgression are more severe but we are less likely to get caught. In this way, young people are socialized into their roles as citizens of a community.

We create governments to craft rules that balance what is required with what is desired, what is ideal with what is real. Compromise is essential. We cannot do as we please without infringing upon the rights of others. Our vision of how things ought to be can never come to fruition because our vision conflicts with the visions of every other person. Remember, sovereignty is never absolute unless one lives completely isolated from all other sovereigns or power holders. Even when we agree on some points, there remain many points on which we do not agree.

We use government as a tool to weave together rules we all can live with without sacrificing our principles or giving up on our dreams. Consensus chooses the colors, weight, and use of the yarn. The yarn not used isn't inferior, it just doesn't work with the design everyone can agree on. The greater the participation, the stronger the resulting fabric will be. Core values and constitutional limits define the warp. The weft is what we put into the enterprise. Every loom has a different pattern. The tapestry is never finished and it is always too complex to fully visualize the design as we work on it. Democracy provides the means for all citizens to contribute to the project and representative democracy insures that there are only so many hands on the shuttle. It is a great undertaking, as any new nation-state can attest. Starting out is difficult if the loom is new and the weavers inexperienced. Fortunately, everyone has a base to begin with in the form of natural laws that are universal to all societies.

Philosophers make a distinction between natural law moral theory and natural law legal theory. Natural law moral theory holds that moral standards arise from objective attributes of rational human beings and the world. This is the natural law understood by the social contract theorists to exist in the state of nature. Since these writers assume God exists and created everything, this natural law, although distinct from divine law, originates from God's plan. That provides all the more reason to undertake the social contract to ensure natural law is enforced.

However, it is not necessary for natural law moral theory to have a divine connection. Grotius, again, saves the day. He argued that the source of natural law was man's rationality and sociability. While clearly stating his belief in God, a rather important point to make during the Thirty Years War with all of those Lutherans and Catholics killing each other over who is more dutiful to God, Grotius posited that natural law would exist even if there was no God. Natural law springs from human nature. Humans are moral creatures. This goes hand in hand with the idea that individuals do not give up their natural rights in order to enter into the social contract. The condition of humans as rational, independent beings with free will, as sovereigns, requires that natural rights are unalienable and natural law is immutable because the source of natural rights and natural law are those rational beings. This also underscores the basic theory of equality: we all have the same natural rights and are guided by the same natural law.

On the other hand, natural law legal theory holds that legislation sometimes obtains its authority from the moral standards of natural law. Legislation also obtains its authority in other ways: the process by which it is enacted, its adherence to social expectations and ideas of fairness, the existence of coercive tools to enforce it, and the fact that it issues from the sovereign state. It may be heart-warming to recognize the morality of some laws, but morality is not critical. Part of the problem lies in the presumption that a law based in morality is just. In order for a moral law to be just, the moral standard on which it is based must be universal. It therefore must be a moral standard arising from natural law rather than a particular religious or philosophical viewpoint.

One of the most classic interpretations of this is in *Jacobellis v. Ohio*, where Justice Potter Stewart of the United States Supreme Court stated in his concurring opinion "I know it when I see it" to explain his definition of hardcore pornography. Stewart was faced with trying to identify what he saw as legally unprotected expression: films, books, and pictures that can be banned. This is no small task since freedom of expression is bound so closely to our innate urge to create, an urge that revolts at the thought of limitation. Springing from this natural right are the freedoms of press, expression, and speech established by the First Amendment to the Constitution.

Potter's role as a member of the Supreme Court was to provide guidance to lower courts when applying the law. The law prohibited the manufacture, sale, and distribution of obscene materials. Typically, the Court in its opinions clearly states tests, definitions, and principles. Stewart could only go so far as to equate obscene materials to hardcore pornography. Then he posited that the identification of hardcore pornography is intuitive. "I know it when I see it." As humans, we can tell in our gut if something is wrong. We may not be able to verbalize it, but we feel it. That sense of wrong is the foundation of moral conscience from which springs moral standards that are expressed in natural law.

While laws based on universal moral standards are just, we cannot say that a law not based in morality is *ipso facto* unjust.

Traffic laws are not based on any moral principles, but they are just. Generally speaking they are based on common sense, i.e. the most obvious way of avoiding problems. They apply equally to all drivers, are easily understood, promote safety and orderly use of roads, and reduce the costs of accidents to individuals and society. We rarely go through all the reasons to obey a traffic law, consciously or subconsciously, while driving, riding, running, or walking. The exception is when a light turns yellow. That situation aside, we unconsciously follow the laws taught to us almost every step of the way to the extent we were taught and remember them.

Any law promulgated through constitutional means by the sovereign state is given the benefit of a doubt. Otherwise, conformity to and observance of laws must be thrown out the window like the Holy Roman Emperor's representatives, whose defenestration from Prague Castle in 1618 started the Thirty Years War. Indeed, the famed tossing of the emperor's officials out the window demonstrates just how badly things can turn out when laws are broken.

The Emperor's Regents in Bohemia, Count Vilem Slavata of Chlum and Count Jaroslav Borzita of Martinice, and Philip Fabricius, the secretary to the Regents, admitted to the representatives of the Bohemian estates they had stopped construction of or closed Protestant chapels on Imperial properties on orders of the Emperor's hand-picked heir, Ferdinand of Styria, who was elected King of Bohemia in 1617 to succeed the Emperor in that position. Count von Thurn, the leader of the Bohemian estates, denounced the Regents as enemies and agitators for the imposition of Catholicism because the letter overrode the Letter of Majesty of 1609 that the previous Emperor had issued granting the Bohemians the right to build the chapels. He further claimed the Regents could no longer be trusted to do justice to the Bohemian people and ought to be killed. With that, the two Regents and their secretary were defenestrated from the third floor, approximately 70 feet up.

One of four things happened: the men were saved by angels; the Virgin Mary caught them; they landed in a conveniently located and sized dung or garbage heap that none of the eyewitnesses noticed; or, most unlikely of all, they miraculously hit the ground in just such a way as none of them received any serious injury. The grateful Emperor ennobled Philip Fabricius, giving him the title Baron von Hohenfall ("Baron of Highfall"—look it up) before dying in 1619. Ferdinand, now Holy Roman Emperor, was deposed as King of Bohemia. The estates elected the Protestant Frederick V, Elector of the Palatinate. Ferdinand went to war to regain Bohemia. The rest of the 300 or so German states, then almost all of the rest of the European states chose sides. The Thirty Years War destroyed and depopulated most of what is now Germany and the Czech Republic as effectively as the Black Death 260 years earlier. All of that because the Regents implemented an order that violated the law and the Bohemian estates, essentially a representative assembly, decided to punish the Regents ad hoc rather than through more formal channels. Indeed, reports are that the Regents thought they were doing the right thing by admitting their guilt so they could be punished appropriately and move on to resolving the underlying issue.

Many people ignore traffic laws despite the hazards, largely because they know enforcement is haphazard. When enforcement is predictable, such as in a town with a speed trap, the law is usually only ignored by those unaware of the enforcement measures in place. So, conformity and observance may get some support from the fact that laws are enacted properly, but the coercive instruments wielded by the state have an impact. Given that drivers are sovereign individuals, they can do as they please up to the point where their actions negatively affect others, as in the earlier example of traveling in the passing lane, or they are caught by the sovereign state breaking the rules of an ordered society. Thankfully, since most drivers want to avoid arguments and accidents, doing as one pleases on the road for most people consists of following the traffic laws as best as they can under the prevailing conditions. Of course that leads to people who are pulled over complaining that it is unjust for them to be singled out. The inability of authorities to uniformly enforce every law, though, has never been considered reasonable grounds for calling a law unjust.

That said, how can a law be unjust? A law may be unjust if it is imposed by a dominant group of citizens to apply to a segment of the citizenry but not the dominant group, or is otherwise unfair. South Africa's laws instituting apartheid, Nazi Germany's Nuremberg Laws stripping Jews of their citizenship and restricting their activities, and American laws supporting slavery and racial segregation were clearly unjust. Each example identified a population within the state's boundaries and subjugated that population.

Laws prohibiting homosexual sex between consenting adults are moral in the Judeo-Christian tradition, but are clearly unjust in that they criminalize the behavior of a minority. Indeed, some have argued that the Bible approves of slavery and a great many other practices we have rejected as immoral. Yet abolitionists also cited the Bible in making their case to end slavery. This makes it all the more important in states with significant religious minorities or no dominant religion to maintain the separation of church and state when legislating and rely only on moral standards arising from natural law in the civil arena. Too often, moral standards arising from religious scripture and doctrine conflict with one another or are interpreted in more than one way. There hasn't been a supreme and universal arbiter of Christian morals since the Great Schism in 1054, and other religions are equally bereft of conclusive authorities. For example, Iran, Saudi Arabia, and ISIL are Islamic theocracies; each one insists the other two do not implement the teachings of the Quran and Hadiths correctly in applying them as sharia.

Sometimes political partisans question the justness of laws. Republicans in the USA argued the Affordable Healthcare Act with its mandate that Americans purchase health insurance is unjust. They claim it is unfair to require citizens to get something they would not get on their own initiative, particularly given that most citizens get it through their employer or the government. Proponents argued that the law merely attempts to get everyone into the health insurance system to be fair to those who have insurance and reduce the costs for everyone arising from having so many uninsured people. Unfortunately, the act was crafted to appease too many constituencies, some of whom still refused to support it, and its ability to do what proponents claim is murky at best.

The United States Supreme Court determined the issue by declaring the mandate to obtain health insurance a tax. Like them or not, taxes are just unless you are a purist libertarian. They are the price paid to the sovereign state to conduct the activities that are mandated by the social contract. Taxes are specifically noted in the US Constitution, for example. Everyone must pay one's fair share. The legislative process takes care of deciding what a fair share is and how the money will be spent.

If citizens think taxes are too onerous or dispute how taxes are used, they always have a means of voicing their concerns to change the tax rates or budget expenditures. But there is a distinction between thinking a tax is burdensome and deciding it is unjust. Considering all taxes unjust ruptures the fabric of society. It declares one is unwilling to pay the requisite contribution to the benefits everyone receives while still receiving those benefits and disputes the validity of having political representatives decide what those benefits will be. It alleges a breach of the social contract. Indeed, the deciding factor for North American British colonists in their turn away from their parent nation was a tax imposed by a government that did not include their representatives. Finding a tax unjust is a call to rebellion just as surely as the government ignoring its own laws as was the case in Bohemia.

St. Thomas Aquinas and Dr. Martin Luther King, Jr. argued that there is no obligation to obey an unjust law. This is common sense. Why should anyone be required to act unfairly or immorally? However, people do obey unjust laws all the time. Indeed, many people fear the consequences of open nonconformity so greatly they will go along with rather heinous or sacrilegious laws. This is the downside to being a citizen, a term we will discuss later. For now, a significant instance when conforming to the law is needed. The Edict of Caracalla in 212 CE, somewhat confusingly issued as the Constitutio Antoniniana or Edict of Antoninus, tried to strengthen the Empire's hold on its provinces by giving all free adults the same rights as Roman citizens. Suddenly, many more early Christians were faced with actively implementing edicts that required all Roman citizens to demonstrate their fidelity to the gods of the pantheon at least once in their lifetimes to prove they weren't atheists. To Romans monotheists were atheists.

Early Christians up to that point had not distinguished themselves from the pantheistic Romans other than to eventually start calling themselves Christians instead of Nazarenes. Prayer, festivals, and worship all were intertwined into daily, monthly, and annual activities regardless of how many gods one had. Romans, Greeks, Egyptians, Persians, Celts, and everyone other than Jews and Christians never thought about labeling their religious beliefs. There was no distinction between the sacred and profane. As Roman citizens, Christians needed to label the people who observed the pantheist rituals and came up with the term "pagan." Rendering unto Caesar was rendering unto the gods. Isis, Ceres, Demeter, Ishtar and Astarte were just different names representing different aspects of a deity everyone in the Mediterranean world knew as the Divine Mother. To the pantheists, Christians and Jews had no Divine Mother to worship, which meant they were not worshipping all aspects of divinity. Not surprisingly then, Christians at this time started to promote the Virgin Mary, Queen of Heaven, Mother of God depicted in the exact same ways as Isis nursing her child Horus.

Syncretic adoption of pantheist imagery became the hallmark of Christianity and remains so. Most people need to be reminded each year how many pagan customs they follow at Christmas, Easter, and Halloween. The one thing Christians never adopted was the pantheist interpretation of sacrifice. More than anything, sacrifice separated the pagan goats from the Christian sheep. To pantheists, sacrifices at festivals meant even the poorest believers would eat some kind of meat because the specially-bred animals once slaughtered were usually butchered and distributed. The Roman state expected all citizens to either participate in sacrificing animals in temples or at least eat some sacred cow now and then. One reason for imposing this demand was that the authorities knew that Christians worshipped in private, not publicly like respectable people. Worse yet, the central feature of Christian worship is Holy Communion, including at the time transubstantiation of bread and wine into the flesh and blood of the Son of their God. These monsters ate part of the part of God that sacrificed Himself for their salvation! That went deep into the realm of impiety and blasphemy as far as Romans were concerned.

The Romans reasonably thought that this despicable sacrilege could only be offset by Roman citizens averring their reverence of the pantheon by participating in a respectable sacrifice. This legal requirement to demonstrate one was not an atheist created a great split in the early Church. Some bishops insisted that anyone who obeyed the law could not be a Christian. These hardliners felt it was preferable to be identified as an atheist and subject to being seized and sold as a slave or executed than to bow to a human law that contravened God's laws. Others felt that their newly compassionate God, unlike the truculent YWH the Jews had to put up with, would not mind them participating in a pagan ritual just once to prove one's bona fides. Wasn't that what confession and penitence were for?

The problem came to a head in the fourth century when the Roman Empire adopted Christianity as its official religion, then didn't, then did. The flaw in the purists' train of thought was that by becoming martyrs for their version of faith their numbers dwindled rapidly when Constantine's successor reversed course, leaving the sin now, pray later crowd with a majority in the early Church.

St. Thomas and Dr. King both knew they were making themselves targets for retribution just like the hardline bishops and their followers. Noting that fact, the two philosophers decided in for a penny, in for a pound. They claimed that an unjust law is no law at all. Just as Richard III could claim that his brother's marriage was invalid and his nephews were bastards due to Henry VI's promise to marry another woman in order to bed her, Aquinas and King reasoned that immorality and injustice erase a law from the books even though it remains in the books for all to see. That is an ironic conclusion given that Henry VII did the exact same thing, erasing the Titulus Regius Act that Parliament passed in 1484 to legally sanction Richard III's ascension. The problem is that immorality and injustice overlap but they are not the same thing. As we have seen, a law may be just but have no basis in moral standards

Laws are authorized on principles other than morality. These other bases for law are as equally valid as morality. Their legality is not an issue. Indeed, all that needs to make legislation legal is its promulgation from a sovereign authority endowed by the citizens through the social contract. Apartheid, anti-Semitism, segregation, and slavery were legal in their day. People obeyed the laws creating and maintaining them because they were lawfully enacted. Indeed, these laws received substantial popular support from the citizenry, further legitimizing them. It only confuses things to say unjust laws are not laws. Nonetheless, civil disobedience was justified, as some courageously undertook, because the laws were unjust. To their credit, St. Thomas Aquinas and Dr. Martin Luther King, Jr. not only explained unjust laws but also took positive steps to disobey and challenge the unjust laws they had described. The former died shortly after suffering a head injury whilst journeying to defend his reasoning to a church council. The latter followed the path of so many others before him, martyred for a cause he felt was more important than his own life.

One of the earliest cases of civil disobedience appears in Antigone by Sophocles. Antigone's brothers are expected to share the throne of Thebes, alternating each in his turn. The first brother refuses to yield when his first tenure is up, causing the second brother to raise an army against the first brother. Both brothers are killed in the ensuing battle and their uncle, Creon, takes the throne. Antigone violates the decree of Creon that her brother who led the army against the city and was therefore a treasonous rebel shall not be buried. The protagonist breaks the law on the grounds that she has a sacred duty to bury her brother's body. Divine law trumps civil law. She is caught and punished by being walled up in a cave to starve.

The king's son, Haemon, who is betrothed to Antigone, tries to convince his father to relent and set Antigone free. Creon refuses. The king is then advised by a blind prophet that he must revoke his decrees barring the burial and walling up his niece because they have angered the gods. The prophet claims these mistakes will cost the king the life of one of his sons. Creon still refuses. The city elders plead with him to rectify his immoral actions. By then, it is too late. Haemon has gone to the cave and found that Antigone hanged herself rather than wait for death from starvation. Haemon kills himself with a knife in grief. Creon's queen is informed her son has died and kills herself.

Antigone's actions have all the hallmarks of civil disobedience. She defies an unjust, immoral law publicly and fully aware of the consequences. It is interesting that she does not premise her action on the fact that her brother who was barred from burial only took arms against the city because his right to leadership of the city was denied. His actions are not civil disobedience but rebellion. The Greeks had no political theory that justified rebellion. Instead, the loyal sister relies on the argument that duty to the gods comes before duty to the state. When Antigone is caught, she accepts the punishment laid out for breaking the law. She has not denied the legality of the law. Her act of civil disobedience brings forth supporters in the form of Haemon, the blind prophet, and Creon's councilors. Eventually, Creon recognizes his errors, but the harm has already been done. The play ends with Creon gaining wisdom from seeing the results of his unjust rule, but remaining King of Thebes. While losing a wife, son, and niece in one day is devastating, the Greeks believed killing off moral people to punish immoral people and help them find the light made some kind of sense.

Notwithstanding the Greeks' failure to find any valid reasons for rebellion, civil disobedience can be a precursor to efforts to overthrow a government that is pervasively unjust. As has been noted previously, John Locke and the Mandate of Heaven both elucidate reasons for rebellion against an unjust government founded on the notion that a government loses legitimacy when it no longer promotes the common good through its actions.

Thomas Jefferson famously made the case for the right to rebellion in the Declaration of Independence. He enumerated a long list of transgressions by King George III injurious to the welfare of the American colonists. In these cases, the question of morality does not arise; the actions of the government lack fairness and justice to the point where the exercise of rights by the citizens is infringed. Rebellion in some form becomes justified and necessary. The shape rebellion takes depends on whose rights are being infringed, the existence of alternate sources of power to challenge the sovereign government, the appearance of leaders to head the movement, the extent of popular support for change, the structures of government, geography, and many other inputs.

The result can be civil war. Civil war is violent conflict causing substantial casualties within the borders of a sovereign state between the de jure government, i.e. the people legally endowed with sovereign authority, and armed insurgents who gain de facto control of some part of the state's territory. Such has been the case in England in the 1640s, the British American colonies south of Canada and Nova Scotia in the 1770s and 80s, France and Haiti in the 1790s, Spanish America in the 1810s and 20s, Greece in the 1820s, China in the 1850s and 60s, the United States in the 1860s, Mexico and Russia in the 1910s, Spain in the 1930s, China in the 1920s through 1940s, Cuba in the 1950s, Sudan in the 1950s to 2000s, Nicaragua, Nigeria, and Pakistan in the 1970s, Lebanon in the 1970s and 80s, Afghanistan in the 1980s, Russia, Moldova, Rwanda, and Yugoslavia in the 1990s, Serbia in the 2000s, and Iraq, Libya, Nigeria, and Syria in the 2010s. This is a partial list.

Approximately 70 civil wars have occurred since the end of World War II, involving more than one-third of the states in existence. Many of those states were created when colonialism ended in the 1940s through 1970s. In the cases where civil war erupted in newly independent countries the primary cause was the sudden absence of the colonial sovereign replaced by a rather impromptu government that had not acquired the consent of the governed but rather was handed the reins of sovereign power. There had been no development of an indigenous state apparatus either. The legitimacy of the new sovereign was weak. Factions based on ethnicity or ideology claimed to represent the popular will better than the new government. With no democratic traditions to sort things out, the claimants used violence to confront the post-colonial authorities.

Civil war seeks not only a change of government but also a change in the terms of the social contract. Oftentimes, the rebels are based in a part of the state's territory because only the people in that region believe their rights are being endangered by the national government. They have historical claims to an identity separate from the majority of the country's population. They use armed conflict to secede from the state to form their own sovereign polity. Such was the case in the British North American colonies that became the United States, Haiti, Spanish America, Sudan, Nigeria, Pakistan, Russia in the 1990s, Moldova, Yugoslavia, Serbia, Syria, and Iraq. If successful, the rebels create their own sovereign state with a constitution laying out the framework of a new government. It is in this moment that the social contract becomes an observable phenomenon. The best known example is the formation of the United States, first under the Articles of Confederation and then, when that agreement was deemed ineffective, the Constitution.

When secession isn't sought in civil war, as occurred in England, France, Mexico, Russia in the 1910s, China, Spain, Lebanon, Afghanistan, and most of the post-colonial civil wars, the rebels still want to replace the foundational rules that endow the sovereign with its authority. They seek a new constitutional order. Success in changing the constitutional order through rebellion is called revolution. All non-secession based civil wars that end in the rebels winning are revolutions. Some rebellions lead to a change in the constitutional order but do not result in civil war or even significant bloodshed; they are still revolutions. Significant instances of revolution without civil war (or at least significant military engagements) include England in 1688, France in 1830, 1848, and 1871, Japan in 1868, China in 1912, Russia in 1917 (twice), Thailand in 1932, Iran in 1979, the Philippines in 1986, Eastern Europe in 1989, and the Soviet Union in 1991.

Theories of revolution are a complex field of study due to the multiple factors that give rise to revolution and the attempts of almost all theorists to explain the civil wars that sometimes accompany revolutions as part of the revolution rather than distinguishing between the two events. The trouble with that approach is it leaves the cases of revolution without civil war as outliers. Fortunately, every theory implicitly or explicitly sees revolution as a change in the social contract arising from rebellion against the sovereign by citizens. And that is sufficient. In an environment where only the rare individualist lives outside society, our only hope of seeing the social contract put into place is in those circumstances where the contract has been broken and a new one must be formulated. As we have seen, this occurs in cases of secession. It also happens in cases of revolution. That is what makes revolutions so interesting.

A somewhat less interesting type of change in government is the coup d'état. Coups occur when a group of elites force out the leaders of the state but maintain pretty much all of the governmental structures and processes. Think of it as an amendment to the social contract achieved by violence or the threat of violence. The constitution may be suspended and the new leaders may stay in power for a long time, but there is no further effort to change the social contract. Coups occur because the government is corrupt or inept, too democratic for the liking of the elites, or someone is hungry for power. It is up to the coup leaders to establish they will govern justly, albeit with their own maintenance of power always in the forefront. If not, another coup or a rebellion is likely.

Some countries become known for the relative frequency of their coups, such as Afghanistan, Bolivia, Haiti, Mauritania, Nigeria, and Thailand. Of course, saying Mauritania is known is a stretch. Others go through periods of political instability with many coups in one or two decades, such as China in the 1910s and 20s, Syria in the 1950s and 60s, South Vietnam in the 1960s, Ghana from 1966 to 1981, Bangladesh and Uganda in the 1970s and 80s, Burkina Faso in the 1980s, and Sierra Leone in the 1990s.

Interestingly for the prospects of democracy, coups have been falling out of favor and many military leaders that established governments by coup have turned over the selection of leaders to the citizens since the 1980s and not intervened since. Thailand is an interesting exception, where the middle class and elites of Bangkok and the south have benefited from military coups. The target of their ire is a populist party that has a very wealthy but corrupt leader who, even in exile, managed his party to victory with the help of the working class and rural north, the people who have benefited the most from his policies.

Coups even occur without a change in leadership, when a constitutionally elected head of government decides to suspend the constitution and rule by fiat. These self-coups have occurred under Charles Louis Napoleon Bonaparte in France, Benito Mussolini in Italy, Adolf Hitler in Germany, Mohammad Reza Pahlavi in Iran, Indira Gandhi in India, Ferdinand Marcos in the Philippines, Alberto Fujimori in Peru, and Pervez Musharraf in Pakistan, to name a few. Actually, there haven't been many self-coups in the last two centuries. The count is just over 100, which is not much given the number of times states have changed governments. This rarity demonstrates the stability of constitutional structures and the loyalty of legally installed leaders to those structures. The social contract is sturdy.

Chapter 8—Constitutions

EVIDENCE FOR THE social contract is found in the constitution that every country in the world has. We have mentioned constitutions quite a bit but need to explore what they are. Essentially they are the blueprint for constructing a national government. James Madison, architect of the US Constitution, thought that was sufficient. He and others convinced the delegates to the Constitutional Convention. However, Madison and his allies were not as persuasive once the document was completed. One of the deciding factors in getting enough state ratifying conventions to accept the Constitution of the United States of America was a push beginning in Massachusetts by Elbridge Gerry (of gerrymandering fame) to agree only if amendments were proposed to clarify what rights the people and states retained. The authors of the Constitution assumed everyone knew what their rights were, thought they were well established in state constitutions, argued the federal government's powers were enumerated clearly enough to bar attempts to reach for more, and hesitated to create a list that might not be complete. Regardless, the citizens of the new nation and their representatives in the ratifying conventions thought it best if they were spelled out.

The matter became so important that Madison promised in his campaign for a seat in the House of Representatives from Virginia that this would be his first order of business if elected. If nothing else, the demand for a bill of rights serves to underline the contractual nature of a constitution. Written contracts are meant to contain the entire agreement between the parties with no assumptions left unspecified. Historians and political scientists have agreed, finding the absence of a bill of rights in the original draft of the Constitution the convention's one serious error.

Contracts have a lengthy history going back to the origins of society or even further. A contract is an agreement. It takes a minimum of two people to form an agreement, despite some evidence that our subconscious minds continually agree or disagree with our conscious minds. A contractual agreement is a mutual exchange of promises. At its simplest, one person gives something of value in exchange for a good or service the other person has, with both agreeing that the good or service has the same value as the something. They both promise to trade with one another. This situation can balloon up very quickly if the number of parties or promises increases or if time becomes a factor in the agreement. Nonetheless, humans have been agreeing to exchanges with each other for so long, in so many circumstances, that making a contract is as natural as eating or breathing. We do it every time we purchase a fast food meal, which is far too often.

A common contract is one that establishes a business. With all the bells and whistles, this sort of agreement can be quite complex. Lawyers trained to write contracts are hired. Many moving parts mean more discussion, more decisions, and more deals. But the result remains the same, an agreement between parties to exchange promises. Businesses can take many forms, but they are all creatures of the law. They can employ thousands of workers, have dozens of offices, and produce millions of profits, but they are all words on a page conforming to rules established by people. Unlike humans, who cannot be redefined or lose their natural rights, businesses are only what we say they are and only have the powers we say they have.

The same is true for states. The state is a creature of the

body politic called into existence with words. That existence derives from the impetus to order and safeguard society, to nurture and spread prosperity, and to preserve and defend the polity of the citizens that made it. The state is also a tool to accomplish certain tasks powered by the contributions of all who benefit from the completion of those tasks. Whether a creature or tool, the state owes its being to the agreement of its makers. For many centuries, states evolved organically; little effort was made to write down these agreements. Everyone knew who the ruler was and who the subjects were. If a new polity was set up, the new ruler would be quick to advertise that fact and defend the territory and people of the polity.

The first true written agreement establishing a polity was the Constitution of Medina, written by the Prophet Muhammad after the Hijra in 622 and agreed upon with the leaders of the families of Medina. The Constitution sets out rules for governance, taxation, and courts, methods to decrease intertribal violence, protect religious freedoms, and improve personal safety, and terms for dealing with other polities. It is clearly and consciously a social contract creating the *ummah* or community of Islam for the first time.

Hywel was king of Wales in the 940s when he called a council to review existing laws on government and codify them in a single document. Henry I of England issued a Charter of Liberties in 1100 that limned his relationships with the clergy and nobility. Then in 1215 the barons of England demanded that King John sign the Great Charter (or Magna Carta), setting forth their rights in relation to the state and eliminating the arbitrary use of sovereign power by the monarch. The idea that a constitution can limit government was born.

Just seven years later, the Hungarian nobility made the same demands and more on King Andrew I through the Golden Bull of 1222. In the interim, Saint Slava devised a constitution called the *Zakonopravilo* in 1219 to regulate the Kingdom of Serbia and establish its relationship to an independent Serbian

Orthodox Church. Also, in 1220, Eike von Repgow began his fifteen-year project of reducing to writing, first into Latin and then into Low German, Holy Roman imperial law in the *Sachsenspiegel* (Mirror of Saxony), which codified among other things, feudal rights, including how the emperor was elected. This document was amended by the Golden Bull of 1356. Other written constitutions popped up in Ethiopia around 1240, Catalonia in 1283, China in 1375, Sardinia in 1392, San Marino in 1600, England in 1655, Corsica in 1755, and Sweden in 1772. Considering how many sovereign states existed throughout those centuries and how often dynasties rose and fell or governments changed dramatically, that ain't many. The scarcity of written constitutions well into the modern age is testament to the conservative nature of societies.

That all changed in 1776 when the United States of America declared independence. The members of the Continental Congress knew full well they were embarking on a great experiment. They were consciously creating a sovereign state. The fact that the members of that congress represented thirteen distinct colonies, each with its own government, was not lost upon them. Independence meant that each of the several colonies became a sovereign state in its own right. Those sovereign states were working in concert to cast off their common British master. The states agreed with each other to wage a war of independence directed by the Congress. They also agreed to work together on matters best not left to go in thirteen directions.

Within days of declaring independence, the Continental Congress drafted the Articles of Confederation. Then they sat on them for over a year, finally adopting the Articles on November 15, 1777. The Articles would not become operational until every state ratified them. All but three states did so by July 1778. The other three saw no urgency in forming a national government. Two caved. Finally, Maryland ratified the Articles on March 1, 1781, making it unanimous.

The first Article of Confederation names the nation "the United States of America." The second Article states: "Each state retains its sovereignty, freedom, and independence, and every Power, Jurisdiction, and right, which is not by this confederation expressly delegated to the United States, in Congress assembled." No clearer enunciation of a social contract can be made.

However, as the citizens and governments of the states soon discovered, they had not given their federal state sufficient authority to be equal to the sovereign states of Europe. In casting off the shackles of oppression, they had gone too far and created a weak substitute for the British monarch acting through parliament. Each state and the citizens therein retained too much sovereignty to make the United States a plausible actor on the international stage or as a worthy director of the interplay among the states. So, just under six years after they went into force, on February 21, 1787, the United States Congress decided to call a convention to revise the Articles of Confederation. Experiments do not necessarily go right the first time round.

The delegates to the Constitutional Convention set two precedents of enormous consequence. They chose to work in private and they decided they had the authority to shelve the Articles of Confederation entirely and come up with something completely new. As for the first, one would think that the people's business should be open for all to see. Indeed, a lot of effort has gone into passing Sunshine and Freedom of Information laws in the United States aimed at making the workings of government more transparent. Executive inaction, the demise of journalistic integrity, and equating money with speech has eviscerated these laws. Nonetheless, the goal usually is for the public's business to be conducted in public. However, as then is now, it is best to open Pandora's Box in a confined setting. This is where the second surprise comes in.

From the start, leading delegates had in mind that they

would propose starting anew in building a federal political structure. They would not get very far if everyone on the outside started debating the wisdom of casting off what they had for some unknown creation. Discussion would focus on how to fancy up the Articles of Confederation when a whole new wardrobe was needed. In order to have everyone think outside the box, they had to close the doors. Time would tell if they had done the right thing. Even if they could reach consensus on a new document, they would still have to convince those thirteen sovereign states and the citizens they represented. It was a bold step, but probably necessary.

Therein lays one of the paradoxes of democracy. Sometimes the greater good can only be accomplished if the people's delegates are sequestered to avoid the world intruding on their work. It is a matter of routine with juries and no one quibbles about that. Unfortunately, politicians have done such a fine job of making themselves untrustworthy, no one likes the idea of them making decisions *in camera*.

Ever since the United States worked out its Constitution, states have found the wisdom in codifying their foundational rules. It does make things easier. A constitution is no different than any other agreement to form a business; a state differs little from a business with one significant exception. The parties to business contracts never endow their creations with sovereignty. Businesses can never do as they please. They have no life. They are animated solely by the laws that permit their creation and the documents that describe their purpose and structure.

States, however, are provided sovereignty from the citizens who form them. Sovereignty animates states. They are equal players with every other state, having much the same range of action in international affairs as sovereign human beings have in dealing with one another. Businesses do not have this luxury. Yes, they can interact with other businesses, with humans, and with states. However, every action they take is governed one hundred percent by some combination of contractual clauses, legislative laws, policy protocols, regulatory rules or judicial judgments. No matter how minimally society supervises businesses, they must always refer to some superior authority to do anything. They are like computers restricted to doing only what their programming permits. States and humans always have unfettered freedom to exercise their sovereign wills with the awareness that all actions have consequences.

The state acts using the structures of government. In the modern era, government has usually been laid out in the same constitution that formally creates the state. All but five countries have single documents to view that provide the world with knowledge of what the state is and how it is governed. The hold-outs are Canada, Israel, New Zealand, Saudi Arabia, and the United Kingdom. The U.K. famously has an "unwritten" constitution that consists of all the acts of Parliament, the laws set down by monarchs that haven't been changed by Parliament, and the common law as determined over the centuries in decisions by the courts. There has been no question that Parliament acts on behalf of the Crown and is sovereign since 1688-89 when noble leaders of that body invited a Dutch invasion to rid the country of James II and set forth a Bill of Rights in what became known as the Glorious Revolution.

Canada and New Zealand have Constitution Acts passed by their respective legislatures, but these only give directions for where to look for the rules establishing the state and government. Otherwise, they follow in the footsteps of their parent state, the U.K. Israel's declaration of independence set a deadline for writing a constitution, but the war that erupted when Israel declared its independence put the kibosh on that. Israel's parliament, the Knesset, is sovereign and has issued a number of Basic Laws that serve as the bones of a constitution. King Fahd of Saudi Arabia decreed a Basic Law of Governance in 1992 that begins by saying "God's Book and the Sunnah of His Prophet" are the constitution of the state. The Basic Law goes on to set out the structures and principles of the government.

The fact that the King of Saudi Arabia decreed what the constitution of the state is makes abundantly clear that he is the sovereign and the Kingdom is not a democracy in any way, shape, or form. Going back to the Constitutional Convention convened by the United States, we have almost the exact opposite. The delegates to the Convention were individuals who represented the states making up the United States. Each voted within his delegation and the majority within the delegation decided how the state would vote on any matter before the Convention.

Since the Convention met in private, no one knows how individual delegates voted. James Madison recorded what happened in the Convention. However, he was concerned with how various measures were getting along, so the state votes mattered to him, not the votes of each delegate. This was probably a good thing, since he focused on the consensus built rather than the squabbles diverting attention from the grand project. The delegates were present because they had been chosen by the legislatures of the states to represent the states, whose degree of sovereignty was immediately at issue in the discussions. The citizens of the states had been represented by the members of the legislatures that chose the delegates. In this way, democracy was served, albeit twice removed.

Interestingly, the delegates were not too concerned about the sovereign rights of the citizens of the states they represented. This is a quirk springing from the federal nature of the state whose government was being redesigned. Typically, the delegates to a constitutional convention are chosen much as representatives are elected to legislatures. They represent the citizens who are agreeing to form a state and government or revise the terms of a previous agreement. The citizens have given up something very important, a part of their sovereignty, and they will want to insure that their pooled sovereignty is used in their best interests. But when the delegates to the United States Constitutional Convention were chosen, it was more like sending ambassadors to a treaty negotiation. Every state had its own identity and guarded its sovereignty and the rights that flowed from having that sovereignty.

The mission of the delegates was to avoid surrendering too much more of that state sovereignty than had already been given under the Articles of Confederation, but surrendering enough so the problems that manifested themselves under the Articles could be mitigated. They wanted a stronger federal state, but not too strong. In any case, citizens of the states would not be called upon to give up more of their sovereignty to make the United States work. Despite the fact that the states negotiated and approved the final document in the Convention, the fact that the new national government was a contract entered by all citizens was made clear by the opening three words: We the People.

The trouble is that when setting an agreement in parchment one hopes will be well preserved, the parties must be careful to include all aspects of the arrangement in the terms. What became apparent toward the end of writing the Constitution was that not much had been done to address the relationship between the federal state and the citizens of the thirteen states. Part of the problem lay in the view that citizens identified with their state, not some fledgling nation. Indeed, although there are a few references to citizens in this briefest of all constitutions in terms of who qualifies for federal office, it doesn't even define what a citizen is.

The federal government was empowered to naturalize immigrants and that was it. Finally, in 1868, the Fourteenth Amendment to the US Constitution recognized that anyone born in the United States or who became naturalized is both a citizen of the United States and of the state in which the person resides. The importance of addressing who is and is not a citizen will be dealt with in the next chapter. Suffice it to say little was considered regarding the impact of the new federal government on the lives of the people. Yet, the drafters of the constitution were creating a stronger national government that would be touching the lives of everyone.

People tend to think of national governments as many-eyed, multi-limbed, overweight leviathans. They prefer it if their government stays at a distance. A Russian proverb states "God is high above and the tsar is far away." What use is it to workers in the fields to worry about national policies that do not help bring in the harvest or otherwise affect their day-to-day lives? Aside from paying taxes, their only interaction with the Russian state might be the obligation to carry official documents from one point to another in relay if they lived near a post road. The tsar certainly wasn't going to pay for postage with so many serfs about.

But the popular sentiment was right. Russia, as early as the eighteenth century, was a police state producing reams of orders, reports, and inquiries. Despite not having enough personnel to really follow up on anything, the tsar's government tried its best to be every bit as observant as the National Security Administration of the United States was shown to be by Edward Snowden. It helped that there was little need in Russia, even up to the Bolshevik takeover in 1917, to spy on residents of the vast countryside. The focus was primarily on those urban and urbane intellectuals who either had gone abroad for some reason or kept up with foreign ideas. Mother Russia did not need outsiders telling her children what to think.

The Chinese empire, on the other hand, instituted a sort of neighborhood watch policy guided by local elders to police villages and city blocks. The actual government itself only went down to the county magistrate level and there could easily be 10,000 households in a county. Along these terms, it is quite easy for most people to go on with their lives never worrying about the heavy hand of government infringing on what they were doing. Come to think of it, they weren't doing much other than trying to survive.

The United States in 1787 only had four million residents,

but they were divided into thirteen states that had towns, cities, and counties, each with their own governing authorities. In 1776, their Continental Congress had made quite a big deal over the onerous burdens placed on the colonists and the essential liberties ignored by their far off monarch. The Declaration of Independence is a petition of redress listing many grievances, but instead of asking the government to do anything about those issues, the Congress used the document to assert its own remedy. Congress determined that the United States would take care of the issues provided King George III backed off. It helped that active rebellion had already begun the year before. Eleven years later at the Constitutional Convention in Philadelphia, the last thing anyone wanted was to establish a new government that could be just as annoying if the opportunity arose. The rights of the people needed to be spelled out.

As was mentioned earlier, James Madison promised that one of the first things on the agenda of the new federal legislature would be amendments to the Constitution to do just that. He delivered on his promise, submitting 39 amendments to the first federal congress, 12 of which were approved by Congress, and 10 of which were ratified by the states quite quickly. One of the twelve left out eventually snuck in almost 203 years later. Before marveling at a politician keeping a campaign promise, it should be noted that Madison feared that if he did not try to control the amendment process, those opposed to the Constitution might succeed in calling a second constitutional convention. He set aside his feelings that a bill of rights was just words on the page and every man knew well enough to assert his rights when necessary. Of course, the idea that women were human beings endowed with the same natural rights as men escaped his notice.

The enumerated rights in those first ten amendments are not extraordinary. In fact, it is a rather short and conservative list lifted from ideas going back to the Magna Carta. The last two, the Ninth and Tenth Amendments, are really a belt and suspenders way of overcoming the fears of those that thought a list of rights would be interpreted to be exhaustive or the source of those rights. The Ninth Amendment says the listed rights in the Constitution do not include every right, are not more important than those left off, and do not void the missing. The Tenth Amendment says the listed powers and prohibitions in the Constitution are complete and any other powers remain to be exercised by the states or the citizens.

This all presumes that the citizens are sovereign individuals who can do as they please except when they agree to restrict their range of action through the social contract, the states are sovereign polities created by those citizens through the social contract that are endowed with certain rights and powers, and those states gave up some of the sovereignty and powers they got from the citizens to create a superior sovereign state with certain powers best wielded by a coordinating authority. The national state has no rights vis-à-vis the states and citizens, having been given none. It was brought into being explicitly to serve the people. The only rights it has are those recognized in international law to conduct relations with other sovereign, national states.

Madison was correct to be concerned that a bill of rights would be interpreted as all-inclusive and make people focus on the words used rather than the principles represented. The United States Supreme Court waited until sexual relations became a topic before it tapped into the Ninth Amendment. Even then, the right of privacy it found protected appeared in the "penumbras" of enumerated rights. Many people thought the robed geezers were making things up. No one was, or to this day is, willing to enunciate what unwritten rights are retained by citizens of the USA. Tea Party extremists, for all their much ballyhooed embrace of liberties, aren't very creative when it comes to promoting these reserved rights. That begs the question whether any rights were left out that citizens enjoyed.

A good source would be the Universal Declaration of

Human Rights. Not only does it cover all of the rights set out in the Constitution, it also recognizes the right to representative democracy through free elections, the rights to education, employment and movement, the right to having basic needs met, the right to marry, the right to own property, and rights to enjoy leisure, culture, arts, and sciences. It is a compendium of the rights human beings can claim as their own whether a constitution mentions them specifically or not. Article 29 states:

> Everyone has duties to the community in which alone the free and full development of his personality is possible.
>
> In the exercise of his rights and freedoms, everyone shall be subject only to such limitations as are determined by law solely for the purpose of securing due recognition and respect for the rights and freedoms of others and of meeting the just requirements of morality, public order and the general welfare in a democratic society.

That second bit is the most lucid and thorough statement of the relationship of sovereign individuals to society imaginable in the English language. At its root, everything springs from the complete sovereignty originally held by individual human beings, the exchange of some of that sovereignty for the promises of order, protection, and prosperity through the social contract, and the individual accepting responsibility for participating in society in order to become the person the individual is meant to be. That is the foundation for all human communities. The next steps are to define who the members of a community are, how non-members are treated, and what rules are made to determine who can do what.

Chapter 9—Citizenship and Equality

ONLY FULL CITIZENS are parties to the social contract. Since not all residents of a state are full citizens, not everyone in a country has consented to be governed under the constitution established by the social contract. There are several different groups to which this applies. Minors who meet other qualifications become citizens upon reaching adulthood. Immigrants become citizens through the legal process of naturalization. Entire groups become citizens as a result of changes to the social contract. Former male slaves became citizens of the United States with the ratification of the Fourteenth Amendment to the United States Constitution and women moved up from economy to first class citizenship with the ratification of the Nineteenth Amendment. Annexation of a territory, although rare it just happened in Crimea, changes the citizenship of the population residing in that territory. Also rare is people stripped of their citizenship, but this did occur to the Jewish population of Germany under the Nuremberg Laws. And groups of people within a defined territory can change their citizenship through a successful effort at secession. Generally speaking, however, the citizen rolls remain fairly constant, as do the categories of people who are not citizens.

To form the social contract, sovereign individuals consent along with other sovereign individuals in a defined geographical territory to relinquish a certain portion of their sovereignty to a sovereign state created by a constitution that will make rules for the governance, safety, and welfare of the inhabitants of that territory. The sovereign individuals become citizens of the new sovereign state. If, on the other hand, the sovereign individuals grant all of their sovereignty to the state, they become subjects of the state. Thomas Hobbes, looking squarely at the English model of absolute sovereignty vested in either the king or parliament, thought this always was the case. To be fair, midway through the seventeenth century Hobbes could canvass the seven seas and the four corners of the world and have great difficulty finding citizens rather than subjects except in Switzerland, a few northern Italian republics, and tribal societies. By then, unfortunately, even most of the First Nations of the Americas had all been made subjects of one European monarch or another on paper at least.

Some libertarians argue that since the United States Constitution starts off with "We the People" and only cites "citizen" without defining it in reference to the requirements for holding federal office and the power to make naturalized citizens, the rebellious British subjects became citizens of their states once King George III was off their backs but not citizens of the United States of America. Then they take issue with how the Fourteenth Amendment to the US Constitution, which defines who is a citizen of the USA, was ratified by former Confederate states as a condition of being accepted back into the Union to further question the constitutionality of such a creature as an American citizen. All of that to argue Americans remain sovereign individuals.

This refers to the idea that there is no social contract to which libertarians have pledged a portion of their sovereignty to the national state. It ignores the fact that the citizens of the original thirteen sovereign states through their duly elected legislatures sent delegates to a Constitutional Convention held in Philadelphia in 1787 that created a sovereign nation just as all other sovereign nations are created through an agreement that hands over part of the citizens' sovereignty to empower the new polity. In this case, that sovereignty had been given to each of the thirteen states and some of that was now passed along to the national state. The citizens of the thirteen states made themselves dual citizens by adding national citizenship as a result of that process, a fact that is clearly, if belatedly, stated in the Fourteenth Amendment. Nothing points to the uses of "citizen" in the Constitution or Bill of Rights as meaning anything other than citizens of the nation, since every instance involves federal offices, powers, or limits. Then, Congress passed a naturalization bill in 1790 to accommodate new immigrants who wanted to become citizens of the United States, not citizens of a state. Finally, the Fourteenth Amendment opened the door to apply the freedoms set out in the Bill of Rights to actions of the individual states.

The libertarian position is unusual and arises from the federative nature of the USA and ambiguous failure to define citizenship in the US Constitution. All states take citizenship seriously. A sovereign state, particularly a democratic one, means nothing without a loyal populace involved enough in civic affairs to express popular will. Otherwise, the state becomes disconnected from the individuals whose sovereignty created it. Even the most repressive, autocratic governments have adhered to the wishes of some segment of the citizenry and oftentimes have engaged in elaborate efforts to promote loyalty and support for the regime. On the other hand, leaders and factions have just as often used non-citizen groups as targets for blame when conditions worsen. Such has been the case with people entering the USA without the required documents or overstaying their visas.

A citizen is a sovereign individual resident of the territory of a sovereign state who enjoys all of the rights and responsibilities of citizenship under the constitution of the state and expresses allegiance to that state by using those rights and undertaking those responsibilities. Citizenship generally entails the rights to participate in public life, to equal protection under and application of all laws compared to other citizens, to choose representatives to and officers of the state if it is any form of democracy, to serve on juries or otherwise join in the application and enforcement of laws, to own real property, and to obtain a passport that allows re-entry to the country if the citizen leave its borders. Citizens have the right to hold public office if they meet age qualifications. They also have the right to exercise the sovereignty they have not given up under the social contract, which is any authority not given the state through the constitution. Citizenship also comes with the responsibility to pay taxes established by agreed processes, to observe the laws and regulations adopted to order society, to be knowledgeable enough to participate in public life, to make contributions to society to the extent allowed by ability and means, and to act loyally toward the state or, from the negative side, to not commit treason.

Enjoying these rights and undertaking these responsibilities reaffirm the conditions of the social contract. Citizens, being sovereign individuals, can ignore these rights and responsibilities and do as they please. In fact, citizens sometimes go out of their way to avoid some of their rights and responsibilities such as jury duty and paying taxes. This prompts governments to impose penalties for failing to fulfill these aspects of citizenship. As noted earlier, some countries even have passed laws requiring citizens to vote in elections precisely because citizens ignore that responsibility.

Fortunately, everyone at some time or another must take action that demonstrates consent, however grudging, to membership in society. Submitting to the requirements to obtain a driver's license or paying sales taxes qualifies. Some may say no one has much choice in these matters. That is untrue. Anyone can refuse to obtain a driver's license or refuse to pay the sales tax on even a lollipop. It does not mean he will get his way. The dissenter will face substantial hurdles without a license, as voter ID laws intend, aside from breaking the law if the dissenter chooses to operate a motor vehicle. Most vendors will deny service to anyone who refuses to pay sales tax since the vendor not the customer is liable.

Business owners agree to serve as the state's agent in collecting sales tax as part of the process registering their businesses. Pretty much any business save "individual's name dba business name" requires registration. People learned long ago that they needed to protect their personal assets from seizure to satisfy a claim brought by customers, vendors, or others they do business with. One tragic accident can wipe out a person if she is not protected by law from personal liability for incidents that occur at her place of business. To protect business owners, states enacted laws describing fictional creatures that go by abbreviations and acronyms like LLP, Co., LC, or Inc. The odd thing is that many larger businesses have no problem benefiting from these laws and doing odd jobs for the government like collecting sales tax, but do everything they can to avoid paying taxes on their revenues. Some have gone so far as to arrange for companies established outside the USA to "buy" them so the company on paper is not a USA company subject to USA taxes. Then they use the money they have saved in taxes to fund Super PACs and otherwise influence elections. As far as being good citizens, they ain't.

Human citizens who are deeply unsatisfied and have the means can emigrate elsewhere. However, such people remain citizens of their home country unless and until they go through the process of naturalization in their new home country and renounce their old citizenship. Naturally there are many people who live in countries legally but retain their citizenship in another country. The USA and Eritrea are the only countries in the world that insist all citizens wherever they permanently reside must file an income tax return annually. Income Americans receive while permanently residing in another country is not taxed, but the government still wants to know how much that income was.

The federal government recently made it much more difficult for expatriate citizens to live overseas. A new law severely penalizes any bank with business in the USA for not reporting data relating to its USA customers' accounts. The penalties for noncompliance, which given the terms of the law could easily happen by accident, are so severe that banks have stopped allowing American citizens living abroad from setting up accounts or keeping existing accounts. As a result, American expats started renouncing their citizenship solely to be able to continue to have a bank account. The government, rather than seeing the problem and trying to fix it, quadrupled the fees for renouncing one's citizenship. It now seems easier to free oneself from mob ties than to free oneself from Uncle Sam's grasp.

Émigrés and expats renouncing their citizenship still will have to agree to a social contract wherever they live. Given the pervasiveness of modern states, the parts of Antarctica not under the jurisdiction of parties to the Antarctic Treaty and the open oceans are the only places on Earth where one can go to avoid having to be part of a social contract. Even then, it would be impossible for a human being to live in solitude in those locations, although having to do so unintentionally on Mars or a remote island have made good stories. A solitary human being needs help to survive and that requires an agreement to interact and order ones' affairs with other human beings. Even the simplest arrangements of human community echo the social contract. Indeed, there is a reason why the most common form of social interaction is called a marriage contract. That is why social contract theory is so vigorous. It is replicated in so many ways at so many levels in societies.

The United States and Canada are the only countries in the world that unconditionally grant citizenship to anyone born within their territories, otherwise known as *jus soli*. Another 30 countries, mostly in the Western Hemisphere, automatically grant citizenship *jus soli* to anyone born in their territories to a mother legally in the country. *Jus sanguinis*, which is the precept applied everywhere else, grants citizenship to persons with at least one parent who is a citizen of the state. Naturally, *jus soli* jurisdictions also recognize *jus sanguinis*. Adults may change their country of residence and take the path of naturalization, whereby they satisfy whatever requirements are established by the sovereign state to demonstrate they understand the social contract accepted by natural born citizens. Speaking of which, the Constitution specifies that the President and ergo the Vice President must be natural born citizens (and, unlike royal succession rules, does not prohibit bastards from filling those offices). No one doubts that *jus soli* citizens are natural born. Even Senator John McCain's birth in the Panama Canal Zone gave him *jus soli* citizenship. The problem is that no court has ever had to rule whether *jus sanguinis* citizens are and if so, whether that is automatic or subject to following regulations governing documenting births outside the USA to American citizens. That question over Senator Ted Cruz's qualifications was something, regrettably, that was not resolved.

Marriage in almost all cultures is monogamous. Citizenship follows the same pattern to a certain extent. Sovereign individuals may swear allegiance to more than one sovereign state and thus become dual citizens unless one state requires renunciation of other citizenship. Almost all countries require renunciation of former citizenship as part of the naturalization process, which makes sense given the individual is making a choice to start fresh in a new country. Therefore, dual citizenship is primarily the result of someone having claims to citizenship in more than one state due to both birthplace and blood or parents with two different citizenships. Only a minority of countries permit dual citizenship, mostly in the Western Hemisphere where in-migration was a deciding factor in the growth and prosperity of nations and many European countries where out-migration flowed to the New World. Some countries do not recognize renunciation of their citizenship at all or only recognize renunciation under specified circumstances even while prohibiting dual citizenship. The War of 1812 began, in part, due to the United Kingdom's impressment of men into its navy who had become naturalized citizens of the United States but continued to be claimed by the United Kingdom as citizens of its own.

A citizen of the United States or Nigeria may renounce his or her citizenship without having another citizenship in place, leaving the person stateless. Other countries do not allow their citizens to renounce their citizenship or only permit it if they have lined up a new state in which to be a citizen. Entire groups of people in some countries are stateless because national law does not recognize them as citizens, such as Bedouin people in some Arab states and non-Malay people in Brunei. The Romani or gypsies were stateless for centuries due to their peregrinations throughout Europe, although some countries had official policies aimed at settling and absorbing them. Palestinians living in the West Bank and Gaza have no state recognized by the entire international community, although some countries recognize Palestine. The residents of Western Sahara and Northern Cyprus are stateless due to their residence in territories claiming to be sovereign states but are not recognized. Many people were temporarily stateless when the Soviet Union and Yugoslavia disintegrated but soon became citizens of the resulting new states.

Statelessness is a concern in international affairs since it means legally no country can protect the person, leaving the person to the whims of whatever country he or she ends up in. Accordingly, two international conventions have been written to guide governments in helping to make statelessness difficult to acquire or keep. The Office of the United Nations High Commissioner on Refugees keeps tabs on the estimated 10 million stateless persons in the world and works to reduce statelessness. Unfortunately, neither convention has been ratified by more than half the states in the world, indicating it is not a pressing concern in domestic policy. Why should it? A stateless person cannot be a citizen and therefore makes no demands on the governments in the countries in which they reside that really need to be addressed. The resources they consume are negligible in the scheme of things. They are not partners in the social contract. A man could live in Charles de Gaulle Airport in France for 18 years without a home to go to but with a dream his story would someday be the idea for a film starring Tom Hanks.

The concept of citizenship has been around at least since the days of ancient Athenian democracy. One of the interesting characteristics about Athenian citizenship was the expectation that every citizen would participate in politics. That is not to say that everyone then was more involved than people now. Indeed, a term used for those who did not participate became the modern word "idiot." Recent political discourse sometimes suggests that word is coming to mean the opposite of its ancient Greek meaning.

Although the laws changed, a citizen basically was any male born in Athens who had reached the age of 20, had an Athenian father, and had completed military training. This ruled out women, children, and foreigners, including slaves. Evidence points to the cheapness of holding barbarian slaves as a reason democracy took off. This, coupled with the treatment of women, including wives, almost as property, freed even the poorer male native inhabitants from enough work to pay attention to public affairs. Not that the men wanted to use their free time in politics. Some effort, for a time, was put into herding men from the agora to the assembly on the days the assembly met to conduct the city's business. After a hundred years, citizens were paid to attend the assembly, which made it so popular citizens had to be turned away from participating. With Athenian men hanging out in town while their wives and slaves worked together all day, one wonders if anyone ever questioned whether their wives were actually bearing children who fully qualified to be the next generation of citizens.

Because sovereignty was vested in the citizenry or *demos*, the assembly was the supreme authority in the city-state. The majority that approved any decision made by the assembly could do no wrong, unlike a king, such as in Thebes, who being a fallible individual could transgress divine law. No, the assembly weighed the facts and chose correctly every time. If a poor decision was made, such as going to war with Sparta or condemning Socrates, it was not the fault of the *demos*. Rather, the people must have been misled by those who presented the facts. This fiction was maintained because admitting errors in judgment would cast the entire political system into question.

Why on earth would anyone look upon this as a model for government? Three-quarters of the population had no say and were treated as chattel or unworthy aliens. It is unlikely participants in the assembly could tell much of what was going on to vote intelligently when a quorum was 6000. Matters of state had to wait until an assembly was called, which was about once every ten days. The testimony from writers of the day, most famously Plato, is that the poorer citizens held a monopoly on vote outcomes as they made up the most members of the citizenry. Plato echoed Churchill in claiming the voters were not terribly well informed, educated, or principled. Those voters demonstrated these characteristics by approving quite a high number of items on their agendas that turned out badly for the city. If this sounds a lot like the poorly educated supporters Donald Trump proudly and happily calls his own, *plus ça change, plus c'est la même chose*.

The only positive attribute of Athenian democracy not gainsaid by the record is the relative number of people involved in the political life of the city compared to other forms of government in that time. In fact, that is the one thing political theorists and philosophers have clung to in holding up Athens as a beacon of enlightenment. The experience proves that direct democracy is a very difficult thing to achieve successfully and may not be the panacea for political ills that some have thought.

In modern times, direct democracy primarily takes the form of referenda or ballot measures put to the voters. The results are not terribly more encouraging than those in Athens. A prime example is the rush in the United States during the 1990s and 2000s to pass measures restricting marriage to a man and a woman. The concept of same-sex marriage needed some time to be digested properly, even by homosexuals, given the all-encompassing heterosexual culture in families, media, religion, and politics. Unlike heterosexual fish, homosexual fish know they are swimming in water and can't do much to change their environment. Given that environment, most voters think it's a no-brainer that marriage should involve a man and a woman. If homosexuals want to pair up monogamously, that is fine, but it isn't marriage. Knowing that marriage comes with a long list of benefits supported by law, a few progressive states passed laws to recognize civil unions between same-sex partners.

With astonishing speed, however, the tide turned. The question was reframed as a matter of equality under the law, a right with which every citizen in a democracy is endowed. Civil unions fell into the category of separate but equal accommodations that the US Supreme Court determined to be unconstitutional discrimination in 1954. Marriage was recognized as a human right. A majority is not supposed to be able to deny human rights to a minority in a democratic society. All citizens are equally sovereign and must be treated equally under the law.

To their credit, a majority of Americans understood this and popular opinion changed to embrace marriage equality. Some courts and legislatures made it official and the ball was rolling back. Holdouts remained, all of which were challenged by lawsuits, but the arguments of ban supporters all seemed to be based on scripture, which cannot be a source of law according to the First Amendment. Of course, the people who voted to restrict the definition of marriage could always claim, as did the

Athenians, that they weren't given enough information to vote correctly, so it wasn't their fault.

The Supreme Court finally took up the matter, striking down same sex marriage bans as unconstitutional violations of equal protection. Stunningly, the response from opponents was to attack the Supreme Court for "legislating" and call for judicial reform or some means of allowing states to ignore Supreme Court rulings. These were mostly the same people who applauded innovations like giving businesses rights to free speech and exercise of religion as if they were natural persons and deciding spending money is a form of speech. Expanding protections to things and actions created by law is fine but expanding protections to a historically maligned group of human citizens is overreaching. This illogical response mocked the definition of citizenship.

The Athenian definition of citizen placed three-quarters of the city's population outside that category. Everyone else was a resident of some type. Before pooh-poohing the prohibition against participation in public affairs by so many, we must remember that the United States had a population of 3.9 million in 1790 of which about 807,000 were free white males over the age of 16, or just under 21 percent of the population, making the percentage of the population capable of voting in federal elections even smaller than that of ancient Athens. Indeed, only a bit more than 43,000 of those adult males voted in the first presidential election in 1788, which is less than half again as much as the size of the entire number of Athenian citizens in the democratic period of that city. Democracies include many more people in settling the affairs of the polity than other forms of government, such as monarchy or oligarchy, but they are far from perfect in reflecting the true popular will judging from participation rates or citizenship definitions. Nor are they intended to do so. They are devised to represent the wishes of those people deemed to be full parties to the social contract who actively participate in the political system.

This leads to the inevitable fact that classes of people who are not full parties to the social contract are not treated as equals to those that are. They are not citizens. Some of these classes of people are citizens in the broad sense of being nationals of the country and may be defined as such under citizenship laws. However, they are not citizens in the strict sense we are using. So who are non-citizens? Minors fall into this category. Slaves fell into this category when slavery existed. Women stopped falling into this category in the twentieth century as they won the right to vote and no longer faced laws restricting their right to own property and do things without the permission of their husbands or fathers.

One of the great objections to the way things are done in the Kingdom of Saudi Arabia is that women cannot drive or engage in many activities without permission of a husband or male relative. However, people forget that the Kingdom is an absolute monarchy and there are no citizens, only subjects. Subjects have no rights and do not have to be treated equally under the law because they have given up their sovereignty. If Saudi subjects do not like the situation, they unfortunately must assert themselves as the English in 1649, the French in 1789 and 1848, the Mexicans in 1823 and 1867, the Chinese in 1911, the Russians in 1917, and many others.

Saudi Arabia is also unique in that it has a high proportion of expatriate residents in the country. People living legally in countries other than their own tend to have many legal rights that are the same as nationals of their country of residence, but are not fully equal under the law to nationals, let alone citizens or even subjects. People living illegally in another country have even fewer rights, most obviously not having the right of residence. Equality under the law has always applied only to citizens with full privileges to participate in public affairs. As the definition of who is a citizen has expanded to include men with little or no property, women, younger people, and former slaves, more people have been equal under the law.

Interestingly, the last Western country to hold out on giving women the right to vote was Switzerland, in which direct democracy is still practiced in cantons and where referenda failed to give women the vote in federal elections until 1971. The two halves of Appenzell, a canton, still refused to grant women the right to vote in cantonal and local assemblies in which citizens meet to make decisions. One half finally gave women the vote in 1989 and women successfully sued for the right to vote in the other. Their success was due to a change in the Federal Constitution by referendum in 1981 that specifically included both men and women as citizens. What this highlights more than anything is the most prominent drawback of direct democracy: minorities and excluded segments of society face an uphill battle to be treated equally by the majority of voters.

The extension of equality under the law to new classes of citizens has not been automatic or effectively practiced, as the history of segregation and continued interest in an equal rights amendment for women in the USA demonstrate. Sometimes the breadth of equality under the law changes, as has occurred with the Supreme Court decision in *United States v. Windsor* wherein the section of the Defense of Marriage Act prohibiting federal recognition of marriages of two people of the same sex was deemed in violation of the Fifth Amendment protection to equality under the law. This resulted in the rapid increase in lower federal courts striking down state marriage laws and constitutional amendments mentioned above. Opposition to these judicial findings relied, in part, on the argument that restrictive marriage laws and constitutional amendments have borne the imprimatur of democratic actions such as referenda and approval by legislative representatives.

This argument ignores the precepts that human rights should not be denied to a minority by the majority, laws failing to extend rights to minority populations are unjust, and equal protection under the law for all citizens is fundamental to the legitimacy and success of a democratic social contract. These points were thoroughly and conclusively debated and agreed to by the nation as a result of the struggle for civil rights by African-Americans. As events in Ferguson, Missouri in August 2014 and many other places since have demonstrated, the attainment of complete civil rights remains caught in the web of distrust and ignorance that constitutes racism in America today. Equality of all citizens in theory does not represent reality and will never do so as long as human beings fail to treat one another with dignity and care foremost in their hearts regardless of any characteristics that distinguish them from one another.

What justifies the failure to extend equality under the law to non-citizens? The quick answer is they are not parties to the social contract although they benefit from it by virtue of their residence within the state. Full equality among citizens is one of those rights endowed to citizens by virtue of their agreement to the terms of the social contract. Only adult white males participated in the drafting of the United States Constitution. Only adult white males, as citizens of the various states, chose members of state conventions that ratified the Constitution. Only adult white males became full citizens of the United States under the Constitution.

When Thomas Jefferson was faced with a choice of language in writing the Declaration of Independence's most famous passage, he did not chose the words "human" or "people" to describe who is equal. He said, "All men are created equal." While it is possible "men" in this context could be a synonym for the other two terms, the choice is indicative of the mindset of the eighteenth century.

Fortunately for women, freed slaves, and legal residents from other countries, the Bill of Rights contains restrictions on the federal government's actions regardless of who is the target of those actions; it does not confine its scope to actions taken against or regarding citizens only. Indeed, the Ninth and Tenth Amendments refer specifically to the rights of "people" rather than "citizens." Such expansiveness annoys reactionary elements who think individuals with no right to residence ought not to expect due process protections. Of course, these same people equate people without proper documents with all criminals and think criminals are coddled as a result of due process.

Why do non-citizens enjoy so many of the benefits of the social contract without being parties to it? Obviously, in times when citizenship was limited to adult white males, they alone could not operationalize all of the benefits possible from forming a community nor could they manage to continue the social contract beyond one generation. A very long time ago, human beings began dividing the workload to survive between men and women. Over the millennia, women became associated with duties involving upkeep of the household and raising children while men hunted, fought, and traded. In agricultural settlements, fields were tended by the entire family in many cases. Men also took responsibility for working together to manage the affairs of the community, although some societies gave women a role and some even turned the affairs over to women completely.

Generally though, when it came time to form governments over larger populations in the period of recorded history, men decided the forms of government and chose men to serve as leaders. As we saw with England into the Early Modern Period, women sometimes were given great authority to serve as regents while their royal husbands went off to war. Having a queen regnant had to wait until no men existed in the first ten slots of the line of succession after Edward VI. Female leaders were rare. One thinks of Boudica of the Iceni in Roman Brittania, memorialized by a statue outside the Palace of Westminster, and Eleanor, Duchess of Aquitaine in her own right as well as Queen Consort of England and duchess or countess of many more territories through her husband Henry II. Both rebelled against the existing government, Eleanor against her husband.

The capital charge against Jehanne d'Arc, La Pucelle

d'Orléans, depended exclusively on her going back to dressing in a male soldier's clothes during her trial since that would make her a relapsed heretic. According to the witnesses at the hearing ordered decades later by the pope to reverse her conviction, her captors arranged so she had no choice but to wear the male military attire made for her; it was the only thing that protected her from rape by the guards. St. Thomas Aquinas had said that women were never guilty of heresy for cross-dressing if it was necessary for their protection. Men in leadership positions who worked to vindicate her did St. Joan little good so many years after men in leadership positions cheated to take vengeance on a teenage girl who had proven to be a more inspiring leader of men than they. She was vindicated though and stands as one of the most admired women and military strategists in history.

Chapter 10—Leadership

AS NOTED ALREADY and bears repeating, a female political leader is rare in any culture prior to the twentieth century. When the English were first faced with the idea in the 1100s, most of the magnates were not ready for a queen regnant, particularly one with a husband they didn't like. They had sworn an oath of loyalty to Henry I that they would recognize his daughter, Matilda, widow of the Holy Roman Emperor and wife of the Count of Anjou. Once Henry was gone, they had second thoughts about that oath. Instead, they sided with Stephen of Blois as their king, whose mother, Adela, was Henry's sister, over the direct bloodline claim of his cousin.

Empress Matilda actually had served as regent for her first husband in Italy as had Adela over her husband's territories while he participated in the First Crusade. Matilda had enough support to wage a civil war to attempt to upend the decision, even taking Stephen captive. However, she was prevented from being crowned and anointed at Westminster due to the London crowds' opposition. Popular will stepped in to choose a sovereign. Except this time it was to deny the rightful heir her crown primarily because she was a woman and secondarily because she was married to a despised man. Four centuries later, Londoners demanded the rightful heir when the choice was between two women and later regretted their decision when she decided to marry a despised man.

After Matilda's half-brother was captured by Stephen's

forces and redeemed in exchange for Stephen, the civil war petered out with both sides controlling large parts of England. Fighting was renewed by Matilda's son from her second marriage, Henry Fitz Empress, when he came of age. He fought well enough to negotiate an agreement that recognized him as the next heir to the throne after Stephen, ignoring Stephen's younger, surviving son. He became Henry II in 1154 and his family name, Plantagenet, became the name of the dynasty that ruled England until another Henry, surnamed Tudor, defeated Richard III in battle in 1485 and became Henry VII.

This episode is another instance demonstrating that sovereigns of kingdoms are chosen by centers of power rather than inheriting them without question. No one complained that Stephen's claim came through a daughter of William the Conqueror rather than his son, Henry I. No one seemed to care that Matilda had experience managing affairs of state. Stephen grasped the concern over having a woman ruling England and one married to a powerful count at that. That England's peers and the residents of London refused to accept Matilda as their lawful sovereign was sexist and personal. That they made the decision against the wishes of a substantial portion of the population outside the capital resulted in the civil war that ran throughout much of Stephen's reign. The result ended up being just what it probably would have been had the peers and cockneys accepted Matilda in the first place except the country would not have had to suffer so much devastation. As with the choice between Lady Jane Dudley and Princess Mary Tudor, the decision makers chose unwisely, a result that happens not only in royal successions but also democratic elections.

Edward VI's death in 1553 as an unwed teenage lad left women in the first ten slots in the line of succession for the English crown. England was going to be ruled by a queen like it or not. Even at that, the succession was marred by a faction made up of men trying to get the most pliable candidate chosen so the queen regnant would just be a showpiece. It is no wonder that after Elizabeth I got to the throne five years later, she not only ultimately rejected marriage but often remarked she was the daughter of Henry VIII and made much of her masculine traits. Of course, her insistence on being the Virgin Queen meant she was going to be the last Tudor to reign yet immortalized in the names of two US states. Her decision made the next step far more complicated than most transfers of authority.

As an aside, Charles I equaled Elizabeth's feat when Carolina split North and South in 1729 most likely not in memory of the king's head being split from his body in 1649 despite that sounding vaguely plausible. His wife Henrietta Maria, a French Catholic Queen Consort, was also honored when Lord Baltimore founded Henriettaland (sic) to provide a safe haven for English Catholics just before the Puritan Revolution. Of course, there couldn't be more colonies named after queens than kings, so George II had a state named after him (guess which one) to make the score 3-3.

New Amsterdam, New Netherland was renamed New York, New York and Fort Orange was renamed Albany in 1664 after the British acquired the colony from the Dutch in honor of the heir apparent, James, Duke of York and Albany. Since he was forced off the thrones of England and Scotland 24 years later when he was James II & VII, the colony was not renamed New England or Nova Scotia, a lucky break since those names were taken and New York, New York was already silly enough. However, one of the finer boulevards in Albany, state capital of New York, is New Scotland Avenue. Fun stuff? Having dipped our toes into the cesspool of useless information, we will now wade into the quagmire of alternate history for a moment. Refreshments will be served after.

By all appearances, Elizabeth I did not much mind England being ruled by her three part Scots, one part French cousin. At least he had been raised outside the Catholic Church. The problem was she refused to officially name King James VI of the

Scots her heir apparent although she mentioned his name quite a bit followed by "hint, hint" after 1598. Remember that year. Her failure to be clear made the closer at hand descendants of Lady Jane Grey Dudley's mother and aunt legally next line per the terms of Henry VIII's will, which had used the old question of foreign-born people being prohibited from owning English land to exclude the Scottish line. The will, which had determined Mary I's and Elizabeth I's claims to the throne despite their still being legally illegitimate, put Lady Jane's sister Catherine and her descendants followed by her childless sister Mary and their first cousin Margaret and her descendants ahead of James VI of Scotland.

Heirs to the throne must receive the monarch's consent to marry since marriage had dynastic and political implications. Both of Lady Jane's sisters married secretly without Elizabeth I's permission. While this did not legally remove them from the line of succession, it made any offspring they had illegitimate because their husbands were automatically traitors and ticked off Elizabeth enough to reserve the newlywed suite in the Tower of London for them. Lady Catherine had two sons by her husband whilst residing in the Tower. James I & VI eventually legitimized them, the younger one posthumously. The older son, ennobled by James, ended up starting a line that led to the birth of the present Queen's mother. See how tricky the consequences can get?

Lady Jane's cousin, Margaret Stanley, Countess of Derby, ended up as Elizabeth I's heir presumptive in 1578 per Henry's will although Mary, Queen of Scots was, at the time, senior claimant by right of descent. Lady Margaret died in 1596, nine years after Mary was executed and seven years before Elizabeth died in bed. Margaret's older son Ferdinando (wouldn't that have been a great name for an English monarch) had predeceased her, so his daughter, Anne Stanley, Countess of Castlehaven, was heir presumptive, followed by her uncle, William Stanley, 6th Earl of Derby, Ferdinando's younger brother.

Elizabeth I's Privy Council decided to set aside Henry VIII's will and did the exact same thing Edward VI's had done initially. They rapidly sent two couriers to inform the Council's preferred choice that he was their sovereign. So, ironically it was Henry VIII's sister Margaret's great grandson who took over after all, half a century after his sister Mary's granddaughter had been offered and rejected. All of that to avoid having a third queen regnant in a row per the terms of Henry's will.

Had the will been upheld by the Privy Council, as some Legitimists claim it should have been, and nothing else changed (not likely) Lady Anne, an English Queen Anne 98 years ahead of schedule, would have had descendants on the throne until 1828. After 1828, the next claimant, a descendant of her sister, would have led to George Child Villiers, 9th Earl of Jersey, who died in 1998, followed by his daughter. Lady Caroline Ogilvy, the heir apparent being her son, Timothy Elliot-Murray-Kynynmound, 7th Earl of Minto. History would have completely bypassed the House of Hannover, the House of Saxe-Coburg-Gotha, and the name substitution to House of Windsor during World War I when the British suddenly decided having largely German monarchs on their throne was politically incorrect but did not warrant ending the monarchy or inviting a usurper as was done in 1603 and 1688.

This "what if" scenario would make for an interesting series of novels, quite the brain tease given that it requires no English law passed since 1603 be valid and Scotland remaining an independent kingdom under the increasingly Catholic Stuarts. The Stanley claim to the throne of England demonstrates the extent to which political machinations based on immediate needs rather than future interests profoundly influence the evolution of a polity. Despite being so remote and different, the outcomes are a lesson on how shortsightedness, prejudice, and disregard for legal principles on any issue—female leadership, climate change, resource exploitation, medical research, et cetera—aren't improvements over honesty, integrity, and playing by the rules.

The selection of James I & VI in 1603 resulted in a tumultuous century that was far more painful than the sporadic bloodiness of the Wars of the Roses or the Hundred Years War. The choice led to even greater change than the Danish occupation or Norman invasion because it thoroughly and irrevocably broke and reframed the British Constitution. Historians looking back tend to agree that the outcome provided the foundations for the great British Empire of the following two centuries. However, might the same result have occurred with much less carnage if an unprepossessing countess had taken the throne rather than an already anointed king who had written the book on the rights of an absolute monarch? The concerns about having a sturdy male Protestant evaporated quickly when James infuriated the English nobility with his Scottish coterie and handsome favorites and then his son, Charles I, married a Catholic and took his father's book on kingship to heart. Then the British repeated the error by bringing back the deposed and executed king's Catholic-leaning and Catholic sons to rule and ended up asking for help via a Dutch invasion, the Dutch only recently having been their enemies in a long trade war.

At the start of the eighteenth century, Parliament found it necessary to look past more than 50 Catholic heirs to designate the wholly German Electress Sophia of Hannover as Queen Anne's successor. At that point about a decade and a half after James II was ejected the heir's religion was far more important than the heir's sex or nationality. Dog forbid they should look to the Stanley claim though because that would be admitting their mistake in 1603. Better to have some far-distant descendant of James I than raise an English noble to the throne now. Sophia had the misfortune of dying shortly before Anne, leaving the crown of the now United Kingdom to her son George who never bothered to learn English in his twelve years as king. Why does a king need to speak the language of his subjects anyway? Well, for starters, they are more like citizens by now but that concept was still a few score decades away.

By the end of the eighteenth century, when the concept of citizenship became central to three revolutions (USA, France and Haiti), the differing responsibilities between the sexes were pretty much set in stone. John Adams is well known for the respect and affection he had for his wife Abigail. But even he among the Founders did not propose a role for women as citizens in the new republic. Women could be commended for their ability to manage a household, but no one thought twice about involving them in the affairs of state. The same was true around the world. Despite the examples of Queen Anne of Great Britain, Empress Maria Theresa of the Holy Roman Empire, and Catherine I, Anna, Elizabeth, and Catherine II (the Great), Empresses of All Russia, the eighteenth century was not keen on giving women political power. Indeed, much of Europe fell into war for eight years over the accession of Maria Theresa as Archduchess of Austria because the King of Prussia thought he could grab Silesia from a female ruler without much trouble and had his eye on Bohemia as well.

Radical politics didn't help women much. The French Revolution got off to a good start and then cut women off from politics with more than just the guillotine. Women were involved in the public protests that brought down the monarchy in 1789. Political opinion at first thought that women should receive more education than they did under the ancien régime but still remain in the home. The Marquis de Condorcet made a splash in 1790 with a newspaper essay promoting complete women's equality in public affairs. A year later, Marie Gouze, under the pseudonym Olympe de Gouges, wrote the Declaration of the Rights of Woman and the Female Citizen, which pointed out the sexist deficiencies that flowed from the Declaration of the Rights of Man and Citizen. Women's political clubs took off and laws were passed making divorce easier and giving women the right to inherit property.

Everything came to a head in 1793. The National

Convention considered, then dismissed, giving women the right to vote and hold office. Charlotte Corday assassinated Jean-Paul Marat in his bath for Marat's denunciation of moderate voices such as Condorcet. The revolutionary government banned women's political clubs a few months later. Days after that Marie Gouze, who had argued that women should have the right to hold office if they also could be executed for political offenses, was guillotined for calling for a national referendum to determine France's government.

The final straw took place in 1795, when women incited riots over inflationary prices, leading to a takeover of the National Convention and death of one deputy. When order was restored, the government banned women from any political activity and prohibited groups of more than five women from meeting. Ironically, every symbol of the revolution portraying the female gendered nouns *Liberté*, *Égalité*, and *Patrie* (but not *Fraternité*, obviously) was a woman in a toga, often bare-breasted. These icons were stirring perhaps, but far from any representation of real French women. French women finally got the right to vote only in 1944.

The nineteenth century was almost worse for women in the political world with the only queen regnant of any significance, Victoria of the United Kingdom and Ireland, Empress of India, making her mark as the model of respectable domesticity and widowhood. Women in the USA met for the first time in 1848 in Seneca Falls, New York to stake out a plan to gain legal and political rights, but even there the idea of women voting was controversial. Susan B. Anthony, Elizabeth Cady Stanton, and others spent the next seven decades fighting for the political rights of women, touching all bases. They endorsed the temperance movement because the laws made it impossible for women to gain control of family finances from or get out of a marriage to an alcoholic husband. They became ardent abolitionists in the hope that women could ride a tide to political rights with freed slaves.

They even supported the Republican Party and its Fourteenth and Fifteenth Amendments only to have a federal judge direct a jury to find Anthony was not a full citizen with a right to vote within the meaning of those additions to the Constitution. Since defendants were not allowed to testify in their trials under federal criminal procedure at the time, Anthony had to wait until she was asked to make a statement before sentencing to give the judge and everyone else in the court an earful about how every right of a citizen was being swept aside on account of her sex. Perhaps to get back at Anthony for her tirade, the judge refused to imprison her for not paying the fine imposed upon her, thereby cutting off her right of appeal, yet another oddity of yesteryear's criminal procedure.

The question of women's suffrage under these amendments was fully put to rest in *Minor v. Happersett*, decided by the Supreme Court in 1875. The unanimous Court took the curious step of opining that, while women like Virginia Minor are citizens of the United States, voting is not one of the "rights and privileges" of citizenship in a democratic republic. The Court's reasoning was that the Constitution does not expressly grant citizens the right to vote and that the original thirteen states restricted voting based variously on sex, race, age, and property ownership (they overlooked religion). It did not occur to the justices that the restrictions based on sex and race had been wrongheaded and not universal. Moreover, New Jersey gave women the right to vote until 1808 and several states allowed free blacks to vote.

Age is always a factor in determining legal rights and obligations. Every state that had religious restrictions eliminated them by 1828 and property qualifications by 1856, demonstrating a progressive trend toward opening the franchise that was capped by amending the Constitution to give freed, male slaves the right to vote. Last and most important, the Ninth and Tenth Amendments stated that not all rights of the people had been spelled out. The Court missed every argument.

Accordingly, women waited 45 years until the passage of the Nineteenth Amendment before they could vote throughout the United States. Another 40 years after that, the Supreme Court quietly started to ignore its decision in *Minor v. Happersett* and considered the right to vote a fundamental part of being a full citizen in the context of striking down barriers to voting by African-Americans. Nonetheless, a woman's right to equality under the law remains unprotected under the Equal Protection Clause of the Fourteenth Amendment, providing justification for the Equal Rights Amendment.

Having won the right to vote almost everywhere in the twentieth century, women made gains, but not strides, in filling offices of government. Since World War II, fewer than 60 countries have had elected or appointed female heads of government, with 20 being the more or less steady number for several years, just about ten percent of all states. The record is 24 women holding high office at one time. They have been well distributed. Europe has done the best, with San Marino and Switzerland leading in the number of women rising to the top. All four South Asian, four Southeast Asian, half of East Asian, and almost half of Latin American states have had female leaders. The record is improving for conservative Africa, where leadership turnover is infrequent and unstable in many places.

On the other hand, only 17 percent of government ministers worldwide are women. By 2014, 21.8 per cent of the members of national legislatures were female, a rise from 11.3 per cent in 1995. At least half of the parliamentarians in Rwanda and Andorra are women and the Nordic countries average around 42 percent inclusion. Twenty-five countries have ten percent or less female representation, including seven countries with no female legislators at all. Interestingly, 10 of these laggards are very small island states and three more (Bahrain, Haiti, and Papua New Guinea) are somewhat larger island nations. Only Seychelles, Timor-Leste, and Trinidad and Tobago among low population island states have above average female participation in parliaments. However, almost all of the independent and autonomous Caribbean islands have had female prime ministers.

The United States, which led by example in forming a representative democracy, has been slower than the rest of the world in electing women to public office. Less than half of the states have elected female governors, with only five having female governors in 2014. Fourteen states had no women in their congressional delegations in 2014 (Delaware, Iowa, Mississippi, and Vermont have never sent a woman to Congress). Only eighteen percent of the members of the House of Representatives and twenty percent of the Senators are women, the highest rates to date and still below the global average. Money is an issue. Women in office, particularly in the Senate, have recently been more active in leading efforts to raise campaign donations to support other women. They have a long way ahead.

Indeed, it is remarkable that to date the only female candidate for president considered to have enough experience for the role came to prominence as the strongly supportive wife of a governor and president and uses her activities as a first lady, an unelected, unofficial position, as part of her credentials. This is not to say that a first lady does not have substantive responsibilities or that particular experience is irrelevant. However, it underscores a sexist double-standard if the only perceived viable female candidate is someone who did not rise independently of her spouse.

Finding female candidates is a problem. Governors like to become United States senators, but with so few women running states Barack Obama decimated their population by hiring two for his first cabinet. State legislatures are a frequent source to fill congressional opportunities, but just 24.2 percent of the seats in those bodies are filled by women. Only four states are over one-third representation while another four are under one-sixth. With these paltry records, it can't be surprising that only three women have been on a major political party's national ticket in the United States, vice presidential candidates Geraldine Ferraro in 1984 and Sarah Palin in 2008 and presidential candidate Hilary Clinton in 2016. As just mentioned, the only woman to come close to being nominated for president, Clinton, first helped her husband build his political base for two successful presidential campaigns. If that is what it really takes to seriously consider a woman for US president, sea levels may be rising noticeably before one is elected without any family connections.

Like their monarchical forbearers, many of the first women in positions of power were wives or daughters of male office holders, succeeding as widows or taking over the father's political connections when no sons were around. Dead men create opportunities for women. This is true even for women not related by blood or marriage to the deceased politico. A very real problem for women trying to enter politics is the paucity of open seats available for anyone. Public service once was a dilettante's game, available to upper class sorts with time, interest, and independent means of support, since the pay for elected office was never great. As legislatures became more powerful, government activities increased, and lobbying afterward became lucrative, career politicians were born. Although the opportunities for corrupt earnings might be possible, legal options to gain from one's position were readily available, too.

Acquiring authority to influence or make decisions became in and of itself a splendid aphrodisiacal addiction. Once in the corridors of power, almost no one wanted to leave. Incumbents found that the longer they stayed in office, the easier it was to get things done, including getting re-elected. They have greater chances to retain their positions for many reasons, not the least of which is being already known to the voters. This applies primarily in countries that use electoral districts to choose legislators. Many of these advantages are lost when legislators are elected through proportional representation by political party. Regardless, women face an uphill battle to find open seats, challenge incumbents, or climb the party lists. Stagnation reigns while equality in female representation slowly progresses.

The Roman Empire offers an example in which women had many legal rights, such as freedom to divorce without cause, property ownership, inheritance equal to male siblings, and freedom of action vis-à-vis their husbands. In a change from earlier times, women remained their father's daughter after marriage, and did not become a husband's wife, as far as permission to do things was concerned. Augustus Caesar's second wife, Livia, is famed for her influence on her husband's political affairs. She also managed household affairs, like any wife, although her household with many slaves, servants, and extended family members was much like a good-sized business. Women were considered citizens but could not vote or hold office. However, being a citizen was no small thing in Rome.

The Roman Empire is notable for how it used citizenship first to distinguish members of the political class and then to lure new populations into becoming more closely allied with the government. Roman citizenship came with a number of substantive legal privileges that could gain families power and prosperity if used properly by the *pater familias*. The six major rights were voting, public office holding, accessing courts, contract making, marrying, and migrating. As noted, female citizens did not have the first two. These rights are notable in that they represent key activities vital to the functioning and development of the state. With these rights came responsibilities to engage in these activities at appropriate times for the benefit not only of the citizen and his family but society as well. Romans knew that the more active citizens were in using their rights, the more vibrant and prosperous Rome would be.

Roman citizens could not be whipped or tortured, nor executed except for treason. If charged with treason, they had a right to a trial in Rome and, if guilty, could not be executed by crucifixion. Traitors were beheaded. Compared to the execution of male traitors in England until 1814 (drawn on the ground behind a horse, hanged until not quite dead, emasculated, disemboweled, burned, beheaded, and cut into quarters), Romans got off easy. The English held quite a strong view about betraying the sovereign. In part, this harkens back to the fact that Jesus was betrayed by Judas. Jesus, of course, was crucified under Roman law for the treason of being called the King of the Jews. Christianity would look quite different if Judean Jews had been eligible to be Roman citizens since Jesus would not have died on a cross.

By the time Caracalla made all free men of the empire citizens of Rome in 212, Jews had been dispersed from Judea and Judea had become Palestine. An argument can be made that Jews would reject Roman citizenship anyway because it implied adopting the Roman gods. As God's chosen people, Jews had (and still have) an identity bound up with monotheism. The prime reason the Romans persecuted Christians was their belief that monotheism and atheism were the same thing. Everyone within the Roman Empire except the Jews had been happy to adopt Roman gods as parallels to their own. The Romans just as happily adopted the gods worshipped by people they conquered as being parallels of Roman gods. The Romans didn't understand Judaism because they could not grasp the monotheist concept. As a result, they let the Jews keep their king and keep their priestly hierarchy that eventually decided Jesus of Nazareth was too dangerous to their continued autonomy. Cooperating with the Roman governor to identify a traitor to Caesar was just the thing to do to maintain that autonomy.

Unlike the Jews who were happy to be left more or less alone, Christians were not organized enough for some time to reach the same accommodation. By the time they were becoming more coherent, they had gone through a very disruptive debate about whether Christians had to practice Jewish Old Testament laws, in essence whether Christians had to be Jews first. As mentioned previously, the early Christians came up with the idea of paganism to distinguish themselves from everyone else worshipping dozens of gods. It didn't matter to Christians if the gods were Roman, Greek, Egyptian, or even Persian.

This saved time later on when Christianity butted up against Celtic, Germanic, and Slavic gods with many more to come, because everyone already knew their followers must be pagans. The world was divided into Christians and pagans with Jews being unredeemed Christians who didn't really matter too much after their rebellion against Rome was crushed in 70 CE. This we/they way groups identify themselves, which was hardly original to Christians, has a fundamental role in the social contract and democracy.

Chapter 11—National Identity and Democratic Development

ONE OF THE reasons Athenian democracy came into being is the state was a city and it's near environs with the same families as residents over the centuries. Athens was relatively compact, everyone had much the same interests and prayed to the same gods; the degrees of separation within the population were low. Outsiders, "foreigners" from other city-states or slaves, were kept at a distance socially and politically. Homogeneity predominated. Athens got into trouble when it dabbled in wider Greek affairs or built an empire. Athenian citizens were used to commonalities. Difficulties arose when easy consensus could not be found.

Small is definitely better for the direct democracy Athens used. Anything larger becomes too unwieldy to manage. There is always the problem of getting the points of discussion across with too many ears and voices not loud enough. In modern times, direct democracy for much larger, more heterogeneous populations, uses referenda. Ballot issues can be easily managed from a logistical point of view, but getting everyone's attention and allowing funding from dubious sources to amplify voices cause frustrating problems that undermine the value of making decisions this way. The larger the group deciding, the smaller the proportion of deciders who understand all of the facts and arguments well enough to form a reasoned opinion. It is much easier to insure everyone in a small seminar class learns everything than in a large lecture class.

Matters do not improve much if representative democracy is used. The many voices are still there, representatives can get mixed signals, and money spent on advertising substitutes for personal interactions. If the people are supposed to direct policy, there are precious few avenues for making clear what the people want to guide politicians. Even then, opinion is always split, sometimes into several strands. In 2016, Denmark, a relatively small country that does the best of any to insure all citizens' opinions are represented proportionately, had eight political parties in the national legislature, twelve counting the ones holding seats for the Faroe Islands and Greenland. Scaling up any form of democracy has its risks and complications.

City-states like Athens make good democracies not only due to their size but also due to the similarities among citizens. Japan is uniquely homogeneous and had been isolated from almost all foreign influences in the modern era up until the 1850s, less than a century before members of the American occupying forces wrote a constitution for Japan in 1946 based on the principles of popular sovereignty, representative democracy, and the protection of human rights. Most famously, this document forever rejects the use of war as an instrument of government policy.

Aside from a few changes made before it was adopted, that constitution has not been amended and Japan has developed into a rather healthy democracy. This democracy was built on a history of feudalism until 1868, followed by oligarchy with heavy military influence, a very brief period when political parties seemed to be gaining control, ending with a takeover of government by the military in 1932. The success of imposed democracy in Japan is the result of the near purity of the country's ethnic composition and the shared cultural values that were used explicitly to promote nationalist sentiment during Japan's transformation to a modern, international actor from

1868 to 1912 under the Emperor Meiji.

In the last twelve years, the Liberal Democratic Party of Japan (LDP), the party that has governed most of the time since 1955, has twice offered amendments to the 1946 constitution. In 2005, the amendments were mainly to give Japan more room to use its self-defense forces internationally and to make it easier to amend the constitution. By the time enabling legislation to hold a referendum required for amendment was enacted, public opinion no longer supported the changes. In 2012, many more amendments were put on the table on top of those from 2005. The LDP, among other things, suggested limiting human rights when needed for "public order," expanding the obligations of citizens to balance the number of rights they have, making the enumerated human rights state granted rather than naturally endowed, and deleting the article that defines the constitution as the supreme law of Japan because it guarantees human rights.

It doesn't take much to figure out that these suggested amendments aim to transfer more sovereignty from the citizens to the state. Indeed, Prime Minister Shinzo Abe said the changes would make Japan fully sovereign in part because they make Japan's social contract, which was not written by Japanese citizens, more Japanese. However, the Japanese people know they have not only embraced their imposed constitution, but built a stable, prosperous, respected society using its principles of government. The constitution's exceptional renunciation of war and definition of human rights as an inalienable aspect of individual sovereignty are fully part of Japanese identity now. Few Japanese bought Mr. Abe's argument.

There are all sizes and shapes of countries that developed monarchical forms of government first and either evolved democratic, representative principles, like Denmark, or adopted them upon achieving independence from an occupying power, like Japan. Many newly independent states fell into autocracy, monarchy without the tiaras, when difficulties arose. Trying to sort out popular will can be particularly frustrating when the people aren't used to having their voices heard. When decisions must be made quickly, debate is a nuisance. In a crisis, the first thing to go is democratic processes. Vigorous leadership edges out coalition building and silences naysayers. Usually, heads of democratic governments have enough authority to manage when situations pop up in day-to-day administration. They are quick to seek more power when things get out of control. Japan was developing parliamentary democracy in 1912-26 during the reign of the Taishō Emperor, culminating in the passage of a universal male suffrage law in 1925. However, progress fell apart when the growing pains from Japan's economic boom, opportunities for further expansion in China, and, finally, the worldwide depression arose at the start of the succeeding Shōwa reign. The military stepped in shortly after its successful invasion of Manchuria.

Until the Glorious Revolution in England, monarchies tended to be autocratic. Indeed, the tsars of Russia had autocrat as one of their titles. However, as we have seen and will see again, monarchs and non-royal autocrats typically must pay attention to the economic, social, and political elites and always run the risk of behaving so badly that the common folk rise in rebellion. Rarely in the modern period has an autocrat had sufficient independent power to dictate every rule, law, and decision. Dictators are, thankfully, uncommon. Most often, elites control the direction of policy, albeit broken into factions that compete for the attention of the ruler. This form of government, in which elites rule through a leader or group of leaders, is an oligarchy.

Due to the nature of how members of Parliament were chosen in England in 1688, the lords spiritual and temporal and the propertied class ruled as sovereign, the Crown-in-Parliament, for nearly two centuries with two factions, the Whigs and Tories, competing for leadership. Russia today, under Vladimir Putin, is governed by economic elites who use their positions to increase their wealth maximally through public contracts obtained corruptly. Russia is, accordingly, the form of oligarchy known as a kleptocracy. Famous republics from history, such as Florence, Genoa, and Venice, were ruled by the economic elites of their respective cities, the oligarchic form of government called plutocracy. Finally, a theocracy is a form of oligarchy in which religious elites are the ultimate authority and all laws must comport with religious prescriptions. Iran, Saudi Arabia, and Vatican City are examples of this kind of government. A handful of other countries (Afghanistan, Mauritania, Pakistan, Somalia, Sudan, and Yemen) have established Islamic law (sharia) as the supreme law of the land but do not have the same kind of state institutions, other than a supreme religious court, enforcing compliance.

Democracy, oligarchy (and its sub-types), monarchy, and autocracy are forms of government defined by whose voice primarily determines policy and who is sovereign. They represent a continuum from the widest base of possible citizen participation to rule by one person. Another continuum defines the extent to which the state is limited by civil liberties and individual sovereignty versus individuals limited by state intrusion in their affairs. Variants of democracy (liberal, social, and illiberal) constitute one end of the spectrum while totalitarianism occupies the other end. In between, anocracy (repressive regimes with democratic characteristics) and authoritarianism (repressive regimes with window-dressing democratic features) complete the sequence.

One of the interesting aspects of having these two continuums is the limited number of variations possible, 42 to be exact. Some combinations would seem to be out of bounds, such as a liberal democratic autocracy or a totalitarian democracy. Yet, an autocrat can create laws that protect the civil liberties of the populace and a totalitarian regime can reflect the will of the people in its decisions and actions. Moreover, if these are true continuums, the forms of government and limitations on the state blend from one to the next, leaving very few "pure" examples. Most importantly for our purposes, democracies can and do allow elements of other forms of government and other kinds of regimes to crop up.

Even well-entrenched democracies take on characteristics of autocracy in a crunch. Look at the response of the USA to the Islamic State. First, the danger was largely ignored until two Americans were executed in 2014. Suddenly, something had to be done. The President submitted a plan of action to Congress and said there was no time to waste. It was just weeks before a federal election and the nation's elected representatives had a more pressing concern: their own re-election. After perfunctory hearings with some noise that they should look into this further after the election, Congress rubber stamped the President's request. No thoughtful discussion. No checks on executive action.

That Congress had the worst record of legislative achievement in recent memory until the next one. The deadlock that continued pushed the President to attempt to move ahead with policy initiatives using executive orders. The House of Representatives authorized a first-ever lawsuit against the President for overstepping his executive authority. Now they were giving him carte blanche in response to the threat posed by the Islamic State. That is not governing responsibly in a democratic republic. But it provides an excellent example of how autocracies move more quickly than democracies.

Agility and speed are not the sole reasons autocracies govern large states well, although Russia's use of serf transport and labor to move official documents at low cost represents one of many ways empires have sought to tie the emperor to the remotest outposts. Rome did so famously with its roads; France under the Bourbon kings is a less well known example. The emphasis on communications with far-flung provinces has become much easier as new technologies have blossomed. Indeed, another key aspect of autocracy is the ability to control the messages distributed regarding policies and loyalties. Unlike democracies, wherein many parties are trying to convince voters of the correctness of their platforms, autocracies usually hide any disputes among supporting factions and enunciate unchallenged messages. This uniformity in communications helps to keep the populace focused on the government's agenda.

The problem endemic to almost all larger states is that they do not have homogeneous populations. Japan is exceptional, the result of a long history of unifying cultural symbols coupled with centuries of isolation from outside influences. As noted previously, homogeneity has made it easier for democracy to take root despite having been imposed. Even so, the current government of Japan considers giving more sovereignty to the state and limiting popular sovereignty in the process a turn toward making their political structures more Japanese. Prior to the oligarchic period from 1868 to 1946, Japan had been an autocracy with either direct rule of an absolute sovereign emperor or, in the last few centuries before 1868, a military dictator called the shogun ruling as the de facto sovereign while the emperor remained the de jure sovereign.

Other large states may be homogeneous in some regards, such as China having an ethnic Han Chinese population so large that the other 55 ethnic groups (Tibetan, Uighur, Mongolian, etc.) constitute less than nine percent of the population. The Han all use the same written language but speak seven main varieties of Chinese that are mutually unintelligible and fourteen additional dialects of those varieties. Beyond a certain point, any human population will exhibit signs of heterogeneity. The differences among a population may take many forms. As Charles de Gaulle famously said, "*Comment voulez-vous gouverner un pays qui a deux cent quarante-six variétés de fromage?*" ("How can you govern a country which has two hundred forty-six varieties of cheese?") Apparently one starts by counting exactly how many types of cheese are produced by that population. However, the differences that most affect the ability to govern are ethnicity, language, religion, history, and geography.

Japan is the quintessential nation-state. Despite having a mountainous geography stretched over several islands, the Japanese people share the same ethnicity, language, religion, and history. Their culture has developed over centuries. The unifying features of that culture were used to develop a nationalist ideology after the Meiji Restoration that was reinforced by military successes against China, Russia, Germany, and China again from 1895 to 1931. It culminated in the substantial support the military received to expand the Japanese Empire further in China beginning in 1937, leading to the simultaneous attacks on Pearl Harbor, Singapore, and Hong Kong at the end of 1941 that laid the groundwork for invading all American, British, Dutch, and French colonies and Thailand in Southeast Asia. Such vigorous and aggressive nationalism also lay at the root of Germany and Italy's invasions that brought war to Ethiopia in 1935, Europe in 1939, and North Africa in 1940.

Nationalism has a Dr. Jekyll and Mr. Hyde duality as World War II proved in spades. Adolf Hitler's policies aimed at purifying the German people (*Reinigung des Volk*), incorporating all German speakers into one state (*Großer Deutschland*), and providing this Greater Germany with the land and resources needed to reach its full potential (*Lebensraum*). The Japanese military leaders only sought the last goal. Nonetheless, they understood that Japan was the only Asian country that had been proven equal or superior to Western states and therefore the Japanese nation was superior to its neighbors and the natural leader of an economic empire. The ruthless aggression required to realize these goals certainly demonstrated the extremity to which nationalism can go in its Mr. Hyde persona.

Conversely, the Dr. Jekyll side stresses the unforced commonalities that people share within an ethnic group or long-time residents of a particular region. The Danes, for example, understood very quickly that Germany's invasion of their country would result in policies that were abhorrent to Danish morals. It was not a secret that the Jewish population would be rounded up and, at the very least, ghettoized as had happened in Poland. Fishermen risked their lives moving Danish Jews to neutral Sweden. In most countries, that assistance is the end of the story. However, after the war concluded Danish Jews returned to find that their neighbors had carefully protected their belongings and done what they could to maintain their properties. It would be one thing if this had happened here or there, but it was done everywhere. Danes are not scavengers or opportunists.

That is the much less well known story. The one much better known is the rallying together of the English during the darkest hour to the finest hour. Everyone made do and chipped in to manage throughout the Battle of Britain. One of the most popular episodes was Queen Elizabeth's (mother of the present monarch) remark after Buckingham Palace had been hit by German bombs, "I'm glad we've been bombed. It makes me feel I can look the East End in the face." The Queen Consort had been concerned that the poorer areas of London and therefore the poorer English people might not believe the royal family was experiencing what the nation was experiencing.

The connection of royalty to the people, a two-way signal of identification, was an early manifestation of national identity all around the world. When philosophers and statesmen were really beginning to wrap their heads around the idea of a nation, Elizabeth I commented, "There is nothing about which I am more anxious than my country, and for its sake I am willing to die ten deaths, if that be possible." How much easier it is to unite the residents of a land when their sovereign head of state sets herself out as the embodiment of that land. Indeed, communal identification in tribes, nations, or peoples often includes a core myth of a single founder whose descendants see reflected in their leaders.

The United Kingdom (or its component parts), Denmark, Japan, and China all have very lengthy histories as political units. Nationalism is almost second nature because of the many events, individuals, and traditions that pretty much every citizen can look to in common with every other citizen. Something of the same can be said for the other Eurasian states, whether they are amalgams of smaller states (Afghanistan, Belgium, Burma, France, Germany, India, Indonesia, Italy, Malaysia, Pakistan, Philippines, Romania, Saudi Arabia, Spain, and United Arab Emirates), reborn earlier states (Armenia, Cyprus, Czech Republic, Georgia, Greece, Israel, Jordan, Korea, Macedonia, Mongolia, Poland, Serbia, Syria, and Ukraine), old states that have kept their identities (Andorra, Austria, Bahrain, Bhutan, Brunei, Cambodia, Hungary, Iceland, Iran, Kuwait, Lichtenstein, Lithuania, Luxembourg, Malta, Monaco, Nepal, The Netherlands, Oman, Portugal, Qatar, San Marino, Sri Lanka, Sweden, Switzerland, Thailand, Vatican City, Vietnam, and Yemen) or new states that reflect Woodrow Wilson's ideals of bringing together people with common languages, histories, and cultures (Azerbaijan, Belarus, Bulgaria, Estonia, Finland, Kazakhstan, Kyrgyzstan, Latvia, Laos, Lebanon, Moldova, Norway, Palestine, Slovakia, Tajikistan, Turkey, Turkmenistan, and Uzbekistan). The borders were drawn in a manner that generally avoided coloring outside the lines, with the lines being applied around nationalities.

No more so is this less true than in the two remaining Eurasian countries: Iraq and Singapore. We already have discussed the irrationality of the Great Powers creating Iraq after World War I. It would have been far better to create Kurdistan, expand Syria and Jordan to take in the Sunni Arabs in Mesopotamia, and expand Kuwait to take in the Shi'a Arabs.

Singapore, on the other hand, is unique as a multinational city-state. It tried to participate in the Malaysian experiment and backed out in 1965. Since then the entrepôt has been a democracy in name that functioned more as a benevolent autocracy in practice under longtime Prime Minister Lee Kwan Yu and remains a rather disciplined system. Malay, Chinese, and Indian citizens have maintained distinct ethnic communities with westerners both staying apart and mixing. No one is ascendant and everyone benefits from government policies. Some attention has been drawn to Singapore's draconian drug trafficking laws and paternalism regarding minor practices such as banning chewing gum. Nonetheless, the old British colony has succeeded in attracting continuing admiration as a modern, civil society. Indeed, Singapore likely has come closest to Plato's vision of a city-state governed by a philosopher-king in The Republic.

Unlike the states of Eurasia, the rest of the world, save some Pacific island nations and a few in Africa, are primarily amalgams of ethnic groups either indigenous to the territory in the case of most of Africa, a mix of indigenous and immigrant populations like most of Central and South America, or primarily immigrant populations that have pushed indigenous ethnic groups to the margins as in North America, the Caribbean, Australia, and New Zealand.

Like all of Asia, none of these states was a party to the Treaty of Westphalia. They all had the principles of international law and national sovereignty imposed on them as they were colonized and became independent. Nonetheless, they have accepted those principles in order to derive the benefits of sovereignty. What they all have struggled to accomplish, some more successfully than others, is a homogeneous national identity not linked to ethnicity or even culture, but only derived from shared history, economy, politics, and language. They have forged new identities for their citizens to use.

Those identities are clearly on display at the Modern Olympic Games, the FIFA World Cup, the Miss Universe Pageant, and many other events and venues. They are reinforced by history classes, national days, symbols, national anthems, and plenty of small reminders that everyone living in the state is a part of a united whole. And they are legally defined by the ability of a resident to receive a passport or vote or do or have anything else restricted to citizens. States rely on citizens to prove the state is sovereign and speaks for all, just as the citizens rely on the state to provide security, infrastructure, and all of the other benefits derived from a people joining together in a social contract. The bargain is quite clear. The question, dating back to Plato, is what forms of input will the citizens have to insure the state provides what they need.

What Plato was unable to see was technological improvements and philosophical developments would enable more people to serve as citizens and require more states to seek input. Singapore works wonderfully well because it is exactly like the polities Plato knew and admired. Indeed, Plato created Atlantis as a large fictional state to endorse the idea that states become unruly and prone to tyranny and anarchy if they got too large. He posed Atlantis against Athens in order to demonstrate how a smallish city-state under a philosopher-king was the best sort of political system for everyone.

Plato, like most Greek thinkers, thought in terms of the natural world. The air in a city-state circulates as through a temple in which the leader can sniff out what the people need and the people can feel a pleasant breeze when the leader governs well. Persia exemplified the stuffiness of a large, old barn in which the ruler's best hope was to find the right perfumes and oils so at least he and those closest to him could ignore the stench. However, Plato had to create Atlantis so as not to use an example already burdened with so much negativity by the Greeks as Persia. What if Plato had other examples of large states to play with?

Chapter 12—The Readiness Question

PLATO CERTAINLY WOULD have found Russia and China fascinating case studies. Two of the largest and least disciplined polities in the world, they appear to be governed best by philosopher-kings of the kind Plato approved, except they are two contrasting examples of philosopher-kings. The bad raps these two countries have are based on the notion that their leaders, the actual decision makers, stand atop machines that work to keep everyone else in his or her place while giving some appearance that citizens actually have a say in who leads them and what decisions are made. In China that machine is the Communist Party and in Russia it is the political network created by Vladimir Putin.

Both countries have authoritarian political systems. They both have long histories of having authoritarian political systems. Individual rights, civil society, and citizen participation never fully evolved in these countries. Some elites have tried since the late nineteenth century to introduce western conceptions of liberal democracy. Resistance came not just from the entrenched powers that did not want to turn their fate over to the hands of an electorate. The people who would have made up that proposed electorate also rejected it. Generally speaking, they had no interest in being burdened with choosing political leaders when they were already burdened with trying to survive.

What observers fail to grasp is that places like England and the United States had average standards of living in the eighteenth century that people in Russia and China did not achieve until after 1950. Political participation in eighteenth century England and US was restricted to landowning white male citizens. While they were nascent democracies along the lines of ancient Athens, they certainly did not embrace universal suffrage and had very strong sentiments about not allowing the rabble to be involved in the nation's business other than to be productive and pay taxes. Early liberal democracies looked pretty much the same as what China and Russia look like today. A large but by no means representative or disinterested group of mostly men, an aristocracy in the original meaning of that word, provide direct support to a government controlled by a much smaller group, an oligarchy, that tries to establish policies that will provide enough benefits to the population for the citizenry to be happy and enough benefits to the elites for them to stay in power for the foreseeable future. Note that the policies must be benevolent. Popular support remains necessary.

Just because these countries are now so closely connected with the rest of the world and their citizens have incredibly broad access to information even with governmental restrictions, from the perspective of who has the time to pay attention and participate in politics the people of those countries have more vital things to do to survive than exercise civil liberties. It does not mean they aren't entitled to them or aren't ready for them. It means one can't eat freedom. If the choice is between doing something that provides food versus doing something that expands freedom of speech, which would most people choose? A similar phenomenon is the low voter participation rate among the poorest members of society in the USA. Voting has dubious value if the candidates will not endorse providing basic necessities or equal opportunity.

People promoting western conceptions of democracy tend to place more value on civil liberties on the assumption that citizens can be most productive and therefore best off if they are free. They rarely consider that political freedom is useless unless one also has economic and cultural freedom. As the money in politics debate in the USA has shown, extending political freedom to everyone, even legal fictions like corporations, does absolutely nothing to promote the equality of participation that proponents claim. Those with more money can participate more. Indeed, according to the Supreme Court, they are speaking more since spending money is the equivalent of speech. That automatically means that you are undermining the equal voice of every citizen in the political arena. Being able to buy more visibility for your point of view is not democracy. If spending = speaking, Super PACs and wealthy individuals who bundle campaign donations have all the bull horns, candidates with big money donors and corporations have all of the microphones, and voters have only their natural voices. Some of them are screaming to be heard but are not.

The actors who buy that extra visibility are doing so by reaping the benefits of owning the means of production and thereby control how much their employees can participate. If money is speech, isn't failing to increase wages when productivity increases suppression of speech? Growing income inequality necessarily results in a widening gap in how much the parties on either side of the gap can participate in politics. As economic freedom diminishes, so does political freedom. What China has been doing since the 1980s in building a middle class is to lay the groundwork for giving more political freedom just as England and the US did into the twentieth century by expanding the franchise and breaking down other barriers. Yet, as the earlier discussion on women described and as discussions on racism demonstrate, cultural freedom remains quite unevenly allocated. Full use of civil liberties requires more equality in the economic and cultural spheres.

The funny thing is that this is the exact same bad rap given to the political structure in the State of New York and several others and is precisely the way the US House of Representatives has been run under a GOP majority. Sure, voters vote for the governor of New York but there is a long history of governors not doing the things they promised to do if elected. More importantly, voters have no input in deciding who the leaders of the state assembly and senate are. When it comes time to create a budget, which is by far the most important piece of legislation enacted each year for determining policies, only three people are involved, the governor and the two legislative leaders, what is called "three men in a room." There are no hearings, no debates. This is supposed to be democracy in the State of New York.

Governor Andrew Cuomo proudly announced that the state budget was completed on time by means of a rule that allows overriding curing a bill for three days, supposedly to give legislators a chance to read it and think about it before voting. No need for elected representatives to know what they are yea'ing or nay'ing about. Just vote so we can say we got the job done on time. Just like Mussolini got the trains to run on time. Almost all citizens of the State of New York are nonplussed being ruled by a triumvirate. Now we know the real reason New York is the Empire State. Hurrah for Cuomo! He's DINO might!

The assumption by almost everyone in the developed West is that people want a direct hand in the affairs of government (direct democracy) or know direct involvement is impractical so want a direct hand in choosing people to handle the affairs of government (representative democracy). Rarely does anyone stop to think that the very low levels of actual political engagement seen in much of the developed West indicate that this assumption is incorrect.

Most people contend they have enough to worry about or deal with or take care of to be bothered to pay attention all that much to political issues. They have better things to do, better meaning more closely related to their day-to-day lives. That will not stop them from becoming agitated about certain political issues whenever they are raised or from having opinions about every political issue. Yes, a big segment of any population is going to be truly apathetic and never want to discuss politics or do anything that amounts to the least bit of participation. That still leaves quite a lot of people who pay enough attention to know what the issues are and have just enough knowledge to be dangerously self-assured they know enough to draw conclusions to voice whenever the situation arises to have one's say.

Political scientists and others have fretted for decades over the question of whether a population is "ready" for democracy. By this they are not meaning are the people intelligent enough, educated enough, or rational enough to have a say in shaping national policies. That was certainly the thinking in deciding when to give greater self-rule to colonies in which the population was not pinkish. Moreover it was precisely the thinking among the aristocracy and landed elites in the United Kingdom and USA, not to mention many more countries throughout history, when the discussion came around to whether the hoi polloi ought to be given the right to vote or run for office. Throughout history, time and again, nobles, magnates, and wealthy others who knew they had a voice in government regardless of the political system dismissed the idea of asking the workmen, traders, farmers, and peasants their opinions on how to run the country on the grounds that they had neither the knowledge nor intellect to say anything sensible.

It didn't matter if the king was insane or the great landowner couldn't read, while the butcher had accumulated years of wisdom and the merchant had picked up Latin and French in his travels. In an eerie echo of the putdowns used against the poor today, the upper classes knew that if the lower classes had any redeeming qualities they would not be lower class. Their station in life had nothing to do with the economic and political systems working in tandem with social norms to insure that only on rare occasion would someone be able to raise himself. Even then it would have to be by his own bootstraps while Fortune was smiling and Lady Luck was distracting everyone else on the ladder of success with her fan dance.

Class prejudice has existed wherever humans have adopted the idea of private property and produced a surplus that could be converted into wealth. The stories in which people overcome class disadvantages to rise have always been popular. Remember Cinderella and the miller's daughter in Rumpelstiltskin? They provide hope to everyone else that it can be done. Lottery officials publicize people winning jackpots because they need to demonstrate that people who look just like their target demographic win. Otherwise, people will lose hope and not participate. The masses will continue to play and justify playing despite the substantial odds against winning a jackpot only as long as they know it is possible. What happens after those people win is always ignored.

More recently, mega-churches have started eliciting donations by telling their followers that their donations will bless them in the eyes of the Lord. If they continue to donate and pray and donate and hate "them" and donate and praise the Lord and donate maybe magic Jesus will strike them rich for being so faithful. The church owners (and that is what they are) become wealthy while they dole out door prizes and parting gifts to make it appear the donors are getting something in return. At least lotteries pay out cash.

It behooves elites to trumpet the feats of self-made men and women for the same reason. Horatio Alger success stories inspired people to work harder. Welcome to the American Dream! What is never trumpeted is the number of people who do all of the same things and get nowhere. After people rise to the top their stories continue to further fan hope unless a fall follows. Then the whole thing becomes the story of Icarus who took too much pride in being able to fly. Yet we still have those wonderful few who made it and lasted. Just gather enough feathers, make those wings, and hope for a good tail wind.

One of the most enduring stories of someone rising to the top nearly always excludes the other person without whom it never would have happened. The two men who won the civil war establishing internal peace in Rome were Augustus Caesar and his boyhood friend and schoolmate Marcus Agrippa, both from small towns outside of Rome. Some accounts say that Agrippa acted as a kind of bodyguard for the then Gaius Octavius at school so his friend would not be bullied. Agrippa was intelligent and tough but apparently came from a less wealthy family. By all accounts he truly enjoyed being Augustus' best friend but also knew his talents were nothing without a patron to use them.

Throughout their lives, the patrician families in Rome, including the Claudians who provided Augustus with a wife to increase his social standing, looked down their famously aquiline noses at the man given all of the powers needed to be an emperor and the general he thought might succeed him and to whom he gave his only daughter as a wife. Why? Because they were hicks. Even though they had been schooled in Rome, they never lost their rural accents or their rural ways. They might never have amounted to anything in Roman politics but for Augustus' political skills identified by his great-uncle Julius Caesar and Agrippa's military skills identified by Augustus.

Augustus, who came from an equestrian family (equites or knights were one notch down from patrician in terms of wealth as determined by the census), had that great uncle who combined his and Agrippa's skills in one person. That great-uncle followed Roman tradition and adopted Gaius Octavius as his son and heir. For that reason alone, the greatest success story of all time, founding the Roman Empire, revolves around Augustus. Except even the emperor's widely known reconstruction of Rome from mud and thatch to marble and gold owed as much to Agrippa's generosity as Augustus'. At the time they were a team fighting the decay they claimed had resulted from Julius Caesar's assassination and Marc Anthony's effete ways.

The most amazing thing is that Augustus hid his creation of

a dynasty behind the ancient trappings of the Roman Republic. He would not have had Agrippa's support or the support of anyone else if he had said he was founding an empire. Here is where the readiness principle steps in. The Republic was an oligarchy ruled by a Senate from the patrician class that elected two consuls annually. The plebs elected two tribunes each year whose persons were inviolate and who could present legislation to the Senate requested by the plebs and veto legislation. Citizens of Rome, as mentioned previously, took their responsibilities quite seriously. Augustus knew this and could not openly ask to assume those responsibilities as an autocrat. Rome did not have kings. Rex was a cur's name.

Unfortunately, a few decades of civil war accompanied by some substantial gains in territory (Gaul and Egypt) had left the political system a bit ragged. By law, the Romans ruled themselves. In reality, everyone knew that the social fabric that supported discussion of the issues facing the state and the civil society in which everyone had consistent allies rallying around common principles and perspectives needed mending before it could function properly again. In the meantime, give the winner of the civil war as much power as he needs to run the government with the assistance of the Senate, consuls, tribunes, and the rest of the magistrates. There was precedent in electing a dictator (literally someone who tells everyone else what to do) in a crisis. The problem was dictators had never had a term longer than six months and Rome needed more time than that to recover. So, the Senate and the People of Rome made Augustus dictator for ten years.

The citizens of Rome looked at their situation and decided that their limited form of democracy was not going to work. They no longer had the underlying social networks and other ancillary structures like scroll reading clubs and weaving circles whereby citizens could learn what they needed to know and talk out what they needed to think. They did not feel comfortable taking back responsibility for deciding policies and running provinces if they didn't have the means to do so knowledgeably and rationally. Far better to give the task to one person who clearly knows what he is doing (he won the war, didn't he?) while we clean up the wreckage and figure out who we want to socialize with. Language helped in this regard. Our word "republic" comes from *res publica*, literally "public thing." There was no shame in putting the Republic in the hands of an able man since it would remain the Republic.

Augustus modestly turned the Senate down a few times before he agreed to accept the powers of a tribune, election as consul, and the title of Princeps, the root of "prince" that literally means "first one." Then he went to work strengthening the institutions of the Republic by weeding out the Senate to make it more respectable and honorable again, solidifying the territorial gains in the East made by negotiating a peace agreement with the King of Parthia, and reinforcing border districts while relieving Italians of having their lands expropriated by settling his troops from the civil war on free land far outside Italy. The last was probably the most popular move since ten years earlier he had sowed his soldiers up and down the Italian boot in land holdings that had belonged to the assassins of Julius Caesar and their sympathizers.

Augustus did such a fine job that the Senate just kept extending his powers and granting him new honors. Except he also allocated some of his time to coming up with new ways to strengthen the government and help it run smoothly, like establishing the Praetorian Guards and hiring administrators from the equestrian class to give them a sense of being involved. Before anyone knew it, the political system had become a constitutional monarchy headed by an autocratic emperor who had sufficient power to force the supposedly independent Senate to do whatever he wanted. Given that the Roman constitution never spelled out the rules of succession and two of the next four Caesars appear to have had severe mental illnesses, the machinery Augustus created had to operate regardless of who was in charge. And it did for nearly five centuries in Rome and another nine plus centuries from Constantinople.

Did the citizens of Rome make a mistake? Probably not. They made a rational decision given the information and circumstances. They did not know that Augustus had been far more brutal as a triumvir revenging his adoptive father's death than he would be as Princeps. They took a chance and held their breath. It turned out he was generous to opponents and happily traded personal jibes with anyone. He was adept at choosing excellent people to serve the state, beginning with Agrippa and including his stepson Tiberius Claudius Nero who would become his successor.

Tiberius famously rejected a position in the eastern provinces and then retired to Rhodes, one of the eastern provinces, just to thumb his nose at his stepfather and mother. Far from being nepotism in Augustus offering the post or favoritism in declining to punish him for offending the Princeps, the entire city knew how able Tiberius was as a general and administrator and how unable Caesar was to offend the titular head of the patrician Claudian lineage. The Romans made no mistake. They had put their fate into the hands of an amazingly sharp and skilled politician who needed the leeway he had to be pragmatic when Roman leaders had always been principled.

One example of how Augustus demonstrated an adjustable kind of justice was when he refused to punish the slaves of a senator who killed their owner due to their intolerance of the shame he was bringing to his house with his gender-bending sexual activities. The Princeps, who was by now Pontifex Maximus or chief priest as well, wanted to make a point: the master of a house must give the appearance of being in control or be subject to revolt by the members of his household. Indeed, Augustus had reluctantly accepted the title of *Pater Patriae*, father of the country, just as every householder was *pater familias*. His leniency could have been seen as upsetting the natural order as Romans saw it by allowing slaves to judge their owner. Instead, he managed to offer the lesson that power stems from earned authority much like the Chinese Mandate of Heaven. A leader's actions can cause his legitimate authority to drain away. In this matter, the owner had disregarded how his household, including his slaves, looked to outsiders. Failing to rule in a manner that is beneficial to the whole voids any oath of allegiance.

Augustus himself ruled for the welfare of all. If his decisions also greatly benefited his own status and that of his family, that was a good thing. What better way to demonstrate the weight and wealth of the Roman Empire than by having its Princeps demonstrate those strengths. Even two thousand years ago, spin was necessary to insure everyone received the right message. Augustus certainly was not making a point about sexual indiscretions. He was famous for bedding the wives of senators and others at a time when a cuckolded husband was permitted to execute his wife and emasculate her lover if he caught them in the act. Some evidence suggests Augustus used his predations more often than not to promote policy ideas with his sexual partners who would then pass the Princeps' thoughts to their spouses. And it was not unknown for senators to send their wives to the Palatine Hill in the hope that the women would get the imperator's ear regarding some matter while giving him whatever. Personal habits aside, Augustus Caesar turned out to be the right man at the right time for what Rome needed. He filled the role of philosopher-king perfectly.

Chapter 13—Responsive Authoritarian Regimes

ASIDE FROM THE sex, how was Rome under Augustus any different from Russia at the beginning of the twenty-first century? The country as primary component of the USSR experienced great upheavals in the 1980s ending in it being left standing alone much smaller than the Russian Empire had been from about 1775 to 1918. Great chunks of what had been Russia 75 years before were now independent countries thanks to the Soviet Union's decision to form twelve republics in the 1920s out of what remained of the empire and adding three more in World War II by invading Estonia, Latvia, and Lithuania. The three Baltic Republics reverted back to the independence they enjoyed for two decades between world wars. Suddenly Russia was free!

Except free means limitations and deprivations in the eyes of a people used to things being available at least sporadically or in small quantities. All of the social services, all of the support systems created to approximate communism, shabby as they may have been, no longer functioned. No one could feel safe any longer about their jobs, their living conditions, their pensions, even their lives. Alcoholism skyrocketed, murders and suicides increased, and the average lifespans for men particularly plummeted. People with connections bought the shares of denationalized industries. Any effort to introduce open government, free expression, or unbiased journalism was literally gunned down. And many citizens wondered what was so great about freedom if it meant the people who already had it good could easily accumulate more and those who never had it good needed to learn entirely new ways to survive.

For decades under the Romanovs, acceptance of a distinct civil society in which educated, well-off people could meet to discuss any topic waxed and waned. In the second half of the eighteenth century, Catherine II the Great was disposed to emulate Peter the Great's efforts at the beginning of that century to introduce European styles and tastes in all of the arts. This German woman from the minor nobility who fully embraced every tradition of her adopted country, including successfully conspiring to depose her husband, created the St. Petersburg her illustrious predecessor had imagined when he won the marshy land by the Baltic from the Swedes to create a capital facing Europe. The gilt, colorful city stands today with a few substantial additions by her successors as the preeminent showcase to tourists of a country that stopped just twenty years after her death from looking any longer at Europe as an example. St. Petersburg is a gorgeous relic of an effort halted in 1815 after Russia successfully assisted in defeating the primary fount of European styles: France. The rest of that vast nation never had the opportunity to move away from being dreadful and stolid and a world apart from Europe.

The sense that Russia was mature enough to establish its own fashions might be occasionally interrupted by some project that was too difficult for locals to tackle. For example, the awe-inspiring St. Isaac's Cathedral in St. Petersburg relied upon a French architect who only knew how to build very large Catholic cathedrals. The building's shape and outside appearance look more like St. Peter's in Rome. The inside, however, is pure Russian with elaborate mosaics, semi-precious stone for columns, and lots of gold. Nonetheless, Russian leaders decided after Napoleon that their nation did not need to look to others any longer. As a result, in those periods when salons were permitted and poets, statesmen, composers, and nobles gathered to discuss events of the day and the newest trends in philosophy they stuck pretty close to Russian events and trends. While new ideas could emerge and did, civil society was decidedly not creating the kinds of associations and alliances that prefigured liberal democracy. Russia remained an autocracy.

Skip ahead a century and a few hotheads who had managed to learn a thing or two from Europeans, particularly two Germans named Karl Marx and Friedrich Engels, latched onto the idea of replacing Russia's autocracy with socialism. An embarrassing loss to Japan in war in 1905 resulted in calls for governmental reforms. Half-measures were introduced and even those seemed far too extravagant for the tsar. Instead he tried handing everything off to ministers who had little time or resources to get anything moving before Russia wound up at war in 1914. The tsar thought victory against the German Empire would prove his effectiveness as a leader. That certainly had worked for many monarchies in the past, but only when the monarchs were successful military strategists. Nicholas II was quite handsome in a uniform and we will leave it at that.

Losses led to abdication. Abdication led to instability. Instability gave Vladimir Lenin the opportunity to see if his theory of replacing the autocratic tsarist government with an autocratic one-party government would provide Russia with the means to transform into a socialist paradise leading to communism. The Bolshevik Revolution needed a good four years of civil war to firmly place Lenin's one party in the position to control the entire government and begin planning how to take over the economy. Unfortunately, Lenin died a couple years after that. His devious comrade from the Republic of Georgia, Josef Stalin, decided to use that one party to be his political apparatus for establishing a dictatorship. Within a few years, Stalin had achieved his goal, outmaneuvering all of his potential adversaries.

Stalin was no more or less than a new kind of tsar, a tyrant who identified his being with the Soviet Union. He was unafraid of ordering or causing the deaths of millions first to transform the Soviet Union into a modern industrial state and then to defend the Soviet Union against German efforts to make that industrial state a slave. Being unafraid is not the same thing as being brave. Human lives were part of the equation of costs required for the benefits gained. What westerners habitually fail to realize about Stalin was his goals really were to improve the lot of the citizens of the Soviet Union. Some may say that even recognizing that fact, the means cannot justify the ends. Like all platitudes, that one is most helpful when explaining it is wrong.

The country the Bolsheviks inherited from the Romanovs was so badly behind the modern world after having closed itself off in 1815 that bringing it forward so quickly was going to be violent no matter who tried to achieve it. The citizens of the Soviet Union desired that it be achieved. The tens of millions who died could always be venerated by the grateful several hundred million who finally wound up economically in the twentieth century after World War II. By 1950, the Soviet Union was not only stable but also one of two superpowers in the world. That is a remarkable turnaround for a country that was falling apart everywhere in 1918.

The achievement does not diminish or overlook the reckless savagery used in its making from the viewpoint of its benefactors. Its accomplishment only asks whether any other paths could have been taken that would have been less horrific but led to similar results. Stalin was faced with a Kobayashi Maru test. Like James T. Kirk he simply cheated in order to get the result he calculated would benefit the most people. Observers can accept the no-win scenario leaders face in fiction because the deaths are an abstraction. Yet they still vilify a real world leader who finds a way to win that saves x lives at the cost of y lives when x is many times greater than y.

De-Stalinization was a way for Stalin's successors in the

government to distance themselves from the means while taking full advantage of the ends. Stalin couldn't object. Nikita Khrushchev and Leonid Brezhnev merely continued to use the same political apparatus to maintain power. Aside from the early successes in the space program, the Soviet Union stopped moving forward. Any possible benefit received from Stalin's brutal effort to pull the country forward went toward keeping up militarily with the USA as a superpower.

By the early 1980s, the stagnation had grown so burdensome that something needed to be done. The quick deaths of Brezhnev's immediate successors gave Mikhail Gorbachev the opportunity to fix the problems. Unfortunately, between hardliners who refused change and wanted the government to continue the arms race and dreamers who wanted the shackles removed, Gorbachev couldn't succeed. The moribund state had sapped the ambitions of the approved organizations and prevented the rise of independent groups. The civil society the country needed to ferment and support ideas for change did not exist. Stalin's old machine certainly was not going to do the job. Gorbachev felt he had no choice but to permit an opening of society so that people could start to talk about issues, exchange ideas, and become the foundation for jump-starting the Soviet Union. Gorbachev needed to build the non-governmental civil society Russia never developed. Unfortunately for him, unlike economic development, social and cultural development cannot be sped up.

Some people in the Baltics, Georgia, and Ukraine had begun developing nationalist-based intellectual groups under Khrushchev that had gone underground until Gorbachev adopted *glasnost*, his policy of opening Soviet society. They were tied into the *samizdat* circles in Russia that produced forbidden books and journals. The *samizdat* circles were fractured among nationalists, civil rights activists, and others, providing less of a base for future developments. Even in the republics in which the groups were more united, this was not nearly enough to shake off one-party rule. It did give those segments of the Soviet Union a starting point when the more capable tremors aimed at shaking one-party rule in Eastern Europe began. As a result, Armenia, Estonia, Georgia, Latvia, Lithuania, and Ukraine wound up progressing further toward western-style democracy than their sister soviet republics when the Soviet Union collapsed at the end of 1991. In the other nine republics, leaders from the Communist Party willing to at least put on a show of transitioning to democracy emerged. All of those but the Russian Federation, that still immense stump of the Romanov Empire, quickly turned into autocracies.

In Russia, a very stubborn, intelligent, feisty alcoholic named Boris Yeltsin took charge. He was popular from having been the first person to ever resign from the Soviet Union's leadership group, the Politburo, in 1987. His first few years in office were marked by efforts to make an about face with the West regarding the Cold War and to denationalize all of the businesses and factories operated by the Soviet state. After Yeltsin faced a coup attempt in 1993, it became clear that the insiders buying all of the denationalized industries were forming an oligarchy to run the country for their own benefit. His popularity dropped as Russian citizens steadily felt increasing economic pressures that seemed worse than the way things were under communism. The first round of the presidential election in 1996 showed just how peeved the voters were with Yeltsin and the new, supposedly freer system by putting the candidate from the Communist Party less than four percentage points behind Yeltsin. The oligarchy rallied around Yeltsin to prevent losing him as the country's leader and corrupted the second round.

These were tough choices for Russian citizens regardless: return to communism or accept oligarchy. What was missing was any significant opportunity to try any kind of real democracy. Except the efforts made to promote representative democracy along the lines of the West were largely turned down. They were not turned down by propaganda or threats. They were turned down by people unwilling to shoulder the responsibility of being active citizens. And before anyone says the Russian people never had a chance to try it to see whether they liked it, look at the participation rates among citizens in western democracies. Very few people are clamoring to be more involved.

Democracy is like a gym club membership. Everyone has high hopes that they are going to make good use of it and only a small percentage actually do with any regularity. Are the people who never sign up for a gym club membership because they know they won't get much out of it wrong for not wasting their money? Of course not. Would they like to feel and be healthier? Probably. Are they going to do much about it? Probably not. Welcome to the way a Russian citizen thinks about democracy! I may die a little younger, but I don't have to spend any time or money right now and I have no motivation to do so. If things get really bad, I will do something about it. I promise.

Given Yeltsin's unpopularity, the oligarchs needed someone to replace him. The man they found, Vladimir Putin, was a former member of the KGB and charismatic in a Russian kind of way, exuding confidence, strength, and rough charm. Putin not only smoothly took over from Yeltsin but also managed to develop a political party made up of people attracted to authoritarian discipline used to correct the economic woes they were facing. He put the state back into business to a certain extent by going after oligarchs that opposed him and turning their companies into government corporations. He piggybacked onto China's economic growth by turning Russia into a warehouse of raw materials. He stuck to a very firm foreign policy that echoed the days past when the Soviet Union, with Russia at its center, was a superpower. His popularity skyrocketed and he became known as the world's most powerful person according to some standards.

While cracking down on civil liberties like freedom of the

press, speech, and assembly, Putin has become a beacon of progress for religious freedom, military reform, and environmental issues, particularly endangered species protection. In short, he is a philosopher-king doing his best to provide the sorts of things to the Russian people that matter to them most and demonstrating their lives can be much better under a government controlled by a monopolistic oligarchy than under Lenin's one-party oligarchy. If some people would prefer a more open society, the door to the West is that way. The point is that a majority of the people are genuinely pleased that their government is providing the things they want. Popular will is guiding policy.

Popular will is guiding policy in China as well. In contrast to Russia, China found the means to make the lives of its citizens much better under Lenin's one-party oligarchy. It all began around 1979. Deng Xiaoping managed to secure his place once again among the highest leaders of the country and definitively put out the last embers of the conflagration called the Cultural Revolution. Free at last to implement his vision of how to stabilize and enrich China, Deng began announcing a series of policies collectively called "socialism with Chinese characteristics."

Mao Zedong had held the Communist Party together through decades of civil war, Japanese occupation, and more civil war to found a one-party political system with a socialist economy after defeating the Chinese Nationalists who wanted to found a one-party system with a capitalist economy. In the 1950s, he and other leaders of the revolution, including Deng, tried to sort out installing socialism on what was, essentially, a feudal, mercantile economy. Naturally, there was considerable pushback from the hundreds of millions of peasants who thought the revolution meant they would own their own farms to do with as they pleased without regard to landowners and their consigliere. Mao pushed back harder to enforce collectivization, resulting in a horrific famine.

As Secretary-General of the Communist Party, Deng Xiaoping was among the leaders that worked on rectifying the problems by loosening restrictions on rural land ownership and ending forced collectivization. Still revered within the party and elsewhere for being the political and ideological leader of their victory, Mao responded to this embrace of free market concepts by setting off the greatest self-evaluation exercise ever known in human history. For a decade, the Chinese people were told to look at themselves and look at each other and find the impediments to realizing progress on China's road to greatness through socialism. Tens of millions of people were denounced by others close to them and "sent down to the country," which meant a great deal of physical labor on state-owned farms or in state-owned factories coupled with instruction on what the "correct" principles were. Deng Xiaoping was among those purged.

Deng was saved from oblivion in 1974 by his long-time mentor, Premier Zhou Enlai, a pragmatic leader and architect of China's return to the United Nations and opening with the United States of America. Zhou had cancer and hoped Deng would replace him. Two years later, the Chinese people began wondering whether the Mandate of Heaven had been withdrawn from Communist Party rule. January 1976 saw the death of Zhou. July 1976 brought the death of an estimated 650,000 people as a result of the Tangshan earthquake in northeastern China, the most deadly natural disaster of the twentieth century other than the Spanish influenza pandemic. September 1976 saw the death of Mao. These three blows certainly seemed to indicate some kind of cosmic comment regarding China's course.

Deng had duly taken over the day-to-day duties of the premier upon Zhou's death. However, in April 1976, authorities brusquely removed symbols of mourning for Zhou placed by citizens at a monument in Tiananmen Square before Qingming, a lunar calendar festival for honoring the dead. The faction in the party allied with Mao still pushing the Cultural Revolution blamed Deng for this “rightist” display of grief. They were unnerved by the spontaneous actions of the people, peaceful enough but accompanied by veiled criticisms of that faction contained in poems about ancient leaders everyone knew had been rotten. A supposedly more pliable person was named premier named Hua Guofeng. Deng was retired to essentially house arrest. However, after Mao’s death, the faction no longer had a powerful patron. Premier Hua decided he would prefer to govern without a group of troublemaking radicals trying to tell him what to do. He rallied his allies, rehabilitated Deng Xiaoping, and dropped hints that the three disasters of losing the two greatest leaders of the revolution and such a large part of the population all within nine months meant the universe no longer wanted the leaders behind the Cultural Revolution to stay in power. The faction leaders, known as the Gang of Four, were arrested.

Hua Guofeng had nowhere near the stature of Deng Xiaoping despite everyone’s amusement that “Xiaoping” is a homophone in Chinese for “little bottle,” which aptly described Deng’s height. Zhou Enlai’s actual successor bringing back into government Zhou Enlai’s choice for successor was necessary for Hua to relieve himself of the Gang of Four. However, it left him to fill the role of a ventriloquist’s dummy as Deng finally had unfettered power to implement his vision of how China was going to become a prosperous, stable world power. The key was to gradually give lower level government entities, like cities and provinces, the authority to make economic development decisions with anyone in the world. Once that was working, individual citizens could be granted authority to become entrepreneurs to take advantage of the ancillary aspects of the economic development contracts and provide consumer goods to the people who were going to have higher, steadier incomes than they ever could have under a centrally-planned economy.

This devolution of power was strictly limited to economic

decisions. The Communist Party had to maintain stability and order in a country that had been wracked by rebellions, civil wars, and even a period without any effective national government in the 1920s like Somalia is today. Socialism was still required to insure that all citizens were provided their essential needs under an economic model intended to give the government enough revenue to actually meet those needs. Accordingly, the decision to devolve decision making was not an invitation to question the political system.

The Chinese Communist Party prides itself on a system for gathering popular input in which people in villages and neighborhoods can address their needs and interests to local party and government officials. Those officials are expected to report to the county or city level and county and city level officials report to the provincial level and provincial level officials report to the national level. Policies are adopted at the national level and then sent back down the line. The system is not much different from the way the Chinese Empire was administered. As with all things, how well it functions depends on the quality, motivations, and diligence of officials at each level.

This is true in any political system. American history is replete with instances in which popular demands are stonewalled by local officials or ignored by state officials. As Deng Xiaoping's career path demonstrates, factions at the national level endorse or oppose the need for change that rises from the villages and neighborhoods according to their views on how best to establish a socialist society. While the Soviet Union was noteworthy for the unity of the top leadership established by Stalin and maintained by his successors, China's Communists since their party's founding in 1921 have always embraced debate within the highest ranks to reach policy decisions that then must be presented as though there was never any question what the proper path was. In this way, China looks much more like a parliamentary democracy in which the cabinet ministers duke it out until the prime minister figures out who makes the best case and imposes a united front on everyone.

Just because citizens do not have much choice in who they elect or who makes decisions in a one-party system does not mean that the party can't represent multiple perspectives reflecting the varied opinions within the populace. Nor does it mean that there can't be methods by which citizens can express those opinions. Given China's turbulent and bloody history from around 1835 to 1975, the single most important thing a government can do is provide stability and safety from rebellions and invasions. The next most important thing is to provide everyone with their basic needs in some fashion to end the recurring destructiveness of famine and disease. After that, people want tangible doo-dads and useful machines, employment to purchase those things, and education to prepare them for employment. They want the government to do those things that are to most societies the primary reasons for forming communities and agreeing to the social contract.

One thing they do not want is for government or party officials to enrich themselves or engage in any other forms of corruption. They do not pay taxes so someone can build a nice villa or vacation in Vegas. Unfortunately, granting lower officials the power to approve business contracts and asking them to promote entrepreneurship led to a fair number of public servants and cadres who wanted to benefit substantially from their efforts to improve local economies. One of the few forms of protest the Chinese government permits is for people to petition for investigations into corrupt practices. The party and government want to be seen as agents of the people. They cannot do so if their representatives are getting wealthy from bribes, connected business ventures, and other forms of graft. This is so serious that the penalties for corruption go up to and include capital punishment. From all reports, officials are not falsely accused or railroaded by others who have a score to settle. That is a remarkable indicator of how much the

Communist Party does not want to be seen as anything else but the champion of the Chinese people.

Since these economic reform policies were designed to ultimately help every Chinese citizen prosper in ways that had never been possible, the government did not want to hear about civil liberties and human rights. Remember, you can't eat freedom. While this is a very paternalistic approach, the only difference between it and economic development in capitalist economies is that everyone knows that and knows the government is the one supervising everything. Under capitalism, individuals face the same paternalism from banks, business regulations, and many other authorities that can put up roadblocks to success. Corporations may enjoy expanded civil liberties as putative citizens. However, the millions of people actually producing their products and servicing their customers outside the USA and the millions of employees working for them within the USA have absolutely no liberties vis-à-vis their employers; exercising freedoms of speech, expression, not to incriminate one's self, assembly, even religion result in termination of employment. Americans believe civic freedoms are as essential to humans as air. Objections to China's disregard for civic freedoms take three forms.

Thanks to the Dalai Lama, people know that Buddhist Tibetans have long demanded independence. Less well known is the demand for independence made by Muslim Uighurs north of Tibet in Xinjiang. A few Uighur jihadists have been held at Guantanamo, raising their profile somewhat. Like three other provinces, Tibet and Xinjiang are designated at "autonomous regions" in which the largest minority ethnic group is supposed to have a greater say in provincial affairs. In practice, that autonomy has been watered down by the internal migration of Han Chinese to these areas diluting the power of the minorities. A lot of the small intrusions by the larger state add up to nationalistic frustration. For example, China runs on Beijing time even though Urumqi, the capital of Xinjiang, ought to be three hours behind. Uighurs ignore this by having "mosque" time based on when prayers are called.

Independence is a tough sell to the Chinese government because the Chinese have held those areas as dependencies off and on for two millennia. Activists in the West tend to look only at an ethnic group dominated by a government run by another ethnic group. The actual degree of independence the regions have had in the past is based more on their remoteness from more populous areas. How remote? Urumqi is the largest city in the world so far inland and so far distant from any city of comparable size.

Even if they were given independence they would fall into the same category as several dozen states that have insufficient resources to be economically independent. Prior to the creation of nation-states and international law, a polity that was not economically self-sufficient using its own resources or through trade would never remain independent. Now nationalities can apply to the World Bank, other institutions, and other states for welfare to maintain their sovereignty. Once a state is recognized as independent, sovereignty blocks the use of any remedies to extinguish it. Witness the response to the invasion of Kuwait by Iraq.

Citizens throughout China also take a strong stand against environmental degradation. Protests have grown over the past ten years. The protesters know they are not opposing government policies or party power because the government and party have identified the state of China's environment as a major concern. The problem is that the government and party seem to have been incapable of addressing environmental issues. The policies are not being implemented effectively. To some extent it is the result of corrupt officials. In other cases the officials are just incompetent or haven't the necessary resources. These delays will not do for people who see their children fall ill, the air become so bad everyone must wear face masks, the rivers and lakes still unavailable for fishing or recreation, etc.

The government and party essentially feel that these protests provide an outlet for anger that must not be directed at how the political system is structured and merely criticizes the political system for lack of diligence and skill. If there is any chance for opposition movements in China to succeed, it is most likely going to be one led by the environmentalists.

The third form of opposition is the most dangerous. Most people of a certain age remember the showdown in Tiananmen Square between democracy activists and the People's Liberation Army in 1989. The photo of one man standing in the street facing a column of tanks has become an icon. The protest started in the same way as the Qingming protest in 1976. Students in Beijing wished to mourn Hu Yaobang, the disgraced Communist Party General Secretary who had been managing the degrees of openness needed for the economic reforms with just the right touch until he was dismissed for being too lenient toward political protests. The students wanted to see further opening of the press and other civil rights. They also were concerned that the country was not going to be able to absorb them into the workforce upon graduation given the way the economy looked. The government at first allowed the protest to continue unchallenged. The demonstrators were voicing opinions held by some in the leadership. However, copycat protests erupted in other cities. The demonstration in Beijing embarrassed the government's rapprochement with the Soviet Union by forcing a ceremony welcoming Mikhail Gorbachev to be held at the airport. The protest was clearly attacking the political system.

The only other big display of support for western forms of civil liberties that had occurred in China in the twentieth century began on May 4, 1919. The Chinese Communists, being somewhat prosaic, call it the May Fourth Movement. Likewise, the protest in 1976 is the April Fifth Movement and the one in 1989 is the June Fourth Movement. Of course, calling their biggest national holiday the Fourth of July makes Americans unoriginal first.

Seventy years prior to the large protests in Tiananmen Square, Chinese students and members of the western-influenced middle class took to the streets of Beijing to denounce their government's inability to prevent the Treaty of Versailles from ignoring China's interests. The treaty handed over German territorial concessions in China to Japan. It failed to block the infamous 21 Demands Japan had made in 1915 to take control of Manchuria and make China subservient. It failed to end the most humiliating terms of the unequal treaties China signed the previous century, such as extraterritoriality that suspended Chinese law in parts of Chinese cities held by Western powers. The protesters knew well enough that it was questionable whether China even had a functioning national government eight years after the abdication of the last emperor. They had counted on Woodrow Wilson's idealism about a family of nations and the reigning theory of self-determination to restore China to full sovereignty over its territory. Oddly, those are the exact same principles that Westerners now use to demand independence for Tibetans and Uighurs.

Despite the apparent betrayal by France, the United Kingdom, and the United States to look after China when China could not look after itself, the May Fourth protesters wanted China to form a liberal democratic government, an idea that had been percolating among Chinese intellectuals ever since a few scholars went to study abroad in the 1880s and 1890s. The difficulty, as had happened in Russia, was that western-style democracy with all of the associated freedoms had only been discussed by a very small number of unrepresentative citizens who had the intellect to grasp the best aspects of it. No one else knew anything about democracy and no one really wanted to know.

One can argue that everyone was ignorant in the strict sense of having no knowledge about the subject. How were they going to learn what would be to them alien concepts of individuality, natural law, liberty, responsibility, and the rest of the package that people in democracies learn from a young age? Most people with any political power, including the growing Nationalist Party and the warlords that were divvying up the country among themselves had no desire to instill civic rectitude in a nation of peasants who just wanted enough security and stability to harvest this year's crops. China's history was marked by centuries of prosperity interrupted by decades of turmoil as the Mandate of Heaven changed hands. This was just one of those periods of turmoil and the Chinese people would be quite happy to reverence the newest dynasty once things got sorted out.

During the 1920s, China would see the rise of the Nationalist Party in the south while the rest of the country was governed by regional landlords. Whoever occupied Beijing spoke for China to other states internationally. By 1927, the Nationalists could say they had gathered up the pieces and established a new government. Meanwhile the Chinese Communist Party was born in Shanghai in 1921 and blossomed into a strong movement thanks to some very persuasive leaders. They joined forces with the Nationalists to rid the country of warlords. Once the Nationalists felt secure, they turned on their allies. China was plunged into civil war. The enemy-allies were forced to cooperate with each other after Japan invaded China proper in 1937, having already taken Manchuria in 1931. Once Japan surrendered eight years later, the civil war started up again. The United States seriously tried to create a coalition government. Instead, the Communists steadily defeated the Nationalists and declared victory on October 1, 1949. Although there would be the almost three decades of self-inflicted turmoil after that, the Chinese people knew the Mandate of Heaven had been awarded to Mao Zedong and the Communists.

After stumbling for so long, the Communists seemed to get it right under Deng Xiaoping. The Chinese people began to grow prosperous and their lives changed rapidly. What led to the crackdown on June 4, 1989 in Beijing against the protests was the need to simultaneously make clear that the Communist Party still needed to not be questioned openly about political issues while preventing the Maoists in the leadership from halting the economic reforms. The premier, Zhao Ziyang, went to Tiananmen Square and tried to explain to the demonstrators that this was not the time yet to ask for civil liberties. China was in the midst of an incredible economic and social transformation comparable to what Japan experienced in the 1960s and 1970s. Although civil liberties were enshrined in their American-written constitution, the Japanese people largely accepted not to use those liberties to criticize their government. They continued to vote to keep one party, the Liberal Democrats, in control of the government steadily for decades, having faith based on the evidence that their economic policies were enriching pretty much all of the citizens of the nation. Zhao knew that the Chinese needed to do the same thing the Japanese had done except without a western-style constitution.

The protesters listened but did not take Zhao's advice to disperse. They wanted freedom. Instead, somewhere around 800 or 900 protesters died in Beijing (none actually in Tiananmen Square that can be verified). The decision was made to end the protests by consensus as usual and with Deng's approval. The hardline faction had wanted to use the protests as a means to roll back the reforms. The progressives had been willing to discuss political reforms that would benefit the economic reforms. Instead, the decision was made only to end the protests. Zhao was removed from office and never seen publicly again. With Zhao and a few others gone, no one was around to boost the reforms, but with the world and the Chinese people appalled at the deaths, the Maoists didn't dare try to dismantle them either. Three years later, Deng conducted a widely-publicized tour of the southern provinces. He made clear that China had to continue the economic reforms no matter what.

Deng knew that the Chinese people wanted freedom. They

wanted freedom from want, freedom from poverty, freedom from abusive employers and landowners, freedom to stop doing the laundry by hand, freedom from curable infectious diseases, freedom to earn enough to be tourists in their own country, freedom from bad water and non-existent waste systems, freedom from no electricity, freedom from only having sitting around at night talking for entertainment, freedom from the confinements placed on people whose basic needs are not met and must work constantly just to survive, freedom to improve their lives through diligence and smarts. Hardly any Chinese people had those freedoms in 1949. At least 90 percent of the population had most or all of them when Deng died in 1997.

The biggest problems facing China today, aside from tackling the pollution and other environmental consequences of rapid economic growth, are keeping the Communist Party's officials, government employees, and members of the military from using their positions to make money and finally helping the peripheral areas within China to achieve the same kinds of economic and social progress the rest of the country has achieved. The latter is a consequence of the geopolitics that guided the reforms. Deng started with loosening the strings on economic activity, building four special economic zones along the coast, allowing deal making with foreign investors by the governments of fourteen "open cities" on the coast, expanding that authority to provinces and other municipalities, promoting the financial infrastructure and building the transportation infrastructure needed to support growth, and all of the small steps that add up to a relatively free market. Very little of this activity reached into rural nooks and crannies found in any country, some quite close to booming districts. Occasionally, the small hometowns of individuals who have made it big receive the kind of attention that gratitude offers. The Chinese government eventually realized addressing the needs of the remaining have nots needed to rise to the top of the agenda for the party and government.

What about freedom in the political sense? That depends on how the Chinese people feel. A portion of the population believes China must adopt western-style civil liberties and respect human rights. No one knows whether that portion is larger or smaller than the portion in 1919, 1949, 1976, or 1989. Most likely, it is larger of course. But that begs the question what rights do even this minority of Chinese citizens really want? Western democracies do not agree on what constitutes freedom. Courts in the United States have ruled unconstitutional the kinds of restrictions on hate speech common in Europe. France bans clothing and accessories that draw attention to a person's religion even if that clothing is part of the exercise of religion. Nor do western democracies always stay clear of infringing human rights. The United States tortured prisoners or had others torture them for the USA, but did so outside its territory so as not to run afoul on the prohibition against cruel and unusual punishment. Most amazingly, government officials and others defended the activities as just enhanced interrogation techniques, as though renaming them changed the nature of the agony inflicted on human beings. Same-sex marriage still is not uniformly legal in the West or even accepted as a human right.

That is the issue. Until every state is named Utopia, every state is going to fall short in actively supporting and guaranteeing human rights as agreed upon in the United Nations Declaration of Human Rights. Some of them conflict with the operation of others. All of them conflict when used side by side. Human beings are not each their own independent, self-sufficient universe. So long as we must work together, the best that can be done is for communities to decide for themselves how to observe human rights and which ones take priority over others when resources are limited. China has demonstrated in the last 35 years that what matters most is to provide those freedoms popular will dictates are needed soonest. The chaos and acrimony of free speech, free expression, free press, and all of the other civil liberties are the result of people not thinking twice if they are overindulging or being reckless. The peace and contentment of free access to food, clothing, healthcare, education, electricity, clean water, shelter, employment, and wellbeing are the result of people taking advantage of basic needs being met and the relief from anxiety and frustration.

Chapter 14—Your Freedom, My Freedom

CIVIL LIBERTIES, THOSE freedoms that men and women have fought and died for over many centuries, do not have to be earned or given. Every human being is endowed with the power to decide how, what, who, where, when, and why given the resources available, just like every other living creature on this planet. The difference, we presume, is only that we use a combination of reason, experience, education, and nature to make those decisions while every other life form is guided by its nature, experience, and sometimes the actions of or training by others. Humans have the right to anything and everything within their ken so long as the exercise of that right to anything and everything does not diminish the same right possessed by any other human. Observe squirrels for any period of time and this will be clear.

Exercise of the right is qualified by the requirement of taking responsibility for the consequences. The root of all laws is that an actor is responsible for his or her actions. The actual consequences of an action can never be known until after the action is completed. Accordingly, the actor is stuck with the consequences. The degree of responsibility rests on the degree of intentionality behind the act. We are responsible at some level even if we didn't consciously intend the act. The clear cut cases are those in which the actor made a conscious decision. One can act without asking permission to diminish the other's right and be held liable for that diminishment, ask permission to act and negotiate what, if anything, the other wants in compensation for that diminishment, or choose not to act.

All other forms of life on Earth have worked out ways to regulate those instances when one action impinges on the right of another. Those ways become part of the species DNA or are taught one generation to the next. The reactions can be downright horrific annihilation or mutually-beneficial symbiosis. The reaction can be one squirrel chasing another for ten minutes. Humans chose to regulate the instances when one action impinges on the right of another by forming communities with rules governing behavior. We call it the social contract.

Humans do not give up their freedoms in order to become members of a community; they merely accept certain limitations on the exercise of those freedoms. They recognize that the exercise of freedom within a community results in consequences affecting others in the community. The person generating those consequences must be accountable for generating them. One of the great benefits of belonging to a community is that the community as a whole chooses how to decide if someone's right has been infringed or damaged, how to hold the perpetrator accountable, and how to enforce that accountability. That beats chasing each other around when we have better things to do.

Speech and expression are wonderful examples of how this works. Justice Potter was faced with that difficult question noted earlier of how best to guide lower courts in determining whether a book, film, photograph, or any other form of expression was so pornographic it was no longer protected by the First Amendment. Why should he even care? The general assumption is that pornography is harmful because it objectifies sexual activities and human anatomy. But at what point does a depiction of sexual activity cross the line from just being two (or more) people doing what comes naturally to harmful objectification? And how does one detect the harm caused? Presumably Augustus thought the line is crossed by the time those sexual activities justify slaves murdering their owner.

Justice Potter's solution, to only say he knows hardcore pornography when he sees it, just adds to the dilemma by requiring a definition for "hardcore." The fact is that people's sensitivities vary so greatly regarding the portrayal of sexual activities no line exists. If the line does not exist, then how can the First Amendment intrude to make a line?

In *Miller v. California*, the case that kept Potter up at night, the US Supreme Court decided there is a line. The Court held that speech is unprotected by determining:

a) Whether the "average person applying contemporary community standards" would find that the work, taken as a whole, appeals to the prurient interest;
b) Whether the work depicts or describes, in a patently offensive way, sexual conduct specifically defined by the applicable state law; and
c) Whether the work, taken as a whole, lacks serious literary, artistic, political, or scientific value.

Let us ignore for the moment how many average persons actually know what a prurient interest looks like let alone what its appeal might be.

Since this ruling over forty years ago, contemporary community standards have changed dramatically for some people and very little for others with regard to depictions of violence. Gone are the days that the blood and gore were suggested rather than shown outright at every opportunity. Television programs like *NCIS* revel in depicting traumatized bodies and body parts with great exactitude to demonstrate a reality previous generations were expected to manifest in their imaginations only if they chose to go that far and had some idea of what the specific kind of trauma could do to flesh.

A film like *M*A*S*H* was shocking in its day for showing the blood on white surgical costumes, a shock intended to emphasize the revolting goriness of war that people had only just discovered in news coverage of the American intrusion in Vietnam. Around the same time, the musical *Pippin* sarcastically and erotically depicted warfare in the time of Charlemagne as both a great game for adult men to enjoy and a greater opportunity to glorify masculine leadership. The scene concluded with body parts being thrown onto the stage as a vaudeville rag played, followed by Charlemagne's son Pippin trying to fathom the worthiness of war in a conversation with the decapitated head of one of the combatants.

Nowadays, children as young as five or six play video games that feature myriad ways of dismembering, destroying, and dehumanizing characters designed to look as lifelike as possible. It's hard to imagine the necessity of conducting research on the effects of such activities. Nonetheless substantial research has been done and it overwhelmingly shows that violence in video games negatively influences how children interpret violence in real life. American parents are raising a generation of children careless of the dignity of human life. Despite this enormous raft of evidence, the US Supreme Court ruled 7-2 in 2011 that video game violence was protected speech, in part using the *Miller* test for pornography to strike down California's law banning the sale of such games to anyone under eighteen. The Court went so far as to state that any depiction of violence whatsoever was protected by the First Amendment.

Brown v. Entertainment Merchants Association was a surprisingly harsh blow to organizations that well know almost all parents learn how to parent as they go along using their experiences growing up as a model of what or what not to do. The Supreme Court rejected the clear scientific evidence in favor of the traditional belief that parents know what is best for their children even though the news on any given day will provide multiple examples of parents clearly not knowing what is best for their children.

The only dim light of hope was a note that maybe if video

games begin to look more realistic the Court might have to look at the issue again. Except cable television shows and theatrical movies already show extremely realistic violence and are not deemed unprotected speech. Long gone are the days when films like *A Man for All Seasons* and historical miniseries like *Elizabeth R* used sound and film editing to great effect to show a beheading without showing the beheading. We have returned to the times when crowds went to watch executions both in make believe and in real life through ISIL videos. We have reached the point where we are no longer concerned that the USA's ally, Saudi Arabia, never stopped public executions, mutilations, and whippings after Friday prayers *pour encourager les autres*. Yes, we are all mature enough to decide whether to watch or not. No harm done if one happens to be passing through the family room just as Ducky on *NCIS* gets to work, right?

Individual sovereignty certainly favors giving the benefit of the doubt in all matters to the individual to decide many things so long as the individual takes responsibility for his choices. Whether to have children or not is one of the most private and personal decisions human beings make. It is at the core of the debate regarding a woman's right to decide whether to take a pregnancy to term. As many have pointed out, the people who clamor so loudly to deny women that choice frequently oppose all efforts to support the well-being of a child and its parents once the decision is made to carry to term. How can a society claim to interfere with one of the most profoundly emotional and weightiest financial decisions a person makes and not take responsibility for the consequences of that interference? Ours regrettably does.

The marriage equality debates included the resoundingly ridiculous argument that marriage is intended to promote reproduction that keeps society populated. The argument is so full of holes it is a wonder it stayed afloat for so long. Lots of marriages between men and women result in no children by choice, physiology, age, or dysfunction. Lots of marriages between same sex couples result in children by adoption, surrogacy, or donation. Besides, procreation does not require a marriage certificate. In fact, it requires nothing other than the exchange of DNA. That is a problem. Millennia ago humans recognized that parents need to have people with more expertise teach their children. Yet it occurs to very few parents that they themselves need to be taught how to be parents. Yes, they may ask their parents or friends for advice, but basically they are winging it based on memories of their own upbringing.

An analogous problem exists in higher education. Individuals who go on to obtain PhDs are presumed able to teach the next couple generations their fields of expertise. To obtain a PhD one typically must complete a certain number of graduate seminars in which one not only acquires greater knowledge of the field but also of research and analysis methods. The person may be required to pass comprehensive exams to demonstrate competency in the field of study. Indeed, the person writing this spent four six-hour days doing that in 1985. Then the person chooses a research topic and, guided by an advisor, writes a dissertation on some question or theory that no one else has bothered to look at or just popped up and defends the dissertation before a committee of professors. Nowhere in those four to eight years of graduate work does the PhD candidate ever learn anything at all about how to teach. Nonetheless, about the only requirement for any faculty position at any college or university in the USA is having a PhD in field or expecting to have one within a year of hire. A person does not even need to speak intelligible English. Isn't that obscene?

If parents are guided by their own upbringing, what will happen to the children raised by the children transfixed by violent video games? Is it impossible to put gory, extended violence back in Pandora's X-Box? We have no word equal to prurient to describe an interest in violent activities. Yet because we do have the word prurient we are free to use it to define a category of sexual imagery that we want to think is harmful but have no evidence to confirm is harmful. One might think it is no longer possible to draw the line in this way to leave some depictions of sex unprotected, even depictions of unprotected sex. A small number of sexual fetishes exist that only those who indulge in them do not find them repulsive. If anyone were to produce a book, film, or whatever else depicting those fetishes in action, the audience would be so tiny that it is next to impossible that anyone not involved in that scene could stumble upon it accidentally. In some cases, everyone involved in that scene may have been involved in producing the material. One is infinitely more likely to casually see one of Ducky's mutilated, pale, post-autopsy corpses when passing the television in the family room.

We are a long way from Lieutenant Uhuru kissing Captain Kirk just as the Supreme Court ruled that miscegenation laws were unconstitutional, but many audience members still feel grossed out seeing two men French kiss. We won't discuss why they are not as grossed out about two women doing the same thing. Do two men French kissing violate community standards in Lubbock? Likely, but all the same who is going to admit having a prurient interest? The only line, the bottom line, is that the depiction of sexual activities between consenting adults is not outside the scope of freedoms of speech and expression.

The consenting adults caveat is critical. If pornography is a form of speech or expression, which it must be because it is a form of communication, the sole limitation placed on it is that it must not depict anyone under the age of consent. As a culture we have decided that sexual acts of any kind involving pre-pubescent children is prohibited and we have almost completely restricted sexual acts involving teenagers who have reached puberty but not the legal age of consent to those engaged in by individuals within that age range. Teen romance stories may hint at or describe sexual activities, but they have some literary value that pornography does not have and doesn't aspire to have. Authorities apparently are confused about the literary or artistic value of sexting given that some teens have been charged with misdemeanor violations for sending dick pics and such to friends.

Child pornography is one of many rational limitations on the freedoms of speech and expression. Threats of physical harm, incitement to riot, treasonous statements, plagiarism, defamation, false advertising, perjury, conspiracy, and fraud are all examples in which speech or expression lie outside the scope of these freedoms. Given the current state of affairs in political discourse it may be time to add one more to the pile.

Voters consistently complain about politicians making promises they will never keep and puffing up data to support their policy positions. With the exception of threats, speech dealing with future events cannot be regulated since no one knows at the time whether the speech is accurate or not. On the other hand, a lot could be done to promote trust in elected officials if they were required to use verifiable data when arguing for or against a policy. Indeed, journalists once were trusted for their honesty until many events in the last two decades and one entire network destroyed that trust. Of course, the law cannot punish people for being lazy or sloppy or forgetful in saying things that aren't accurate. Nonetheless, it could be worthwhile to ask candidates, politicians, journalists, and news media sources to voluntarily pledge to have their "facts" scrutinized by an independent organization much the way restaurants in New York City are graded and have their scores made public. The Associated Press already has started doing this after presidential debates.

That raises another civil liberty that sometimes has difficulties: the Fifth Amendment right to not incriminate oneself. Law and order types always like to say that someone "taking the Fifth" must be hiding evidence of their guilt. Innocent people, after all, are willing to spill their guts. The problem is that even innocent people can become anxious under interrogation not because they are involved in whatever is being investigated but because they have other things they would rather not have authorities know about them. The meaner kind insists everyone is guilty of something. Perhaps. More likely, everyone feels guilty about something.

The thesaurus does not have so many synonyms for untrue because people are routinely truthful. Like perfection and imperfection, honesty and dishonesty are not parallel antonyms. Imperfection and dishonesty are each a great field of points, while perfection and honesty are each a single point. There are infinite ways to be imperfect or dishonest. There is exactly one way to be perfect or honest. To be perfectly honest one must make room for all of the other angels on the head of that pin. Everyone feels guilty about something because everyone, no matter who, hides things about themselves. Holding back information is only dishonest if the reason for holding back the information is to prevent the whole truth from coming out. That is why witnesses are sworn to tell the whole truth.

In fact, witnesses swear or affirm to tell the truth, the whole truth, and nothing but the truth. While it may be that thirteenth century Old English had some quirks about repeating words in a sing-song way, the phrase actually is holding the oath taker to three distinct things. The truth is the observations of the witness unclouded as much as possible by prejudice. The whole truth is the complete record of observations relevant to the matter. Nothing but the truth is the absence of any impressions, suppositions, or suggestions—coloring of the observations—by the witness. When these three perspectives are combined, the witness' testimony becomes as factual as an object submitted as evidence. In comparison, a person being interrogated is not reminded of the need to focus his words quite so directly. No, an interrogation is about asking for a story, a narrative that will include objective and subjective elements. It is rarely the truth, the whole truth, and nothing but the truth. That is why the right to remain silent is so important. And that is why investigators do whatever they can to break that silence.

The same holds true for all of the other civil liberties that protect people charged with crimes or found guilty of committing crimes. The concept of innocent before being found guilty barely registers with many people. Once an arrest is made or a suspect identified, story over. Why? One less thing to worry about? Cops don't make mistakes? The evidence is clear?

The world has seen many legal systems in which those charged must prove their innocence. We reasonably recognize that the burden should be placed on the accuser; proving someone did something is far easier than proving someone did not do something. Except civil liberties make it less easy because the people working with the accuser must follow procedures that respect the rights of the accused. Amazingly, many investigators, police, attorneys, and judges think that those burdens are heavier on them prosecuting cases of crime than the burdens on people who are wrongly convicted due to a violation of civil liberties. In other words, being careful and following rules required by your job outweigh the incarceration of individuals who should not have been incarcerated. Yet people get away with this argument because the only people being hurt are criminals who should be locked up for something. That is unless, as DNA evidence has helped uncover, they are not criminals at all.

Recently, the tail end of the Fifth Amendment received an interpretation that raised some eyebrows because the people being hurt were property owners, a group near and dear to the Founders and those in the present who claim to want to interpret the Constitution precisely along the lines those Founders supposedly intended. The last bits of the Fifth Amendment prohibit confiscation of private property without due process of law and without just compensation. Of course, confiscation sounds rather too much like being forced to do something and the actual word used is "deprived." Either way, the aim is to give property owners a satisfactory hearing on why they are being required to hand over their property for government use and how much they are entitled to receive for their loss. One might think this was mighty white of the Founders to protect people from their own government, but the fact was that Mother England had a long history of confiscating properties and rounding up supplies for armies without adequate payment. The Founders would not want their creation to turn to them seeking their private property for public ends.

Jump two centuries ahead or so and the problem is not so much whether the government is going to offer a fair price or provide a fair hearing. Everyone knows the price will be sort of fair market value and the hearing perfunctory. The problem is the reasons why governments want property. For a very long time, public ends were construed mostly to include providing access for private individuals to water sources. Not every farm in the valley may sit by the river, but every farm ought to benefit from the river being there. The public good is served by all farms being productive.

In mid-twentieth century the public ends were expanded to include buying up properties to be sold to a developer whose construction project would benefit the community. That was fine so long as the properties were primarily boarded up buildings and vacant lots with a few still livable residences sprinkled around. The theory goes that the property owners should be glad to get out of a blighted area; everyone wins if the area becomes deblighted (unbloght?).

The Supreme Court took a case in 2005 in which New London, Connecticut sought to buy perfectly good properties because a developer wanted that site. To the great consternation of many, the Court ruled this was all right. Here a corporation created under state law could ask a municipal government in that state to evict living, breathing citizens of that state for its private purposes on the grounds that the city stood to earn more tax revenue. While state supreme courts elsewhere scrambled to rule such findings unconstitutional under their state constitutions, New London bought the properties and leased the tract to the developer once the Supreme Court ruled. The developer failed to use the land and a local company that was hoping to benefit from the development also walked away while it still had tax credits to use from being lured to New London. New London ignored its citizens' property rights, spent a load of tax money taking the case to the US Supreme Court and buying the properties, and wound up in an even worse position with its tax revenues, all to satisfy corporate interests.

The very same members of the Supreme Court that so easily and willingly expanded the definition of public use within the eminent domain clause of the Fifth Amendment also supported the finding in a case finally interpreting the extent of the right to bear arms. The interpretation showed a baffling refusal to read the amendment as written, just as baffling as expanding the definition of public use to include any property development a jurisdiction claims is going to increase its tax revenues.

The Second Amendment very clearly states that the sole purpose of the right to bear arms is to provide for a well-ordered militia. A militia is basically a volunteer fire department except it's for the purpose of mutual defense and protection. The Second Amendment was adopted when real concerns remained of attacks on settlements and homeowners by American Indians everywhere, Spanish from west of the Mississippi and Florida, and British from Canada. Indeed, all three were involved in attacks until 1815. Indians remained a concern until a bit after the Civil War.

The fact was that the Founders had revolted in part against having standing armies and were not going to create a large enough US Army to protect the country's population, just like places now do not have the resources to fund large enough fire departments. Since militias have not been needed for the most part since the Civil War, the purpose of the Second Amendment no longer exists. The paranoid minds of some people think they have to protect themselves against their own government despite there being absolutely no reasonable evidence the government has any intention of creating a police state or military rule. Even if it did have that intention, the right to bear arms is still restricted to militias that are somehow tied to local government.

The Second Amendment clearly does not provide any kind of overarching right to own a gun. The First, Fourth, and Fifth Amendment protections do not provide unhindered freedom to speak, assemble, demand warrants or juries, prevent self-incrimination, etc. In fact, almost every limitation on those freedoms has been established by proponents of law and order. Given that, it is astounding that these same people insist the Second Amendment grants an unlimited right to own guns and insist the lack of reasonable gun control laws is not responsible for enough gun deaths every year to depopulate sizable towns.

If those same 34,000 more or less people were killed all in one act or even one day by terrorists, the law and order folks would not hesitate to insist on restricting our other freedoms. In fact, they did when only about one tenth of that number died on September 11, 2001. The resulting successful infringement of First, Fourth, and Fifth Amendment rights is called, of all things, the Patriot Act, the greatest affront to the men (mostly) who spent seven years under General George Washington's command securing those rights.

If the Second Amendment is unlimited, then shouldn't all of those other rights be unlimited? No evidence in criminal trials ever without a warrant, so no stops for traffic violations or DWI checkpoints. All forms of speech that are not protected (child porn, threats of violence, slander) now protected. No need for permits to hold demonstrations so a town can be prepared. Remove "In God We Trust" as our motto. No confessions can ever be used in criminal cases because that's self-incrimination. Or are we going to be more sensible and recognize that the right to bear arms is limited to possession of guns for the purpose of forming militias?

Given that the Founders knew people needed guns to hunt and protect their property in the day before police departments, a blanket prohibition of gun ownership would be wrong. The law should permit sane adults who show proof of having attended safety classes (as is done for automobiles) and have never been convicted of a violent crime to own firearms for hunting and target practice provided they are not automatic or semi-automatic. The laws can provide that guns and ammo are stored in separate rooms under lock and key, the guns have trigger locks and can be tracked like a licensed vehicle, and ammo has whatever identifying attributes possible for investigations to determine where it came from. Part of that safety course should be a discussion on how other countries have successfully reduced the use of guns in crimes. While guns do not kill people, people with guns kill people, and fewer people with fewer guns thanks to reasonable gun control laws kill fewer people. Another should be on the actual statistics and stories surrounding instances in which people used a lawfully-owned firearm to defend themselves legally.

The purpose of a discussion is for both sides to present their evidence and conclusions on the topic and not bring in irrelevant issues or refuse to provide facts supporting their conclusions. No one in this country is asking for 100 percent confiscation of guns. There is no point whatsoever in discussing a scenario that will never happen. Yet this is precisely the argument made. Scares about gun confiscation have only lined the pockets of gun manufacturers and sellers; any time a rumor of confiscation starts, people run out to buy guns. Is it possible the rumors are started by gun manufacturers and sellers?

Every single mass shooting in the USA is committed by people who are deluded into believing the world is out to deprive them of stuff. The GOP and NRA say that means we should do more to treat mental illness, not enact reasonable gun control legislation. However, they take no steps at all to introduce legislation to increase funding for identification and treatment. In fact, they argue that since others are so concerned about mass shootings it is up to them to introduce such measures. The people most concerned about mass shootings do not see poor treatment of mental illness as the real cause of mass shootings. While they wouldn't oppose such legislation, preparing it would indicate they agree that is the root cause. Incredibly, those who say it is the root cause won't lift a finger to correct the problem they have identified because they are not concerned by mass shootings. And yes, that is exactly what they say.

Quite frankly, anyone in the United States who believes the government wants to confiscate all guns and anyone who believes gun ownership helps them to avoid being victimized by crime sounds paranoid, a personality disorder, a treatable mental illness. There is absolutely no evidence to justify these beliefs; fears that arise from unjustified beliefs are the definition of paranoia. Ergo, if the GOP and NRA declare that guns ought not to be placed in the hands of mentally ill people, their supporters are the very people who ought not to own guns. Unfortunately, the GOP and NRA steadfastly contend that gun ownership protects against aggression from government or criminals and have no interest whatsoever in substantiating that belief.

That brings us back to that pesky problem of belief. So long as people cling to the idea that unsubstantiated, unverifiable belief must be equally respected with evidence-based, logically derived conclusions, discussion of any topic will not be productive. Some people cling to that idea because they have a "right" to their own opinions. No one espousing that idea ever stops to think that view is completely opposite to education. Students traditionally were not allowed to have opinions beyond liking or disliking subjects, teachers, peers, and cafeteria food. Inside a classroom, the only person who had a right to an opinion was the instructor. The instructor had been trained, qualified, and hired on her expertise. Students were expected to respect that expertise.

In the age of the Internet, anyone can be an instructor on any subject regardless of training, qualification, or experience. While everyone quickly recognized one cannot trust everything put into cyberspace as being accurate, that left everyone suspicious of anyone claiming to be an expert, even the actual experts. In fact, actual experts became pedantic, snobby know-it-alls whose well-intentioned efforts to clarify or correct errors are denounced as unwanted, condescending intrusions. Where subject-matter specialists once were the swiftly flowing waters of a river carving away the bedrock of ignorance, the positions have been reversed. A flood of unsubstantiated opinion laced with jealous invective now wears down the solid substance of received knowledge and rational discourse.

Lest anyone think that this is the biased opinion of some bitter Rapunzel cast from her ivory tower her prized locks shorn, remember the Founders themselves worried that voters could be swayed by charlatans and demagogues who might convince them that their myopic, selfish interests deserved priority over the common good. In the end, that is exactly what those who claim all are entitled to their opinions are doing. They are staking their dignity on the proposition that since all humans are equal under the law and as sovereign beings, all humans hold equally valid views. We have done away with the class concept of "betters" and the assumption that someone possessing more of anything was better than those possessing less. And that brings us to the problem with equality. The greatest stumbling block for the Equal Rights Amendment was the argument that women should not be singled out as being equal under the law because we already said everyone was equal under the law. That same stumbling block has been used whenever any minority has sought recognition of its equal rights. You already are equal, opponents say. You're asking for special treatment.

What the people claiming this is special treatment cannot fathom is that women and minorities experience life differently from what has always been the norm for the people who generally have written, executed, and applied the laws. One does not have to sound accusatory to notice how pinkish, male, heterosexual, un-disabled, economically-secure, and Christian the governing class has been since colonies were first settled in North America. It is an historical fact. It is a sociological fact that people with similar backgrounds and experiences build relationships more often than people with differing backgrounds and experiences.

There is absolutely nothing wrong with this naturally occurring segregation of people into circles of like others. The small town of Pittston, Pennsylvania once boasted having Catholic parishes for Slovak, Irish, and Italian immigrants and their descendants. The Slovak and Irish churches sat directly across from each other on the same street. In the former, the Stations of the Cross were in Slovak and the homilies were spoken in Slovak. No one ever gave a second thought to this form of segregation and none of it mattered when everyone went to work in the coal mines or met for national holidays. There is absolutely nothing wrong with segregated circles developing their own cultures, entertainments, and perspectives. Even a community the size of a family has its subcultures. There is absolutely nothing wrong with establishing relationships among people like you.

Nothing wrong that is until some of those circles monopolize or become dominant in making decisions for the community as a whole established in the social contract. For a political system to adequately address the popular will, the people chosen for making decisions must be representative of the experiences and backgrounds in the community. Yes, it is possible for someone to be empathetic and understanding about the experiences of people in other circles. Yes, it is a requirement of representative government that representatives do their best to represent the interests of all of their constituents, even the people who did not vote for them.

George H.W. Bush nobly recognized this in a note to his successor, Bill Clinton. He reminded Clinton that he was the president for all citizens of the USA. However, it is not possible for someone to know what it is like to be someone with a different skin color, different religion, different appearance, different sex, different sexual orientation, etc. Most people never even try to imagine it, trapped in believing that everyone else must be just like them really and if they aren't it's because of some defect in them.

The long dominant, pinkish, male, heterosexual, economically-secure, un-disabled, Christian group believes it has enough knowledge about human beings and enough specific knowledge of females and minorities that it can formulate valid policies for everyone. That position rests on the implausible assumption that since everyone is already equal under the law everyone is already treated equally under the law. The piles of statistical data and plague of anecdotal observations definitely indicate otherwise. It is further made ludicrous by the irredeemably preposterous belief that capitalism in a democratic republic provides everyone with equal opportunities to advance themselves if they are intelligent and diligent enough. The very nature of capitalism and how wealth, access, and information are controlled by the haves to have more decries such idealistic platitudes. No, the governing class does not and cannot know what it is like to be anyone other than themselves.

If we were to manage a large art museum, we would need many people to oversee the collections. We would not hire a palette of curators who all specialized in post-modern art. While they probably all would have the same basic education in the history of art and the various styles, traditions, masters, and genres, they would know a lot about post-modern art and very little about any other period. They could use their basic knowledge to try to handle the impressionist or Renaissance holdings, but they would have no specific knowledge to help them and no experience evaluating works from those eras to determine how best to approach acquisitions, special exhibits, or anything else beyond the most general duties of a curator. That is not to say that people would not jump at the opportunity to accept the offer of employment and try to do the best they could. Jobs aren't that widely available.

On one level, the problem with hiring post-modern scholars to curate all of a museum's collections is reminiscent of the issue of expertise. Some people think that with a basic idea of a subject plus their specific knowledge of other subjects and their educational background they can formulate opinions just as sound as subject-matter experts. It is not to say that is impossible, just very unlikely. Polymaths do exist, but they spend a lot of time grooming unicorns. Most likely, the person forming the benighted opinion can appear confident and reasonable in defending his finding because he or she is used to appearing that way when talking about her own field of expertise. However, she will refuse to believe that knowledge of other subjects and training in other disciplines is largely nontransferable. She knows what she knows but she doesn't. Granted if someone were to form an opinion about something in her field of expertise she would lambaste the offender as not knowing what he is talking about. That's different. People really need to work hard to understand how to analyze problems in their disciplines. Remember, there will be a test and it will last twenty-four hours spread over four days.

Political science is predisposed to being invaded by amateurs because democracy insists that everyone know a little about the subject in order to participate responsibly. The degree to which any citizen actively pursues knowledge of public matters, candidates, and proposed legislation and regulation varies widely. Three things are certain. Citizens by and large do not go beyond collecting just enough information to feel they understand an issue or can feel comfortable choosing a candidate for whom to vote. Their sources of information are frequently dubious by academic standards. And their framework of analysis almost always begins with their political leanings.

For purposes of being an engaged, active citizen there is nothing seriously wrong with this approach given that voters do not have the time to acquire more information, have no control over the biases of the media that supply information, and would not be human if they did not apply a pre-existing preference bias to that information. If we desired better results, we would legislate shorter work-weeks, impose the same mandatory, professional ethics regime on journalists and politicians that is applied to most other professions, and use political messaging to educate voters regarding the soundness of other views rather than demonize them for holding on tightly to irrational opinions. Citizens cannot be expected to make reasonable choices without giving them the proper tools to reason with.

Voters only touch the surface of politics for the most part. That is all they need to do. However, they do not want to be told that their surface understanding is too simple, a bit misleading, or altogether inaccurate. They want to believe that they know all that is needed to form valuable opinions because their vote and therefore their government are derived from their opinions. Just look at ancient Athens where the assembly claimed to be infallible because it was the *demos* expressing its will. Voters certainly do not want to take the removed, theoretical approach required to study politics. Understanding how political systems operate, how policies are developed, and all other aspects of the field require the same professional proficiency as any other in academia. Adopting that perspective requires setting aside the fact the researcher is one of the actors being observed. It also means digging into the mechanics of something voters have been told is natural.

Home cooks learn from a parent or both parents, some other relative, cooking shows, or trial and error. The more enthusiasm and interest one has, the more developed and creative a home cook can be. Some can learn to imitate professional chefs who have gone through extensive apprenticeships in fine restaurants or attended the Culinary Institute of America, Johnson & Wales University, or other exceptional programs. Home cooks generally do not know or care why recipes need to be followed for some dishes, what certain ingredients do, or how their efforts create the results everyone loves. They may know that some of the flavonoids in tomatoes will only dissolve in alcohol, not water, making the addition of wine in Bolognese sauce essential to obtain the full complexity of tastes. They may never realize that forming a bowl of pea-sized clumps by rubbing the pie dough between their hands after adding butter or shortening to the dry ingredients become the flakes of a flaky crust when they are rolled out into a flat mosaic.

Home cooks know how to cook. Great! They do not typically know the first thing about why their dishes turn out so well or why some people depend on boxed mixes and prepared foods to have something edible. A food scientist or cooking school graduate could tell them. For years the Food Network's drawing card was having a variety of fun, interesting chefs explain not only how to prepare dishes but also why ingredients were used, why the recipe steps were in the order they were in, and what utensils and processes worked best. Competitions and personalities eventually replaced the informative programs as so much television entertainment followed the same trajectory away from the short period in which cable networks primarily attempted to broaden viewer's minds and program content that reflected the networks' names.

Competent home cooks were seeing the mechanics of what they had learned organically and informally. It held their attention for a while, but became redundant. It had some practical value but was not going to noticeably raise their game. It was entertaining but not always useful. The people they cooked for did not and would not applaud them any more than they did already for having spent that time acquiring arcane knowledge. They saw it was possible to learn more but didn't see the point of doing so.

The exact same problem occurs with voters and their knowledge of political science. Just how many people in the USA have taken a college course in political science? Not many. Even the most basic concepts as the difference among forms of government, the role and mechanics of political parties, and the distribution and balancing of powers within a political system would be difficult for almost all Americans, or people anywhere, to explain.

Readers at this point have some understanding of democracy, the social contract, civil rights, citizenship, and a few other terms. As we have seen, sometimes the trickiest ones are those that people think are easiest to understand like freedom of speech. There is much more to it than the right to say what you want because that is not an accurate explanation. On the other hand, democracy itself is considered quite difficult to pin down. It isn't. It primarily boils down to whether or not the popular will can be and usually is expressed through policies adopted by the government so long as those policies do not unnecessarily infringe upon the rights of any minority. Given that petitioning the government in a populous country almost never gets any results, the mechanisms used to determine what the popular will is depend principally on local governments and political parties. It helps if the structure of government has several layers.

Chapter 15—Federal Systems and Autonomous Regions

THE WAR BETWEEN the States arose from a flaw in the Union that the Founders were very much aware of and decided to ignore in pursuit of the greater goal of independence. It is a flaw that is found in almost every country in the world and has been addressed in many ways peculiar to the specifics with varying degrees of success. It is a flaw that can rarely be wholly ameliorated except by secession. All too often, governments have addressed it with genocidal warfare. The problem is stepchild culture, a pronounced culture with its own institutions and morals sufficiently different from those of the country's dominant culture as to cause persistent frictions on certain issues. The separate culture may be distinct based on any combination of ethnicity, language, religion, or history. Most always, the economy has decided characteristics that make the members of this culture poorer, richer, or just other than the rest of the country to which it belongs. After the fact it is quite easy to tell what set the part apart from the whole. In the thick of things, one may not be able to tell how great the differences are or whether they can be settled peacefully.

Stepchild cultures come in all shapes and sizes. They can be almost as pervasive as the dominant culture. Generally, the frictions remain so minimal that there is never going to be any fear of a fire starting. Countries typically have some version of red necks, hicks, or assorted other groups of people who are not considered respectable. In France, Parisians think anyone who cannot say which arrondissement he lives in must be *a péquenaud*. The *Français* provincials don't much like Parisians either, but they have never had much of a say in the matter. Then there are the "they" populations; Jews, Roma, Muslims, Aboriginals, First Nations, and all the varieties of others so set apart from the majority that they can easily be made scapegoats or pointed to as troublemakers. Shi'ite Muslims fill this role in Sunni dominant states and vice versa. Catholics and Protestants can play this role, too, most notably in the British Isles. Tensions rise and fall over how citizens of minority cultures are treated.

Unfortunately, the most frequent result is an effort on the part of the dominant culture to assert its dominance due to bigotry. For example, many localities in the USA with large Latino populations are repulsed by the idea of offering Spanish-language services and demand English-only legislation. Compare that to Finland which was for most of its history part of the Kingdom of Sweden. Finland accepts Swedish as an official language despite being spoken by only five percent of the population and, more interestingly, accepts Finland as the country's official English name even though it is the Swedish name for the country the Finns call Suomi. On the other hand, Finland usually tries to pretend it wasn't a Russian duchy for the last century or so before its independence.

The stepchildren that are the most worrisome are the ones that are confined to one region of the country. Whether they will erupt in protest against the Mother Country depends on many factors. Some, like Scotland, Quebec, and Catalonia, seem to have too many links with the greater state and are far too established to justify bloodshed over autonomy or independence. Some unions were justified on the grounds that the parts could not make it independently but together had a chance. Later, things changed and Bangladesh hived off from Pakistan, the Czech Republic and Slovakia divorced, and the pieces of Yugoslavia fought themselves into separation. Eritrea and South Sudan eventually followed suit. The latter tops the list of fragile (formerly "failed") states but its parent state, Sudan, is number four. At least Eritrea is ranked 24th compared to Ethiopia's rank of 20th. Both Eritrea and South Sudan managed to ignore the prohibition on messing with Africa's borders by being large separatist regions clearly victimized by the parent state. Biafra was not as fortunate in trying to secede from Nigeria.

As we discussed previously, many stepchild regions have tried with varying levels of success to secede from their parent state. Typically they have been regions of a unitary state, one in which all policies and laws are directed by a central government. Less commonly, the component polities of a federal state seek independence. Eritrea and South Sudan were groups of subnational states that broke away from their federal systems in the manner the southern states of the USA tried to do. Yugoslavia truly was exceptional in that all of its component parts wanted to be independent and end the South Slav experiment except Serbia, which had long dominated the country. The Soviet Union did itself a favor by having established a federal system. That allowed the fifteen republics to go their separate ways. The largest, the Russian Federation, was a federal state within a federal state and just maintained the same system.

Currently, 26 countries have federal systems of government. Russia has the most subnational units and the most kinds of subnational units (forty-six oblasts, twenty-one republics, nine krais, four autonomous okrugs, three federal cities, one autonomous oblast). The territorially large federal systems aside from Russia are Argentina, Australia, Brazil, Canada, Ethiopia, India, Mexico, Sudan, and the United States. The moderately sized members of the club are Germany, Iraq, Malaysia, Nigeria, Pakistan, South Sudan, and Venezuela. Last, a roster of smaller states uses a federal system: Austria, Belgium,

Bosnia and Herzegovina, Comoros, Federated States of Micronesia, Nepal, Saint Kitts and Nevis, Switzerland, and United Arab Emirates. Size and history play a great role in whether federalism is used. Calculated political marriages similar to the former Czechoslovakia explain some. The oddballs are Nepal and Venezuela. Aside from stunningly diverse geography, neither has a history of being a patchwork of smaller polities, substantial cultural variety among regions, or administrative need that warrants this system.

Not too many of the other 169 states in the world have the characteristics that indicate subnational units endowed with specific legislative powers. The only large country that is not a federation is China, although its autonomous regions and devolution of economic decision-making have provided a bit more power to subnational units than most unitary states. Of course, by that standard the United Kingdom is even closer to a federal system with the glaring exception that England itself has no national parliament. The English only have the British Parliament that includes representatives from the three other components that all have empowered national assemblies. Indonesia, a large country in terms of population scattered across many islands, would seem to be a perfect candidate for federalism. However, precisely because those islands are so far-flung the government tries to emphasize unity.

France and Spain went through much the same process of pulling together sovereign polities into one unified state as Germany and Italy did much later. Germany had been a patchwork of hundreds and then dozens of independent or autonomous states bound together more by language and culture than a specific territory. Most, but not all, German territories owed a feudal obligation to the Holy Roman Emperor until 1806 and then gradually to the Prussian monarchy. After World War II, Germans decided a federal system would be stronger. The monarchs of France and Spain had to work hard to bind the pieces of their kingdoms together into one polity directed by one sovereign. Regions had developed cultures and dialects substantially different under their own sovereigns that required greater direct control to standardize into a unified national identification. The Italians needed only to look back at the earliest achievements of Rome uniting Italy and the centuries of rule by foreigners after 476 CE that fragmented their nation to see their country as a unitary state. Even so, the wide differences between the far south and the north led northerners to form their own political party.

One of the demands made by Russian-speaking Ukrainians has been the desire for a federal system that would provide the eastern regions of Ukraine with more direct control over themselves. That is a sensible argument. Ukraine was created out of pieces that historically had never been unified under one government. The Principality of Kievan Rus created by Vikings built a confederation with other Slav principalities starting in the 800s. While the principality covered the areas now in northern Ukraine, European Russia, and Belarus, Kiev itself was in the southeastern corner of a large polity stretching west to what are now Poland, Germany, Hungary, and Romania. Power shifted thanks to the Mongolian invasions in the 1240s and Muscovy began to dominate the same areas by serving as vassals to the Golden Horde. Muscovy became the Russian Empire which became the Soviet Union. However, by the time the Russian Empire was established, Muscovy had lost most of Kievan Rus to the Polish-Lithuanian Commonwealth. As that polity became weaker and weaker, its lands were divvied up between Russia, Austria, and Prussia.

The parts that the Russian Empire had regained were used in Soviet times to create Belarus and the top half of Ukraine. The bottom half of Ukraine was the steppe lands between Kiev and the Black Sea that had been ruled by Cossacks. Cossack was a status related to participation by registration in a militia applied to people of mixed ethnicity. The Cossacks emerged from the remains of a nomadic people called Cumans who intermarried with East Slavs, or at least that's the best guess. The Cumans had used the robust grasslands and wild herds of the steppe for centuries in a huge territory stretching from the Black Sea almost to China. The Cossacks employed a form of democracy in which fighting-age men could participate. While they were used to working with or warring against neighboring states, their territories had only been brought under somewhat direct authority in the 1700s by Russia. Even then, the tsars indulged their independent streak while paying them handsomely to form a buffer along the southwest border.

In 1919, the Soviet Union pushed together the Cossack lands and the southern Kievan lands under its control to form Ukraine. Then Ukraine gained huge areas to the west from World War II where ethnic Ukrainians had long ago become used to living under Polish, Hungarian, or Romanian governments. On top of that, in 1954 Khrushchev gave Ukraine Crimea, a territory traditionally settled by Tatars until Stalin evicted them and sent in Russians to populate the peninsula. In 1991, independent Ukraine was left with large territories and populations that had no history of association with Kievan Rus. What is more, a long history of looking to Moscow had given most of the eastern half of the country the name "Little Russia" well before the name Ukraine emerged. Kiev was, after all, where the Viking Rus had come to prominence and adopted Christianity. Vladimir Putin has even taken to talking about Little Russia rather than Ukraine in discussions over Crimea and eastern Ukraine.

The conservative nature of international law and the jealousy sovereignty generates twists ideological principles in the oddest ways. Africa is a prime example of a continent that feared if anyone opened the subject of adjusting any national borders the troubles and miseries that sprang from Pandora's Box would look tame in comparison. The idea was that everyone was just going to have to make do and live with the boundaries Europeans drew in the 1880s. Except as already noted regarding

Ethiopia and Sudan, this idea remains fixed in any discussion of ethnic issues within any African state. Africa has good reason to be wary. Wars of the past in South America and the Balkans attest to the consequences of greedy claims. Bolivia would not be referred to as "landlocked" had it not warred with Chile over its province on the Pacific coast. The Former Yugoslav Republic of Macedonia might be part of the Macedonia in Greece the Greeks demand not be confused with the independent state of the same name. Even when objectively it would make sense to adjust borders, no one wants to upset the status quo. Well, almost no one.

Vladimir Putin is largely right in supporting autonomy for the Donbas region in eastern Ukraine or even a vote to be annexed by Russia. His problem is that he was so hasty in holding a vote in Crimea after breaking international law invading the peninsula. He needed the vote to legitimize his invasion ex post facto, but made the vote itself illegitimate by not permitting outside observers to determine the fairness of the referendum. Who is going to trust a referendum in the Donbas would be remotely fair? The Tatars, who rightfully ought to be the primary population in Crimea, are voicing their objections loudly now that the Russian military has backed away a bit. With any luck they might at least obtain some autonomy within the Russian Federation. If Putin had not allowed testosterone to addle his mind, he could very well have made a case for the peaceful transfer of Crimea back to Russia with the support of the Tatars. Instead he and Ukraine are stuck with a mess made by Putin with little chance of sorting things out through negotiation.

. The United States of America created much the same problem in toppling Saddam Hussein on specious grounds. Iraq technically has a federal system under the government established after the USA-led invasion in 2003. Iraq most certainly is a good candidate for federalism. As noted previously, Iraq is as much a mulligatawny stew of cultures as Ukraine except with a few less ingredients. Principally, Iraq has Shia Arabs, Kurds, and Sunni Arabs. For a medium-sized country divided three ways, nineteen provinces indicate the central government does not want any of the subnational units to be too strong. In response to the occupation of much of northern Iraq by the Islamic State of Iraq and the Levant (ISIL or IS, but never ISIS), some realists have gotten the idea that Iraq ought to have three autonomous provinces that do their own thing in most regards *a la* Scotland and look to Baghdad for foreign policy, military coordination, and economic supervision.

Just think what such a proposition would have done for this platypus of a country when it was created after World War I. The British may still have made the mistake of preferring the Sunni Arabs as allies and the monarchy may still have been overthrown as a unifying element. At least the Kurds, Sunnis, and Shi'ites would most likely be strongly encouraged to make the situation work, just as the Swiss cantons did in 1291, the Walloons and Flemings of Belgium in 1830, the Czechs and Slovaks in 1918, and the United Arab Emirates in 1971.

The Swiss are the shining example of federalism doing what it does best: preserving the independence of disparate people who share some cultural and social characteristics both from external threats and internal domination by one group. Without that united front, the Swiss Alps would have long ago been absorbed by the surrounding states based on language. The 26 cantons certainly could not make a go of it as sovereign states in the international system. Strong, dominating leadership along the lines of Louis XIV of France or Charles V of Spain or from one part of the whole as the Kingdoms of Prussia and Piedmont did in Germany and Italy respectively was far too unlikely given how evenly balanced each canton is with the rest. The Swiss simply had no alternative because any alternative would diminish the traditions of direct democracy they were loath to let lapse.

For all its fine features federalism is no more the most effective method of administering a divided country than democracy is the most efficient method of governing according to popular will. However, just like democracy, it looks so great when it is working well people start to think it is better than the other forms of organizing a country's administration. A federal system could have prevented the annexation of Crimea or the horrific consequences of revolt in the Donbas, including the destruction of a Malaysian Airlines flight. It might not have, too. Hardly anyone saw Yugoslavia, much less the Soviet Union, breaking into independent states. A federation works and continues working well only as long as the subnational units feel they have a better deal sticking with their partners than going it alone. Better to void the marriage contract than to be forced to stay together while enmity and frustration build. And that brings us back to the nasty bit of business the Founders of the USA failed to attend to.

No one was mistaken in believing that the American South was a slavery-based culture formed from a slavery-based economy. The South saw absolutely nothing wrong with that. They had the Bible, the Roman Republic, the facts regarding the most efficient methods of producing cotton and tobacco, the states in Africa supplying slaves, and the merchants of the triangle trade all as reliable reasons for maintaining their peculiar institution. None of that would have mattered one bit except for the unique way in which the British had established colonies and dealt legally with those colonies on the Atlantic coast of North America.

Unlike the monopolies granted politically-connected merchants to exploit all of the Indies by many European courts, including England's, or the claims to all lands found asserted by the crowns of Castile and Portugal, the English had issued charters and grants to groups and individuals to establish and operate colonies as they saw fit so long as the king was the sovereign of their inhabitants and the king's parliament was permitted to tax those inhabitants, their activities, and their goods. In short, England was establishing a row of autonomous districts endowed with certain rights and privileges depending on how they were formed and developed. In this way, the Crown had limited liability or responsibility for ensuring the colonies' success, recognized the extent to which English citizens governed themselves with the guidance of their betters, and added to the Stuarts' accomplishments with little effort in a century that saw the monarchy annihilated, restored, and transformed, thereby in great need of accomplishments.

Other colonial empires saw less of a need to actually colonize their holdings in the way that Britain did. The British in North America were not imitating the ancient initiatives of the Phoenicians and Greeks who set up replicas of their city-states on the Mediterranean coasts of Africa, Spain, France, and Italy plus more Greek colonies around the Black Sea. They were more like the Celts, Goths, Slavs, and other Eurasian groups. Those groups spread into the areas north of the Mediterranean basin and sometimes into the Iberian and Italian peninsulas from 800 BCE during the Iron Age up to 800 CE as Europe finally started sorting out who was who. The later Mongols, Bulgars, and Turks similarly shook things up in Eastern Europe and Asia Minor from around 1200 to 1700. These Indo-European peoples known by their root languages that are their lasting mark and distributed among tribes the Romans enjoyed sorting based on height, hairiness, and hair color typically expanded into relatively unused lands or pushed off the people already settled there.

The Celts having been first to apply modern agricultural techniques all through the midsection of today's Europe ended up with the short end of the stick. They were pushed and pushed by succeeding Germanic tribes until they wound up clinging to the frilly fringes of the British Isles, Brittany, and Galicia. A good bit of Adolf Hitler's demands for *lebensraum* in Eastern Europe was founded on the Goths having supplanted the Celts and remaining in that region until the Slavs followed the Huns who scared the Goths west and south. What they all were doing was sending large populations out along with military forces capable of seizing territory, preferably territory that was not heavily populated and could sustain more people.

In many ways this is what the British did in North America. North America, like Europe during the successive great migrations, was populated but only sparsely. The primary difference is the British had evolved a complex political system by the seventeenth century. The Celts, Goths, and Slavs were still using the durable Eurasian model of tribal communities in which warriors selected leaders from candidates put forward by families that had traditionally led the communities. Tribal confederations could quickly rally around a particularly adept leader like Attila of the Huns that just as suddenly fell apart upon the leader's death. Or they could flourish as the Mongols did for a few centuries when Genghis Khan united them and successfully divided his realm among his sons and grandsons, who further expanded it.

For the most part, the Mongols stuck with their established political system as they created khanates from Manchuria across to what is now Ukraine. However, they wisely adopted the elaborate and experienced Chinese political system after they conquered China; they merely slipped themselves in as the Yuan Dynasty. Similarly, the Goths in particular, but also the Celts and Slavs, wound up adopting Roman political forms once they settled into the lands that generations later would become the nations of Europe. The Grand Prince of Muscovy even adopted the Russian translation of Caesar, tsar, as his title in the 1400s and the King of Prussia was proclaimed Germany's Kaiser four centuries after that. Such was the influence of the first European empire.

The British took their political system with them, which morphed into a more democratic form in the colonies due to the absence of great, noble landowners, the much smaller populations in each colony, the narrow range of common interests, and the inability of Parliament and the Crown to effectively rule directly due to the distance and state of communications technology. The colonists gradually became more identified with their colony than with England. When they finally decided to break their bonds with the Mother Country, each colony considered itself to be a sovereign polity with its own citizens. The reality was that no matter how independent each was from the others legally, practically they were linked economically, culturally, and socially. More importantly, even their combined resources were no match for what the English could throw at them should they rebel. They not only had to present a united front but they also needed to find allies as a single entity.

As we all know, the colonies formed a Continental Congress to debate the issues surrounding relations with the Crown and Parliament. The colonies sent representatives to Philadelphia. Notice how the colonists are not doing anything? That is because the problems with the Mother Country were primarily between the assemblies of the colonies and the British government, not between the citizens of the colonies and the British government. The people who cared the most about being taxed by Parliament without being represented in Parliament were the members of the elected bodies in each colony that traditionally had a say in the imposition of taxes and other matters.

Paying taxes was a side issue that was pretty much withdrawn unilaterally by the British when they cancelled most of the new assessments. The bigger issues were who was going to govern each colony, who was going to make policy decisions, and who was going to determine what was best for the colony's development. The politically and economically well-endowed property owners and merchants enriching the colonies, the Crown, and themselves knew they were in the best position to handle these matters. They were big fish in thirteen small ponds and they didn't appreciate interference from across the big pond. Nor did they care too much for interference from a national government once they united. One of the issues this created, however, is that those colonists that were a step removed from the political union of the colonies realized after independence was won that they now had two levels of government to complain about and complain to.

Chapter 16—Expressing Grievances

THOMAS JEFFERSON'S DECLARATION of Independence most frequently is noted for the stirring, Enlightenment-soaked paragraphs at the beginning and the noble, Roman Republic-tinged rhetoric of the conclusion. Most people skip over the bulk of the document, which is a standard issue petition of redress citing the numerous ways in which nasty King George III had infringed upon the liberties of the American colonists. Except that really isn't what the accusations contain. The overwhelming majority of complaints relate to the King's interference in the governance of the colonies, i.e. using his prerogative to decide upon the adoption, execution, and application of laws in place of the assemblies elected by the property owners of each colony and in the Canadian settlements. Another group of grievances focuses on how the colonies are being treated as a rebellious territory with royal and mercenary troops imposed on them. A few mention the deterioration of safeguards to protect individual colonists from due process of law. In sum, the United States of America declared their independence but the American colonists did not.

Best modern estimates are that 40 to 45 percent of the residents of the colonies were Patriots, 15 to 20 percent were Loyalists, and the remainder were pacifists or apolitical. Given the small size of the overall population, perhaps 2.2 million, that left very few men of fighting age to do the work of their political representatives and turn a declaration into actual independence.

As we see today with members of the poorest segments of the citizenry being the most apathetic, the same was largely true back then. What is the point in getting involved if the results are not going to change the fact that one is struggling to survive and obtain basic necessities? These people were not represented in the colonies' assemblies. They had no say in their government as British citizens and for the most part would not have any say in their government as American citizens for quite some time. Why stick one's neck out if the outcome made no difference in what was essential for humans to live and not just high-sounding Enlightenment ideas of liberty?

The British particularly, but the rebels eventually, offered freedom to slaves who volunteered to fight. That was quite a prize that could not be offered to the free white men being asked to enlist. While both sides shamelessly reneged on granting freedom to some, enough freed Loyalists survived to found settlements in Nova Scotia after the war. When the Nova Scotians made clear they did not want former slaves in their colony, the British offered to move the black Loyalists to Sierra Leone in Africa. There they established Freetown in 1792 and, with the aid of abolitionists in Britain, became the ruling class of the territory under British oversight.

While we like to say that the American Revolution struck a blow for liberty and established what would become a model of democratic republican government, it really was a civil war brought on by the secession of the governments of thirteen subnational territories aided eventually by their nation's greatest enemies, France and Spain. How much this was the case can be seen in the terms of the Treaty of Paris ending the war. Benjamin Franklin didn't even bother to tell the French and Spanish he was negotiating the treaty despite being bound to do so under their treaties entering the war. The British generously acknowledged the colonies now owned all of the land west to the Mississippi, north to the Great Lakes, and south to what the British said was Florida. France earned scattered territories lost in the Seven Year's War but certainly not enough to compensate for the amount of money it spent helping the Americans. The Spanish got Florida back from the British but thought the northern and western borders went farther than the British told the Americans. The Spanish were miffed enough to challenge American use of the Mississippi River that the British had promised even though Spain, not Great Britain, owned the right bank lands stretching to the Pacific Ocean. And the reason why the British were so generous to the new country was they wanted to resume the high volume of trade with the former colonies to block France and Spain from using their support of the rebels to gain an advantage.

The independence gained as a result of the War for Independence was specifically and deliberately restricted to the governing merchant and landowning classes of each colony. The Articles of Confederation make clear that the members of those classes did not want to shrug off one superior sovereign for another. Knowing they had to stay united to survive individually, the Continental Congress devised a national government that was not much better than a scapegoat for anything that went wrong. That clearly failed. Unsurprisingly, the delegates to the Constitutional Convention were swayed to close their doors to scrutiny and toss aside their mandate for the necessary task of creating a central government strong enough to establish uniform policies on those areas that required complete cooperation among the states and nothing more. They still did not want a sovereign authority over the states but found they had no choice but to endow a federal government with some of the sovereignty vested in the state governments by their citizens.

The Convention was sufficiently wise to start its deliberations using James Madison's Virginia Plan. Had it instead tried to start from scratch every word would need to be chosen, debated, and decided like any writer facing the blank page. In this case there would be dozens of writers all suggesting the words to choose. The Virginia Plan offered the opportunity to skip over choosing words and go straight to debate. In those debates, Madison gradually wore down his colleagues about leaving too much sovereignty with the states that they could continue to cause turmoil. He was unable to move them as far as he would have liked, which was to clearly centralized government like Britain or France each with its counties and provinces that had some powers due to needing decisions made quickly on some matters. That would be impossible given that the states were each proudly and jealously guarding their independence. The only time a state relinquishes its sovereignty over any territory is if it forced to do so and cannot do otherwise. Ukraine demonstrated that when Russia seized Crimea. Madison was thinking of relieving the states of all of their sovereignty over all of their territory without firing a shot.

What emerged was a balance that the states wanted to believe left them in a good position. Just to be certain, the supporters of states' rights had made clear that slavery was barely mentioned while getting slaves counted as part of the population for determining the size of a state's delegation to the House of Representatives and thus the Electoral College. The Tenth Amendment was icing on the cake. That laid the foundation for a divide over expanding slavery as states were added. Who could choose, the citizens of the territory seeking admission or the federal government?

Increasingly, abolitionists and northerners who just didn't like slaves being counted as fractional citizens when their owners did not consider them to be anything but property thought the federal government should decide. States had been let into the union and were being let into the union with the exact same degree of sovereignty as the original thirteen. Except the new states after Vermont, Kentucky, and Maine were being populated by people who had chosen to abandon their citizenship of one state to live on land that was under the jurisdiction of the federal government. They had taken back whatever sovereignty they had passed to their state governments to offer to whatever territory they settled.

The citizens of a territory seeking statehood made the same bargain the citizens of the original thirteen states did when they elected representatives to vote in favor of the Constitution. They approved becoming citizens of their new state now endowed with some degree of sovereignty and approved that state seeking its equal place among the existing states. What is amazing is that the residents of American Samoa, District of Columbia, Guam, Northern Marianas, Puerto Rico, and US Virgin Islands sit around being told they cannot do the exact same thing. However, remembering the idea of an economic independence test for countries to join the 195 countries currently recognized as sovereign states of the world, it is hardly likely that any of them except the District of Columbia and Puerto Rico could pass the test. Indeed, the Marshall Islands, Micronesia, and Palau are all independent states associated with the USA, meaning dependent upon. If they could not succeed as sovereign states under international law, they perhaps should not be eligible for statehood.

Inserting the fifty states into a list of the world's countries ranked by gross domestic product can, depending on the year, push the Netherlands, Turkey, Saudi Arabia, and Switzerland out of the top 20, replaced by California, Texas, New York, and Florida. Out of the 195+50=245 states, Vermont, the state with the lowest GDP, would still be around 146th with 99 currently independent nation-states with smaller but not always poorer economies. It really doesn't matter where the states of the United States exactly would fall, only that they would certainly fall in the top two-thirds.

While that sounds wonderful and most everyone will ask why there has never been a referendum in all the other states whether Texas should secede, a key element in the US Constitution missing from the Articles of Confederation was the ability of the national government to oversee interstate commerce in a meaningful way. As many of those countries with smaller economies than the Green Mountain state know all too well, and quite a few of the ones with larger economies know as well, smaller economies are more dependent on trade to prosper than large economies. There is a reason the modern city-states of Hong Kong, Macao, and Singapore produce enough to rank in the top half among countries, even though the first two aren't countries. The Phoenician city-states in the ancient world, northern Italian city-states in the Middle Ages, and the Netherlands and Portugal at the beginning of the Modern Era all thrived on moving merchandise great distances for their time periods.

Deng Xiaoping more likely than not got his idea for devolving foreign trade decision making to coastal cities as a means to start enriching China from the long history of success this economic model has had. Remember how Great Britain was so eager to please its rebellious colonies in the Treaty of Paris and subsequently jumped right back in to being those colonies' biggest overseas trade partner? Cut your losses and mend fences quickly before France and Spain have any chance to wiggle in.

Naturally, if one's greatest concerns are economic, what good is there in demanding political control if releasing that control leaves one with fewer expenses and still permits friendly and hopefully growing trade? The jockeying over accepting new states into the Union was as much about creating additional markets, trading partners, and sources of materials for neighboring states as it was about maintaining a balance of slave and free states in Congress. Sending settlers from one state to a territory made certain there were bonds of affinity not only to the politics and culture of the sending states, but also trustworthy lines of creating business deals. As the southern states learned though, their more established and necessary economic ties looked north within the US and east to Britain. That is the aspect of the War Between the States that really upended the rebellion.

The seceding states had much more to lose. Their economy

depended upon slavery to produce materials they depended on the North and Britain to buy. Of course, that was not all of the southern economy but it was the part they were defending against federal intervention. It was the part that mattered culturally and politically. The southern states individually and collectively determined that there was no other path than to continue the economic model developed over almost two centuries that required slavery and made those states dependent upon others for their continued well-being.

Like any sovereign discovering that his de jure right to decide issues was constrained by his de facto lack of real power to see those decisions applied, the slave-holder states tried to seize that power. If they had any question whether they could succeed, they could go back at least as far as Nero, who staged a coup against his mother Agrippina at the age of twenty-one. Just three years after the war ended, the Southern Coalition in Japan backed the Meiji Restoration, which put the emperor back in place as the de facto as well as de jure head of government. However, the Meiji Emperor could not have done this without the support from a faction within the *daimyo* (noble) class ready to order their *samurai* retainers to battle if needed. Sometimes the authority of de jure power is sufficient to overcome a lack of de facto power. Unfortunately, that is like matching wits with brawn in a bar fight. History contains many more instances of impotent sovereigns losing their quests to actually rule. They were not permitted to decide what history said about them and so fell into obscurity.

The southern states claimed to be fighting to defend their individual rights as sovereign states to reject decisions made at the national level. To do so they, like the thirteen colonies, had to unite in war or face defeat separately. However, like the rebellious colonies, the rebellious states formed political institutions to make decisions on behalf of the members that had united. They were not wartime allies coordinating their offensive and defensive efforts as has occurred for centuries when nation-states fight a common enemy. They attempted to create a federal government along the lines they wanted, more like that under the Articles of Confederation. Immediately upon doing so they rejected their asserted *casus belli*. How could they be fighting for states' rights they were so willing to give up to fight for states' rights?

One does not fight for one's sovereign rights within one social contract by offering those sovereign rights to a higher entity of your creation in a similar social contract. All that shows is that the rebellious states were satisfied being subnational units just as long as their interests were supported by the actions of the superior nation-state. But that is not how a federal government operates. The federal government must look to its responsibilities to the entire country, not to one state or region.

The Supremacy Clause is in the Constitution for a reason. The interests of the country as a whole take precedence over the interests of any one state or region. That includes deciding for itself how to interpret and implement the powers it has been given under the Constitution. One of those powers is the regulation of interstate commerce. One of the most substantial results of the War Between the States was the recognition that the federal government could broadly interpret that power to include interfering in the economies of states that were dependent on other states to market what they produced. If the South wanted to continue to sell goods to the North, it would have to abandon slavery as a means of producing those goods.

What the Founders had done was to provide a means for the national government to decide how much sovereignty the states kept for themselves. That is far more reasonable than allowing thirteen going on fifty states to individually decide what rights they had retained. However, by ignoring the issue of slavery, the Founders left it for future generations to prove the national government had this authority through a grievous conflagration. In the 1780s, it was deemed impossible to demonstrate this authority by ending slavery, since that would break the already precariously situated new nation in two. The principled thing to have done was to take that chance if the consequences would result in less human suffering in the short term compared to what slaves endured for almost another eighty years. No one knew and so action was put off.

Even recently, states led by people who have a visceral hatred for Barack Obama insist they can unilaterally determine the extent of states' rights. They have undoubtedly not learned the lessons of the War Between the States much less observed how the Constitution has been construed since the South was defeated through the lens of the three post-war amendments. Unfortunately, this is the frustrating, maddening aspect of American politics that ranks higher than the spending money equals speech formula as the chief reason why the United States is no longer a democracy.

While the plutocratic evidence is quite clear, it came after the far more damaging end to negotiation and compromise within the governing class. Ronald Reagan's assault on government as the source of problems rather than the solution to problems fed neo-conservativism. Neo-conservative tactics morphed into no-holds-barred fighting when the GOP finally found an excuse to pillory Bill Clinton on a legal error committed while trying to defend himself against the totally apolitical non-issue of his extramarital relations with Monica Lewinsky. It is not the business of Congress to investigate a president's infidelity to his wife. The GOP members of the House of Representatives that went after the president were hypocritical not only because it was discovered they were just as unfaithful to their spouses, but also because they clung to the belief that they and only they strictly construed the Constitution.

The GOP was upset that Clinton had successfully shifted the Democrats to business-friendly, law and order, moderate policy positions and achieved a balanced budget. Those were their policies. Since they could not attack him on policy matters, they only had his moral character to work with. Given that Reagan had built such a strong base for the GOP among evangelical Christians, it wasn't difficult to whip up support for an impeachment that rested on a congressional investigation into the president's private life, something way out of bounds for Congress to take up according to a strict reading of the Constitution.

The rancor impeachment brought to Washington only became fiercer as a result of the 2000 presidential elections in which Al Gore received more votes from citizens, but George W. Bush received more votes in the Electoral College after the Supreme Court ruled along partisan lines to stop a thorough recount in Florida. Naturally, the GOP became the more vitriolic camp because they were defending actions of dubious merit that greatly benefited them. If they had to argue these questions logically and legitimately without partisan spin they would have to agree they received a windfall rather than achieved anything by skill and reason.

George W. Bush refused to acknowledge the terrorist attacks on September 11, 2001 may have been avoided but for his transition team's missteps. He had no response to questions about his subsequent use of those attacks and false information about weapons of mass destruction to ask for support to invade Iraq and bring down the government of Saddam Hussein. Their president's positions required the GOP members of Congress to dig their heels in deeper.

Along came the movement for marriage equality. Aside from blatant efforts to impose one religious view on all citizens of the United States, opposition centered on attempts to ignore the results of the War Between the States that clearly placed Constitutional equal protection under the laws above any actions by a state or by the citizens of a state through referendum. The Ninth and Fourteenth Amendments coupled with the Supremacy Clause give teeth to the first eight and several after that in the face of any effort to use the Tenth Amendment or states' rights to claim parochial definitions of freedoms and liberties can be narrower than those established by the nation as a whole. Nor does it matter which orifice the nation uses to manifest its definitions of those freedoms and liberties. The Supreme Court rendering decisions has as much authority as Congress working with the Chief Executive to define them in laws.

What is astounding is the two-faced hypocrisy of neo-conservatives and evangelical Christians when they praise the Supreme Court for expanding the definitions of some rights when the result pleases them and just as vigorously denounce the Court for applying the existing definition of a right to a minority currently not enjoying the protections of that right when the decision displeases them. A court in a democracy cannot be deemed legitimately doing its job only when it rules in your favor.

The denial of civil liberties to any cognizable minority for any reason must be prohibited in any democracy. To do so is gravely immoral in every ethical system consistent with democracy. Protection of the rights of minority populations is an integral feature of democracy given that society's laws are created to represent the popular will of the majority on any given issue. Members of minorities are every bit as much equal participants in the social contract as members of majorities. Once it was established that marriage equality was an equal protection question, opposition from any nonpartisan corners should have ended. The fact that four members of the Supreme Court determined that marriage equality was still about preserving a tradition established by religion demonstrated beyond measure that those four members were no longer applying the Constitution as written and were instead looking for any somewhat plausible arguments they could use to achieve a result consistent with their partisan leanings.

Before that came *Citizens United*, *McCutcheon*, and *Hobby Lobby*. Those cases also demonstrated the same sleight of hand by the neo-conservative wing of the Court. For all of their bluster about adhering to the Founders' intentions in writing the Constitution and Bill of Rights, they used mind-blowingly irrational and unsubstantiated assumptions to broaden the definition of speech and broaden the definition of who was entitled to exercise civil liberties. Indeed, money fuels rigid partisanship. The purity grandstanding of Tea Party activists and shrill denunciations of Moveon.org would not exist but for loads of money. Now it goes even beyond that. Senator Bernie Sanders' rejection of campaign support from Super PAC money and Donald Trump's partial reliance on personal wealth if outside financing weakens created divisions within the Democratic and Republican parties by showing candidates can run viable presidential nomination campaigns without any support from the party establishment. This won't end the usefulness of political parties but it certainly indicates the two major parties are in for a very rough ride.

Chapter 17—Partisan Politics

THE ROLE OF political parties in most of the world, the world with parliamentary style governments in which the prime minister is the leader of the legislature and head of government, is to provide an organization to likeminded people who wish to accomplish a defined policy agenda if enough voters vote for their organization as represented by individual candidates, party leaders, and their party platform. Sometimes, particularly in countries in which one party rules or dominates, the party serves as the debate hall for deciding national policy. In either case, on most matters party members, and particularly elected legislators, are expected to publicly support the policies the party chooses as its own. They are not always forbidden from criticizing those policies, but they may well jeopardize their status within the party and their chances of being selected to represent the party in elected offices. Obviously, if the ruling party is just the tool of an authoritarian head of government, having one's name removed from consideration for political office may be the least of a rebellious party member's concerns.

Even in countries with presidents who are elected separately and have significant powers as head of government not granted the legislature legislative leaders frequently insist that members support the legislative agenda of a president from their party. That is to say, countries not named the United States of America. The USA's political system has the peculiar trait of generally not requiring much in terms of party discipline from its office holding members, much less the rank-and-file. A major reason for this is the duopolistic nature of partisan politics in the country.

Despite warnings to avoid factions, from its earliest days the Republic has generally had two contending political parties of any significance. The one time this was not the case, the Era of Good Feelings in the 1820s, was the result of three Democratic-Republican presidents in the twenty preceding years doing more to demonstrate the strength of the federalist government than the Federalist Party ever managed. It only took Andrew Jackson's populism to cause the Whigs to group up and further divisions among Democrats over slavery for the Grand Old Party to pick up where the Whigs left off. Almost 160 years later, the two parties have done everything possible to prevent any other parties from gathering much strength.

In other countries, even the Anglophone ones that often have two major parties, the rules for getting a political party going and the requirements for it to field candidates on ballots are far less restrictive. This has allowed for strong regional parties to form and even for major parties to see breakaway factions organize and eventually gain representation in legislatures. Countries that award seats in parliament based on the percentage of the vote a party receives or even partly this way like Germany may have up to a dozen parties with legislators. More parties may be trying to exceed the usual five percent or so threshold required. The threshold avoids having lots of small parties with one or two members of parliament, a situation that would create more instability without providing the smallest parties' supporters with much. In such places, voters have a wide variety of policy platforms to choose from and can feel more satisfied their views will be represented. In the USA, voters complain about settling for candidates who meet some of their criteria for support or abstain from voting if neither choice is palatable. Bernie Sanders supporters, for example, were split between voting for the lesser evil and sticking to principles.

Political parties in the USA not only prevent new parties access to the ballot but also use tricks like gerrymandering and choosing where to count prisoners and university students as constituents to protect legislative districts. These are universal problems when candidates run for specific seats rather than being on a party list of who will be selected based on the proportion of the vote received by the party. Not only does this provide one party or the other with a near guaranteed seat, it also breaks up the ability of minority populations to be represented. A conservative Supreme Court has made matters worse. People who defend such rigging of the political system claim that minorities can be represented just as well by thoughtful, concerned representatives from any background. That is patently untrue. The representative from the majority population will not have had any of the personal experiences shared by members of minorities. The majority in the US, for example, will never know what it means to be arrested while being black and a large part of that majority will even claim that doesn't happen. The problem applies equally to the great underrepresented non-minority: females. Men can never know what women experience. Men who think they can also typically think the Equal Rights Amendment is unnecessary on the grounds that men and women are differently able.

While claiming anyone can represent anyone's interests faithfully, in the same breath gerrymandering defenders say that representatives ought to vote based on the desires and interests of a majority of their constituents. If the majority of constituents have views opposite of minority constituents, how can the minority ever be represented? An individual represents the interests of the entire district, not just the people who voted for that individual. If the interests of the constituents in the district are divided, the representative's most ethical approach would be to find out how a compromise can be reached. Some voters may be upset, but a legislator's decisions are not supposed to be based on whether it hurts re-election chances. They are not supposed to be but routinely are.

Along the same lines, the idea of always voting what constituents support is not a sign of leadership. Businesses everywhere impose ridiculously authoritarian rules on employees to the effect that supervisors and managers are always right and employee opposition to this rule is insubordination, a firing offense usually. If undemocratically obeying people higher up at work is demanded, how can anyone claim that a talented politician chosen for his or her abilities cannot make any decisions not supported by constituents? Are voters stupid at work and brilliant when they speak their minds to politicians? Why accept this glaring inconsistency?

Could it be that elected representatives are not as good as corporate managers at making decisions beneficial to all? Does a workplace lose anything significant if employees provide input on decisions? Of course it depends on the issue. All the more reason to suspect that businesses are needlessly authoritarian and voters are needlessly demanding. And it reminds us that political parties in the US are neither. They exist to help candidates win election.

The first thing parties do is choose which candidates to help. Parties are generally strong enough to choose candidates who will withstand any intra-party bickering in primary elections. Oftentimes, there are no opponents to the party's choices. If there are, the office most likely is being or has been vacated leaving room for seedling politicians to compete for sunlight. In that case the party may or may not have a favorite. Instances of a renegade challenging an incumbent in a party primary generally are cases where extremists are dissatisfied with the incumbent, as has been the case with Tea Party activists knocking off establishment Republican incumbents.

Choosing presidential nominees is quite different. The greatest irony of the 2016 presidential race was the roles of the party establishments in the nomination process. Both parties were faced with popular candidates who have little support within their parties' official segment. Both candidates can be rightly cited for not really having been members of their respective parties until they announced their candidacies. Both candidates received their greatest support from what conventional wisdom says is the active base of their parties, the voters that prospective nominees for the last fifty years at least have targeted in the nominating season because they decide the results of poorly attended primaries and caucuses. In the past, successful candidates have used their party organizations to recast themselves for the general election as more generically appealing to armchair party registrants, independents, and dissatisfied folks from the other camp. GOP candidates dip to the right until nominated and Democratic candidates dip to the left.

This go round however, Donald Trump and Bernie Sanders pretty thoroughly soaked up a good bit of their parties' active bases while also bringing in new participants. They showed no signs of wanting to recast themselves once nominated other than Trump sometimes saying his positions are just opening gambits in prospective negotiations. Article after article was written about how the parties' establishments needed or were actively trying to stop these two from being nominated. Then WikiLeaks proved that the Democratic National Committee had indeed been working quite hard to derail Sanders.

What makes this so ironic is that the GOP typically has been the better disciplined party to find a candidate and the Democrats have had trouble zeroing in on their best chance. In 1984 and 1988 the Democrats blew it entirely. This go-round the GOP establishment couldn't decide who of the poor choices remaining to rally behind and coherently work against Trump. The Democratic National Committee pulled out every trick in the book almost to prevent Sanders from defeating Hillary Clinton. The fact that Sanders did not gain the nomination is clearly the result of dirty tricks and his own failure to translate the enthusiastic crowds at rallies into a new political movement. As spring progressed every indicator pointed to Trump and Sanders being nominated because, unlike their opponents, they were working the changed political landscape rather than trying to ignore it.

Almost everyone has viewed this election cycle as though it is no different than previous election cycles, or did until they had to explain why Sanders and Trump were doing so well once the caucuses and primaries began. Hardly anyone was willing to admit or able to see that the political landscape has been reshaped by twenty years of bitter hostility and intransigence reminiscent of the First World War. The lines have been drawn. The trenches have been dug. All hope of a negotiated peace has been lost.

The most resilient forces are the pundits on either side who continued to irrationally believe that Donald Trump would collapse at any moment because in their minds he had to collapse. Except he didn't. He had the resources, support, and mentality to continue to fight through to November. There was not one bit of solid, valid evidence pointing to Trump failing to gain the GOP nomination. The only arguments being made were based on assumptions that no longer apply to presidential nomination battles in this country. The same arguments are still percolating in the blogosphere and pundit-land.

This is also true for the Democrats except for one difference. Senator Bernie Sanders had all of the hallmarks of Trump's ascendance on the other side. He was riding the same wave of virulent disenchantment and insistence on change that was promised and not delivered with President Obama's election. The one thing Sanders did not have was an array of opponents who make the Three Stooges look like a new Roman triumvirate, making it impossible for the establishment to decide who to promote as its candidate. Instead Hillary Clinton had the Democratic National Committee and its chairperson working full-time to push her to the nomination. And this is not just an observation resulting from the WikiLeaks evidence. The author's Ruffbear7 diary on the Daily Kos website contains numerous entries pointing this out and explaining why Trump would win the nomination dating back to August 2015.

Despite all of this, the nattering mob that gets paid to analyze presidential elections assessed the situation as though all of the old assumptions applied. They do not. Mindsets changed. Facts and reason no longer mean anything. Ignorance is as soothingly blissful as a warm, sudsy bath. Voters think they already have come to their senses. We are sailing the North Atlantic and everyone remains below deck in the salons satisfied that the ship of state's bulkheads will protect us from disaster. No one seems concerned about icebergs.

A work of this nature can grow stale as events overtake the analysis. It can become as silly as some of the science-y stuff science fiction writers put into near history stories. The aim here is to explain from within the primary season what analysts could have been finding but refused to try. Consider it a variation of a "what if" analysis conducted before the "what" has happened. Perhaps this is a time capsule newspaper. The following, for example, is from an analysis the author published on September 10, 2015 on Daily Kos:

Donald Trump will become the GOP nominee for president. The odds are in his favor that he will be elected president as well if Hillary Clinton wins the Democratic nomination. The reasons why are:

1. Almost everyone who read those two sentences immediately scoffed. Trump is too…Trump. So? That is why he was and still is leading in the polls. That is why his supporters support him. Tens of millions of people scoffed at Ronald Reagan for being Ronald Reagan. Tens of millions of people scoffed at George W. Bush for being George W. Bush. Candidates resonate with voters when they come across as individuals with distinct personalities.

2. The GOP base has a very strong anti-politician, anti-Congress streak. Mike Huckabee won the Iowa caucuses as a preacher not as a politician. Mitt Romney was chosen by the GOP in 2012 because he ignored his stint as governor of Massachusetts. The GOP pack of senators and governors are virtually indistinguishable. Of the other non-politicians, Ben Carson was picking off much of the support Trump wasn't and Carly Fiorina, well....
3. The GOP, the party of business and people who think they are going to strike it rich someday thanks to magic Jesus (inshallah), prefers successful people. Dwight D. Eisenhower's military success is legendary, as was Herbert Hoover's commercial success (and courage in China during the Boxer Rebellion). Even George H. W. Bush was a successful oil man before he entered politics and his son co-owned a major league baseball team. Failure for the party usually comes when the GOP candidate is "just" a political success. Speaking of failure, what compels a failed CEO and Senate candidate to think she had any chance?
4. The GOP establishment was freaking out about Trump by September 2015. If Republican leaders thought he needed to be stopped then, they had concluded he could realistically win the nomination. Except they decided to cross their fingers and trusted Trump would tumble. Compare that inertia to what Hillary Clinton's campaign did in the face of Bernie Sanders' surge and started doing during Joe Biden's Hamlet imitation.
5. Trump has a non-stick surface reminiscent of the venerated Reagan. It does not matter to his supporters what he says or who he says it to. He has the ability to be confident without looking smug and to be ridiculous without looking crazy to many people. Those many people will not give any credence to everyone else

believing Trump is smug and crazy. The GOP base praises forthright, irrational statements, opinions based on the Bible, bigotry, and bitterness. Sarah Palin still gets air time and she does look smug and crazy.

6. Does anyone really think Trump's second favorite book is Holy Scripture? Yes. A lot of people will not question anyone's opinions if the person says he is guided by God's Word (cue footage from Rowan County, Kentucky). This sort of thing has greater impact when it is a revelation about the candidate rather than something expected.
7. Reagan was elected because of his personality, message, and outstanding oratorical skills, not because he was once governor of the largest state. He asserted that government and the Soviet Union are evil and set about destroying both. His opinions were disturbingly unsubstantiated, but he was too charming for people to critically analyze what he said. Now, those attitudes have hardened within the GOP and parts of the rest of the population, substituting China, Mexico, Russia, etc. for the Soviet Union. Trump has speaking skills equal to Reagan. He is pompous personally, but not condescending to audiences (just everyone else). He even shares weird hair with Reagan.
8. Trump has spent his adult life building and selling the Trump brand. Despite some major bumps, he has been hugely successful at letting the world know what "Trump" means. That brand is not a facade; the real Trump is already standing and lots of people like it. The real Obama was not revealed until after he was elected. No one left in the GOP field seemed real like Trump. As for the Democrats, the real Clinton is there, but way too many people don't believe it, both supporters and critics. Sanders certainly does not hide any aspect of his personality.

9. Trump will do anything to win, including promise not to run a third-party campaign. However, he signed that pledge because he strongly believes he will win the GOP nomination. If the GOP establishment somehow pulls the rug on Trump, he will have ammunition to claim he was the victim of the same old political intrigues that need to be removed from Washington. He will whip his supporters into having him denounce the pledge. That will not be necessary because Trump will win the nomination. He has the skill to outmaneuver the GOP poohbahs. Indeed, the post-Super Tuesday debate found the other candidates being forced to admit they would support Trump. Just no more wire coat hangers, Mommy.
10. At present, Trump would love to see Clinton nominated. She is the anti-Trump on every level. For Clinton to beat someone as genuine as Trump, she would have to do everything Richard Nixon would do in her place and probably a bit more. The problem is that is what Clinton is already doing to chase Sanders away. As a result, the "Bernie or Bust" movement has taken off quite strongly. Whether that would remain solid if Clinton was nominated is unknown. Given the tenor of the discussion, quite a few people would rather a Trump presidency that cannot see his most flamboyant ideas realized without risking impeachment than a Clinton presidency that would brush off opposition, strengthen the status quo, and never face impeachment for any transgression given she would be the first female president. They probably would not vote for Trump but they won't help Clinton either.[1]

[1] http://www.dailykos.com/story/2015/09/10/1420069/-Trump-will-be-the-GOP-nominee

Sanders posed the only true threat to a Trump presidency. Sanders and his grassroots supporters needed to succeed at explaining to voters why the senator's approach to the issues is necessary for the USA to recover from its decades-long decline and offers a clear framework compared to Trump's "I will figure it out when I have to" philosophy of governing. What was most worrisome about Sanders' campaign was its failure to emphasize the importance of supporters going around and convincing people a political revolution is necessary and what role everyone needs to play. The campaign did the traditional canvassing and phone banks. That sort of suasion only touches the surface and lights up the nerve endings in the hope the person will find it a pleasurable experience. It is nowhere near close to the education necessary to move voters from passive interest to active participation in a political movement. Convincing people to engage in revolution is not the same as getting out the vote. Getting out the vote is necessary, but electing one person to one office, even if that is the Oval Office, does not a political revolution make. Frankly, the figures for Democratic turnout in the primaries and caucuses were not all that promising anyway. The prospects for a political revolution were grim so long as Sanders' supporters avoided and continue to avoid door-to-door, face-to-face engagement with people who were undecided or chose Clinton.

Secretary Clinton was unfairly treated by the House GOP and others regarding her State Department emails, Benghazi, all of it (although more email information indicates there are legitimate issues). Most thoughtful people are fully aware of the importance of compromise to create successful policy solutions. Hillary Clinton can work out compromises that create good policy. The GOP members of Congress have demonstrated resoundingly that they are united in opposing any compromises whatsoever. Moreover, as her positive/negative polling indicates, Clinton is a polarizing individual. She has the political skill to chip away at these obstacles and forge consensus eventually. It will use up political capital and goodwill, but she would probably be good enough at it to wind up with a landslide re-election in 2020 against an extremist GOP nominee riding the backlash among folks who will detest seeing Clinton succeed.

The last president to get a lot accomplished despite facing the same obstacles was Richard M. Nixon. That man's long list of policy accomplishments working with Congresses controlled by Democrats remains extraordinary. His party has since turned against all of the wonderful things he created to protect the nation, its people, and its environment and now denounces essentially the very same healthcare insurance policy he had hoped to achieve in his second term. It is unfortunate but necessary for history to balance his achievements against his self-inflicted destruction. Otherwise, we would be hard-pressed to rank him lower than his bête noire, John F. Kennedy, who could have achieved more but for his assassination.

Nixon's political acumen was breathtaking. In his time, this was not a particularly rare feature. However, after Watergate politicians have been wary of being too adept at playing the game, at least publically. Ronald Reagan, Bill Clinton, and Hillary Clinton are the only other people who have sought the presidency since that come close to his ability to outmaneuver opponents. Nixon is visible in Hillary Clinton's actions. She adopted much of Senator Sanders' agenda only after he entered the race. The debate schedule's bias to prevent other candidates from gaining name recognition was obvious. The mess with data access at the DNC had all the hallmarks of the Watergate break-in. Surrogates channeled Spiro Agnew to say the nastiest stuff and leave her clean. Chelsea Clinton criticized Sanders' healthcare insurance proposal before he had announced a proposal, one of the oldest tricks in the book to undermine a political opponent. And Hillary Clinton used coded messaging with ethnic minority voters and others to imply Sanders would not support their interests just as Nixon did with Yellow Dog

Democrats in his Southern Strategy.

Hillary Clinton did whatever it took to avoid being shut out of the White House a second time. This is when those political instincts no longer benefit the party, the candidates down the ticket, or the voters. They benefited Hillary Clinton only. Richard Nixon's campaigns did absolutely nothing to help his party. Given the shape the Democratic Party is in on all levels, the Democrats could not afford to have a solo performer at the top of the ticket. But that is what they got.

A huge portion of the American electorate wanted to see politics turned upside down in 2016, not continued on the way they have been. Senator Bernie Sanders has a long and distinguished record of accomplishments in Congress on many issues. Sanders has all of the strengths that Clinton has. He does not have the baggage of having ever been vilified by a large segment of the public. That makes him more capable of putting this country on a progressive track. He certainly has a more consistent record of voting based on principles rather than political expediency.

This is most clearly and damningly exemplified by the vote to authorize the Iraq War. Clinton voted to authorize war against Iraq. Bernie Sanders did not. That was the single point in the last fifty years in which every member of Congress was asked to demonstrate true leadership by not repeating the mistake made with the Gulf of Tonkin Resolution. Clinton has made a life out of following the crowd. The Iraq War authorization was the one moment that she could have demonstrated that would not always be the case. Instead, she admitted during the campaign for the presidential nomination of her party that she owed George W. Bush her vote, a vote that was going to cost hundreds of thousands of lives, in exchange for money the state she represented deserved without any quid pro quo. She did exactly what politicians do. She log rolled. She exchanged one favor for another rather than making a decision based on what was right or best for her constituents, state, and country and what was moral.

And what about the fact that must not be spoken? The USA is far past the time one of the two highest offices should have been filled by a woman. That was not a reason to choose Clinton, but it was a reason to insist that the Democrats have a woman on the ticket. Since many good candidates for vice president exist, not to mention the binders full of fair to poor candidates, let's look at someone who was never part of the conversation and yet may have been the perfect choice. Janet Napolitano was governor of Arizona, a state with one huge metropolis (unlike Vermont), a sizable number of Latino residents (unlike Vermont), and no preferred party (unlike Vermont). She was a member of President Obama's cabinet, giving her additional, federal executive experience. Her role was Secretary for Homeland Security, a position that gave her the opportunity to be involved with foreign affairs, defense matters, and other areas under federal jurisdiction. She has shrugged off controversies and, although not exactly laid back, engaged gamely in banter on television programs favored by progressives. Her public service appears selfless, and she left government to lead one of the nation's greatest state university systems. Napolitano's experience and favorable qualities easily equal Clinton's.

The reason why Hillary Clinton gets up every morning wanting to lead the USA is she feels she deserves it after losing the nomination battle to Barack Obama in 2008 and the Electoral College vote in 2016. It is the same reason Richard Nixon got up every morning in 1968. Clinton has and Nixon had all of the experience and qualities one wants in the President of the United States. Clinton's stalwart supporters stop there. But Clinton has and Nixon had further qualities that make one want to recoil in horror from the idea of reliving that kind of national anguish.

Clinton has the Democratic Party establishment on her side. The political party establishments do not work alone. They use the resources they know best to sway public opinion away from Trump and toward Clinton. The New York Times editorial board demonstrated its deep-seated involvement in the establishment by endorsing Hillary Clinton and John Kasich solely because they were the most traditional candidates. Rather than consider how Trump, Carson, and Sanders awakened opposition to career politicians and entrenched interests, they dismissed Trump and Sanders as unrealistic for two distinct reasons and just ignored Carson. If Sanders and Trump are that unrealistic, why did they garner so much support? Their supporters clearly do not consider these two outsiders as presenting unrealistic agendas. The editorial board ignored that policies should be representative of what the majority wants unless what the majority wants is a clear infringement of minority rights that will harm that minority. That is the core of the liberal democracy the USA was built upon.

Trump is unpalatable to a very large swath of the American public, but so is broccoli. That does not mean we denounce people who like broccoli. We either ignore them or try to figure out what they like about something we find so distasteful so we can at least understand their point of view. The broccoli aficionados can try making broccoli with cheddar cheese sauce or something else that makes it more palatable to more people. That is up to them to convince us. Regardless, one does not just reject out of hand such a large group of people for approving of something we do not.

Similarly, Sanders supporters (who mostly continue to identify as such) are like vegetarians trying to convince omnivores why a vegetarian diet is healthier. Everyone is used to eating meat and many people really like it. The omnivores are only showing that they feel threatened by vegetarians or subconsciously know the vegetarians are right when omnivores ridicule the idea of putting aside meat. Rationally they have to admit the science and economics supports vegetarianism as preferable. Emotionally and selfishly, they do not want to give up something they are used to and find tasty and satisfying. The vegetarians are going to blunder a bit by pushing soy substitutes that aren't prepared well. It is their responsibility to educate the omnivores about the great benefits of vegetarianism and also create recipes omnivores will find just as satisfying as ones with meat and lead them to realize they can do without meat.

At some point the vegetarians ought to recognize that the broccoli lovers are promoting something that could help vegetarians in the long run. Unfortunately, a lot of vegetarians don't like broccoli and others do not see the point in focusing on broccoli. If the NYT editorial board wanted to be truly realistic, it would have helped the broccoli lovers and vegetarians to realize they actually agree on some things and can possibly work together in the future rather than waging their own separate campaigns. For example, they could show how Sanders and Trump supporters both agree that the establishment, so vividly represented by the NYT editorial board, needs to be removed from power. Regrettably, the biggest sticking point may not be the fight the establishment will put up but rather the intransigence of a part of the public that believes it already has elected the people needed to fix things and are becoming more and more frustrated their representatives aren't getting anywhere despite their best efforts.

The United States government is established so that the majority voice of the people directs public policy and legislation. That is the essence of a democracy. However, for eight years governing came almost to a halt due to the actions and arguments of a minority faction within the GOP that demonstrated its ability to upend establishment candidates. They are the Tea Party. Although their existence may be tied to corporate money being used in 2010, 2012, and 2014 to support them, they represent the Reagan Revolution distilled down to its most purely irrational essence, an unfathomable hatred of government action other than going to war, securing the nation's borders, and deporting all people residing in the US in violation of the law. This extreme form of libertarianism is breathtaking in its inability to fathom that almost all of the good things in the lives of its proponents are the result of government action. The fact the Tea Party movement has succeeded in getting so many people elected to Congress who agree with their philosophy makes one wonder how anyone can view Donald Trump's success as an aberration.

When a minority like the Tea Party in the House or the filibustering GOP in the Senate obstruct the majority will for no reason other than to be obstructionist, they violate the principles upon which the Republic was founded. It is not politics or governing; it is blackmail and terrorism. They are using the rules set down to order how laws are prepared in Congress to sow disorder. It is a rebellion against representative democracy. People that cherish the ideals and structures that have worked for two centuries are prohibited from using those ideals and structures because a small group of extremists want to demolish those ideals and structures.

They have little to offer to replace what they want to destroy. They do not put forward ideas. They criticize and protest. President Obama did all he could to circumvent the gridlock caused by these obstructions. Their response was to sue him for allegedly not doing his job when they weren't doing their jobs as elected officials of the United States. They are not following the Constitution. They obey Grover Norquist and his reprehensible no new taxes pledge. They certainly have won accolades from their constituents for standing up to any law or appointment they find unacceptable. Their representatives promised as candidates to do this and they did. Not many voters can say that. Now they are getting antsy that their agenda of slicing up the government isn't progressing very well. One Speaker of the House is gone for failing them. His replacement came in reluctantly and had the gall to say he wanted a guarantee of having time for his family when he has opposed every effort to help voters get more time with their families. He claimed he would see to it that everything the Tea Party House members promised their constituents would get a vote. However, a vote in the House of Representatives, even a passing vote, is just one step in enacting the Tea Party agenda.

While disciplined parties in parliamentary systems frequently enact a good bit of their electoral platform, the only political party that ever fulfilled all of its election promises was the National Socialist Worker's Party of Germany in 1933. Enacting an entire platform means that all of the people who voted for that party get what they want. Everyone else only gets whatever they wanted that is consistent with the majority party's platform. True, majority rule is a part of democracy. True, majority rule can result in the majority deciding it wants to establish a dictatorship. True, doing so infringes on the rights of the minority that don't want a dictatorship. True, protecting the rights of minorities from infringement is also a part of democracy. Now, is it true that protecting the rights of minorities from infringement is inconsistent with majority rule? No. Unfortunately, most times people in the majority just think "we won" and expect legislation they want regardless of its impact on any minority, least of all the minority consisting of all of the voters who had to settle for thinking "we lost."

Yet just like a representative in a district needs to represent the needs of all constituents in the district, a governing party needs to be cognizant of what opponents want. Eventually the governing party is going to be the opposition. Any effort to influence the legislation of the new governing party will look like hypocrisy after the former governing party ignored the opposition. Otherwise, going the route of the Tea Party is all that remains for a minority. Going that route and obstructing all legislation requires demonizing everyone else to the point they probably would not want to negotiate a compromise even if the obstructing minority was open to compromise. Heels are dug in, nothing gets accomplished.

One of the most amazing features of politics today is the

large number of people who embrace hate-filled opinions of President Obama. Regardless of the facts, regardless of the illogical nature of their positions, regardless of the obvious bigotry, one segment of the population has held a consistent view of Obama. That was the foundation from which the GOP built its obstinate refusal to consider any proposal made by the president as a starting point for discussion, much less as a fully formed solution to a problem. Again, how does the GOP leadership not understand why Trump is so popular when it has used the same anger he does to bring government to a halt? Most other people were baffled at the intransigent ignorance behind this characterization of Obama and eventually gave up trying to engage that segment of the electorate. It has been a constant burden and roadblock to accomplishing anything in Washington.

Supporters of Obama dismissed people who reviled him because they were so way off. Supporters of Hillary Clinton dismiss criticism of her because they want a female president, know she has the needed experience and would be good at it, and the GOP has spent almost 25 years blasting her for transgressions that were not transgressions. Supporters of everyone else dismiss Donald Trump and his supporters because Trump is arrogant, narcissistic, and buffoonish among many other rotten things. The rest of the GOP field was dismissed by Democrats as being a bunch of hyenas fighting over the carcass of the Tea Party movement, as well as being hypocrites, misogynists, etc. Everyone not supporting Sanders dismissed him and his supporters as fantasizing dreamers bent on creating in the USA what the Bolsheviks failed to create.

When we dismiss political opponents we make clear we are not going to work with them to negotiate compromises because they are unreasonable people embracing ridiculous positions. Our politics have gotten wound up in the idea that you don't work with people who are clearly wrong because nothing you say will convince them otherwise. Except that tends to only be true if the reason they are wrong is their position is based on racism or religion. No rational, logical, evidence-based argument will ever sway someone whose heart is bound up due to bigotry or belief unless that person is willing to step away from that emotional foundation to consider a scientific analysis. In order to fully address the problems facing the Republic, one thing that must be addressed first is that we can write off people who disagree with us and still address our problems successfully. The roots of our problems are these deep divisions.

It is not possible to bind a serious wound without doing something to pull the two sides together to allow the opening to heal. Demanding your policy proposal be enacted as is does not a compromise make. The automatic defensiveness and shutting down to new inputs is not debate or dialogue and does nothing to advance reconciliation. We must start to believe others can be right no matter how firmly we believe otherwise. Belief is just that. It is not knowledge. We can no longer afford to instantly respond negatively. We must learn to evaluate our positions and the positions of others using facts and reason.

Time to stop dismissing others and instead address why they take the points of view they do. Bernie Sanders appears to know this. Many of his supporters have not grasped this. That, more than Tea Party elements in Congress or wider GOP obstructionism, would have significantly diminished Sanders' ability to move a legislative agenda forward if he was elected president. So long as Clinton and Trump supporters particularly, but anyone else not supporting Sanders, are demons, they will continue to dismiss Sanders and his supporters. The work that needs to be done is to end the derision, look for commonalities, and calmly discuss differences of opinion. Without that, Sanders' political revolution is dead on arrival.

Chapter 18—How It Can Be Done

EUGENE V. DEBS was a remarkable individual. He stood as the presidential nominee of the Socialist Party of America in five of the first six elections of the twentieth century after having served in the Indiana legislature, helped found unions, and led the Pullman strike. His activities and actions consistently supported the expansion of rights for workers in the face of employers' refusals to ease up on their requirements for continued employment. In 1912, running against two men who already had been President of the United States and one man who became President as a result of the election, he garnered just shy of six percent of the votes.

While Debs' chief aim in being on the ballot was to help down ticket candidates win local elections, a fairly successful strategy, his performance stands out principally because all three of the other candidates agreed that progressive legislation begun under Teddy Roosevelt ought to be continued to some extent or another. He was the farthest left on a political spectrum that pretty much stopped soon after it passed center to right. Unfortunately, Debs never spent much time trying to build a coherent organization for the Socialist Party, which was riddled with divisions over what kind of socialism the party represented. After his last bid for the White House in 1920 while serving a ten year prison sentence dropped his vote count to 3.4 percent of the total (still his second best showing), his sentence was commuted by the honorable winner of the election, Warren G.

Harding. Harding even invited Debs to the White House the day after he was released and warmly welcomed him as a great orator and politician.

The health concerns that gave rise to the commutation prevented any further campaigning. Debs died in 1926, the Socialist Party already falling apart. It had endorsed Senator Robert La Follette's candidacy in 1924 under a revived Progressive Party which received seventeen percent of the vote and the thirteen electoral votes of the senator's home state of Wisconsin. Just to be clear, La Follette had been a Republican, had challenged Teddy Roosevelt and William Howard Taft for the Republican nomination in 1912, took up TR's Progressive Party mantle, and was endorsed by the Socialist Party. Eighty-eight years later, La Follette would be considered too progressive for the Democratic Party and Republicans would shrink away from him for fear he might be contagious.

After 1924, the Socialist Party fielded its own presidential nominees for the next eight elections. The candidates never received more than one-seventh percent of the national vote. While it might have shown a revival as a result of the Great Depression, the failure to have established a unified organization under Debs, the draw of the newer Communist Party of America, and the even greater draw of FDR's democratic socialist New Deal policies all prevented the Socialists from taking advantage of Wall Street's selfishness. The party finally called it quits after the 1956 election.

The reason why party organization was so clearly needed may be seen from the trajectory of the British Labour Party over the same period. Labour arose from union leaders' political activities like the American Socialists. They embraced the same basic platform of improving conditions for workers and democratic socialist features like social security, healthcare, and easier access to education. The Liberals, one of the two existing major parties, was fractured over a few issues, most notably Irish home rule, just as the Republicans in the USA were over tariffs and progressive policies.

The Labour Party succeeded in establishing a political organization in the first two decades of the twentieth century. It was that organization, not any one leader that helped the party gain enough support among voters to be in a position to be asked to form His Majesty's Government in 1924. Ironically, the Liberals had their best ever election results in 1906 based on a democratic socialist platform of creating the welfare state not much different from Labour's intentions. The Liberals fatally injured themselves in 1910 by gaining the support of King Edward VII to pack the House of Lords with newly minted barons if the Lords continued to vote down the so-called People's Budget that expanded the welfare state created four years earlier. In order to get the King's approval, the Liberals called two elections to demonstrate the country wanted the welfare state expanded. However, the Liberal Party successively lost seats in the elections and ended up needing to ask the Irish Nationalists in Parliament to support a continued Liberal government. Despite the losses, the party had shown that most British subjects wanted the People's Budget enacted, so Buckingham Palace was obliged to agree to blackmail the House of Lords.

The Liberals limped along due to World War I requiring a united front with the Conservative Party, although shattered further by the Irish Easter Uprising in 1916. The Conservatives changed their allegiance from the Liberal Prime Minister H. H. Asquith to the Liberal Chancellor of the Exchequer David Lloyd George, who gave the Conservatives more cabinet positions. Once the coalition ended in 1922, the Liberal Party floundered in the face of the Labour Party's skill at attracting Liberal voters. It wasn't so much that these two parties had close policy agendas. The Liberals were nowhere close to embracing workers' rights. Rather, the Liberal Party had always been stronger in urban areas with the same kinds of voters that Labour wanted in their column. The Conservatives had always been the "country" party, representing landed interests in the counties.

One of the stated reasons for this book is to guide people back to recognizing that political terminology like "liberal" must have widely agreed upon meanings, not whatever meaning the user wants. The guilty parties can be found not only among politicians and voters, but also in the mainstream media. Indeed, it is a sad commentary on the state of political analysis when someone can have an article published in the Washington Post that sets up a false opposition between capitalism and socialism. It is one thing for citizens generally to not know the difference between political and economic systems. It is quite another for someone posing as a professional to ignore the difference. This is one of thousands of examples in which individuals are justifying their arguments for or against candidates and policies on a thorough lack of understanding of the vocabulary they are using. Sometimes it is just ignorance while other times it is intentional.

The curse of the Tower of Babel applies as much to misunderstood dialogue in a single language as it does to not understanding other languages. Socialism is a broad concept. Many American political programs, such as Social Security, workers' compensation, Medicare, etc., are socialist. They are just as socialist now as they were in the 1880s when Chancellor Otto von Bismarck implemented unemployment insurance and old age pensions to undermine the growing support for the Socialist Party in Imperial Germany. Socialism may involve government ownership of some industries, as was the case in post-war Great Britain and elsewhere. However, none of these forms of socialism substitute for capitalism. Socialist political policies work quite well in capitalist economies. Just look at all of Scandinavia and the Low Countries.

It is wrong to compare Bernie Sanders' socialist propositions to capitalism. He has not been arguing for the appropriation of the means of production from private owners. He has been arguing for tax and regulatory policies that were prevalent in the United States from the mid-1940s to the early 1980s. He has been arguing for the appropriation of political power from the wealthy and corporations who appropriated it from voters in the last three decades. Much as some on the left would like and almost all of his critics contended, Sanders' campaign was not an effort to undermine, replace, or attack capitalism as the Republic's economic system.

Much has been written over the centuries about identifying the Whore of Babylon mentioned in the Revelation of John of Patmos. First it was Rome. Then it couldn't be Rome after the empire was Christianized, so heretics opposed to the Nicene Creed became the whore. Then Islam. Then Catholicism according to Protestants. Any entity that could be warped into being antithetical to Christian teaching was eligible. By that measure, given how far off right-wing evangelicals are from the message of Jesus of Nazareth, they have come to look and smell like the Whore. They use words to spread hate and denounce opponents. They are trying to convince everyone else that their language is accurate. And they have been succeeding.

More than anything else, progressives need to be doing everything possible through every medium available to define the language of debate. For example, why is abortion split between pro-life and pro-choice? Pro-life folks are quite likely to embrace the death penalty, judicial murder, on the grounds that those convicted of capital crimes are not innocent like fetuses. The glaring problem with that argument is the number of convictions overturned by new methods of using DNA evidence. Innocent or, technically speaking, not guilty people have been executed. Pro-choice folks are not anti-life although a case can be made that pro-life folks are anti-choice. If the two categories are inaccurate and not full opposites, what is the point of the labels?

Progressives also need to hammer away at the deceptions and unsubstantiated opinions put forward from the GOP and right. Mudslinging is a singularly appropriate term for the way in which partisans throw accusations and innuendo at their opponents. Not every muddy charge sticks but each one dirties the political arena. Sanders said it best when he pointed out that people are just tired of the Clinton email scandal. Granted, he said that without all the facts being out. Nonetheless, the best response to any question that is unproductive in terms of moving this country forward is to say it is not worth the effort to answer. Unfortunately, most partisans prefer to counterattack rather than allow the biased or false claim stand unchallenged. This is particularly true when the charge is a boldfaced misuse of a term, such as the allegations that President Obama is a socialist. Sometimes, however, a term is misused to describe the person using it.

Hillary Clinton claimed in a debate on February 4, 2016 that Bernie Sanders had made himself the gatekeeper of what progressive means. However, she failed to explain what her definition of progressivism is while Sanders pointed out that progressivism involves reducing income inequality and addressing the lack of real opportunities to succeed caused not only by that inequality but also by the failure of the government to insure that certain basic requirements to personal success are met for all people. The Associated Press, in reporting the debate, stated that the definition of progressivism is no longer agreed upon. So much for unbiased reporting.

The only reason the definition might not be agreed any longer is Ronald Reagan's assault on government actions to improve the lives of the governed. Ever since, the Right has steadily worn down the idea that definitions are facts that may evolve over time but are accepted by all as being what experts tell us they are. Instead, the Right has insisted that the definitions of terms such as progressivism are whatever the user wants them to be. This nonsense is not going to end anytime soon. However, we can start by saying there is a definition for progressivism and Senator Sanders is using the accepted historical definition. That does not make him a gatekeeper; it makes him a definition defender.

Progressivism in American politics holds that the government, using evidence-based, rationally-developed ideas, can improve the lives of citizens and thereby increase their opportunities to enjoy their inalienable rights to life, liberty, and the pursuit of happiness. It rests on the fact that individuals alone are incapable of obtaining all of the information, resources, and skills required to insure certain of their basic needs are met efficiently and effectively. It also rests on the fact that individuals create governments for the purpose of safeguarding their well-being not only from foreign aggressors and criminals, but also anything that can harm their health such as defective products, unsanitary food, environmental pollutants, unlicensed professions, and contaminated water.

Progressives take this one step further and agree with the principles of democratic socialism and the United Nations Declaration on Human Rights. They agree that people's well-being and liberty are undermined if they do not have unhindered access to certain essential necessities such as education to their full potential, healthcare, employment based on merit alone, leisure time, family planning, childcare, food, clothing, and shelter. Typically, the acquisition of these basic needs traps people into an existence overwhelmingly dominated by a job they cannot afford to lose. Without reasonable governmental intervention to insure these basic needs are met for all members of society, the vast majority of the members of society become nothing more than wage slaves, living to work and working to live. Citizens have life but not much liberty and little time to pursue happiness.

Any governmental policy designed to safeguard the well-being of the people, promote the general welfare, or protect equality under the law of a minority in any regard is progressive. Any governmental policy designed to protect the interests of a segment of the population or a narrow interest that does not need any help in obtaining the above-mentioned necessities is not progressive. The universally-recognized method of insuring the basic needs of all members of society are met is to tax the wealthiest members of society and corporations sufficiently to fund programs that provide those needs. The rationale for doing this is that the wealthiest members of society and corporations obtain their wealth primarily from the productivity of everyone else and the stability provided by the government but do not fully compensate everyone else or the government for providing them with the means and environment to acquire their wealth. The imbalance in negotiating strength between owners and employees prevents the one and lobbying and campaign donations prevent the other. The 99 percent can only be guaranteed their basic needs are met if their government enacts laws that tax the 1 percent and corporations to fund those needs.

Progressivism recognizes that all people are equal under the law, all people hold an equal stake in benefiting from society, and all people deserve equal opportunities to realize their full potential. The wealthy and corporations want everyone to believe that they just happen to be better at using the benefits of society. The problem is that they did not start out with the same opportunities that the 99 percent did. They had an advantage due to their prior accumulation of wealth under a much less equal system. The deck is stacked to prohibit any but the rare few with a radically new technology or business process from moving up. The deck has become even more stacked since 1982.

The list of progressive policies enacted in the twentieth century is long. They were supported by Democratic presidents like Wilson, FDR, and LBJ and by Republican presidents like TR, Ike, and Nixon. They were approved by Rockefeller Republicans and liberal Democrats. They were opposed by Yellow Dog Democrats and Goldwater Republicans. Every single program that insures Americans are healthier, safer, less poor, better educated, and treated fairly and the American landscape preserved and appreciated are the result of progressivism.

Progressivism came to a halt with the Reagan Revolution that declared any kind of government intervention bad and Reagan's fulfillment of Nixon's Southern Strategy to sweep bigoted southerners into the GOP. Progressivism nearly died with the advent of the Democratic Leadership Council (DLC) and the extreme Right that falsely equated progressive with liberal. Barack Obama campaigned on the progressive promises of hope and change but he was co-opted by the DLC remnants in 2009 and paralyzed by the Tea Party element in Congress in 2011. His refusal to support marriage equality until Joe Biden forced his hand indicates he is not as progressive as he wanted people to believe.

Many countries have demonstrated that democratic socialism not only can be implemented but also creates the most stable, contented societies in the world. What is stopping the USA? Opposing adoption of the metric system. Keeping dollar bills and pennies in circulation and avoiding two dollar bills and dollar coins. "Believing" evolution isn't real. Insisting the Second Amendment is an absolute right to gun ownership unlimited by its initial clause. Subsidizing profitable oil companies. Claiming substantial speaking fees and campaign donations from Wall Street firms will not prejudice one's decisions. In sum, American exceptionalism, that closeminded deception that the USA is unique among nations, stands in the way.

America already adopted scores of progressive policies, but no one seems to recognize this because this happened before they were born and was couched in language that downplayed the socialist tinge due to antipathy toward communism. The only obstacles to democratic socialism are greed and the libertarian refusal to acknowledge that a democratic republic requires faithfulness to the universal principles that all people are created equal and the full enjoyment of civil liberties only obtains if everyone is guaranteed their basic needs will be met. That last bit is one of the most difficult for people to swallow. American exceptionalism includes a heavy dose of independence and self-reliance, the belief that people must fend for themselves, mythologized by how the country was colonized and expanded.

While there is a certain truth to that still in much of the country west of the Mississippi, the rest of the truth is that people who fend for themselves essentially have the freedom to do little but work, eat, and sleep. The exercise of civil liberties primarily operates as an adjunct to diversions that someone scraping together a living has no time to enjoy. One of the blessings of being a citizen of the USA once was having sufficient income from decent employment coupled with dependable periods outside employment to indulge in all that freedom offered in one's free time. Such is no longer the case by and large. The reason for that is the greed of employers who have demanded increased productivity from fewer employees working longer hours each week and dispensing with vacations or from more employees working less than full time who are not entitled to paid time off or other benefits. That greed has been enhanced by the dismantling of regulatory structures and forms of government bias favoring businesses over human beings.

The extent to which that bias has infiltrated the decisions of the Supreme Court was starkly demonstrated when Dow Chemical Company settled a lawsuit that had been appealed to the Supreme Court days after Justice Scalia died suddenly. Dow's lawyers knew the appeal had much slimmer chances of success with the perfectly reliable, corporation friendly Scalia unable to add the fifth vote. Anyone the least bit uncertain whether justice is being bought in the high court already understood given Scalia's death at an exclusive hunting camp where he had been invited as a non-paying guest. Circumstantial evidence, yes, but also more reasonably scrutinized than the evidence Scalia would not acknowledge in his most tempestuous dissents.

The battle in 2016 was reason over belief. The real surprise is that anyone is surprised that Donald Trump received so much sustained support given that he merely echoed the beliefs of a very large segment of the country's population. The real concern is that no one is concerned that Sanders and his supporters were the only Democrats actively trying to promote reason over emotion, positive action over negative reaction.

Even there, all is not as rosy as it could be. Bernie Sanders, his campaign team, and the majority of his supporters were all working under the supposition that a political revolution to restore the Republic to its citizens consists of electing one man to the highest office in the land through the kind of grassroots effort that faded with the advent of television advertising in campaigns and the corresponding donor base where almost all monetary contributions are small amounts from a lot of people. Except that is not a revolution or revolutionary; it describes a traditional grassroots campaign for a presidential nomination.

Back in the 1970s, when civics was still taught in schools, one of the most interesting classes was the discussion on how citizens participate. What was so startling to any student interested in politics or from a family engaged in politics was the proportion of the population that had absolutely no interest in participating in the political system whatsoever. About three-quarters of eligible voters show enough interest in politics to follow elections to some extent in the news. After 1968, voting in presidential elections has been under sixty percent with a low point of forty-nine percent in 1996, a diminished rate comparable to the 1830s and 1920s-30s. The 1924 election is the only one lower. Going back from 1968 to 1828 (the first election with reliable figures), only one-quarter of presidential elections saw fewer than sixty percent of voters participate. 1876 was the high water mark at 81.8 percent, just edging out the 81.2 percent in the fateful 1860 election. Americans have always been lackluster enthusiasts of exercising the right to vote. In fact, non-presidential election years have been consistently below forty percent since 1974 and rarely broke fifty percent before then.

Counting the number of citizens that engage in some sort of political activity other than voting actually shows that somewhere around 63 percent do something each year, a bit higher than the proportion voting in presidential elections. Citizens oftentimes have no choice but to engage with their local elected officials. In descending order the other forms of political participation include: signing a petition; contacting an elected official (usually local); helping someone else with a problem involving local officials; attending a town meeting or similar; donating money; actively participating in an organization that tries to influence policies; attend a political rally; send a letter to newspaper; volunteer for a campaign; speak publicly on a public issue; or engage in a protest or demonstration. Donating to a campaign is done by less than twenty percent of all eligible voters. The rates go steadily downhill from there. However, whenever anyone goes out to look at what citizens are doing what they find is the same people doing multiple things. More than half the people engaging in activities other than voting only do one or two things in any given year, perhaps one or three hours' worth of engagement out of the 8784 hours in 2016, a leap year. Of the remainder, slightly more than half engage in three or four activities and slightly less than half (about 13 percent of all voters) engage in five or more.

Given these statistics, one might claim that drawing huge crowds at rallies and scoring millions of small donations qualifies as some kind of revolution. Bernie Sanders and his campaign were saying just that. Hillary Clinton was saying no, that is not a political revolution. She was right. Sanders was using traditional, pre-Super PAC, grassroots methods to build his candidacy state by state. His messaging, the pleas for contributions (meaning money, not talent), and particularly the nasty demonization by many of his supporters of anyone daring to point out flaws in his campaign were all consistent with every other hopeful nominee's campaign. If anything, his campaign looked pretty much like Barack Obama's come from behind victory over

Clinton, a point too obvious even for the pundits to ignore.

Sanders needed to do more than just run a campaign to get him elected in order for a political revolution to occur. The grassroots movement had been successful despite a glaring lack of media coverage. His donors felt included. Their donations gave them a stake in the election. Judging from his messaging, his campaign wanted people to think that this outburst of popular support for what many considered a fringe candidate midsummer of 2015 evidenced a new form of political participation. He was describing the groundswell lifting him as though it was some kind of mystical awakening. He was claiming this was the political revolution. Except there was nothing revolutionary about what was happening. Almost all of that enthusiasm rapidly fell away as people pivoted to accept he did not win the nomination. That does not mean a revolution still can't happen, but it is much less likely. When the real work of creating political change begins, what structure will be there to maintain the momentum and rally the people? Sanders' supporters were not going to morph into a revolutionary organization if they already had given up on the sole purpose of the Sanders campaign: to elect him President.

Sanders was getting a lot of people not only to donate but also to volunteer, many of them doing it for the first time. Getting people involved in a political campaign in large numbers is not revolutionary. JFK, RFK, Reagan, Obama, and many others all did the exact same thing. It is the standard model for a populist candidate, not anything new in any way. Just because a lot of people are energized to participate in a campaign for the first time is not in any way revolutionary or evidence of a political revolution. However, there were plenty of ideas the Sanders campaign could have adopted to demonstrate it was more than just a run of the mill grassroots candidacy.

Sanders could have told his supporters he was not going to beg for money at least until after the convention. Instead, he would provide updates on what the campaign was doing, promote events like marches and rallies, and circulate talking points for supporters to explain his policy agenda. He could have reported how much the campaign was taking in and what their goals were but not ask for donations. Sanders could have asked Democracy for America or some other group that endorsed him to work on coordinating the work of all of the progressive organizations so they weren't duplicating efforts and preferably work under one umbrella like ActBlue. Sanders also could have promoted a council or network that had as its sole mission laying the groundwork to obtain maximum support for his legislative agenda to overcome GOP opposition and unify Democrats.

The biggest drawback among progressives is their lack of coordination and discipline. Look at how effective the GOP has been blocking almost everything in Congress solely based on the demands of Tea Party elements and the no tax pledge made to Grover Norquist. They achieved their stated objective of stopping Obama from getting anything done legislatively. Their problem is they cannot push through their own legislative agenda due to the rules they put into place regarding how bills get a vote. They refuse to get rid of those rules in the event they become the minority again in either house. Progressives need to work from the same page and be prepared to attract as much support as possible. That is not happening. Yet a progressive agenda is precisely what the country needs to maintain a role as a world leader.

For quite some time the USA has been a world leader only in military spending, prison population, and economic output from employees who have seen their real wages shrink. The USA remains exceptional in terms of its refusal to adopt any of the social welfare programs other countries have had for decades, the metric system and large denomination coins, and reasonable gun control legislation. The ridiculous thing is that if the USA stopped spending so much money on its military, stopped incarcerating so many people for minor drug offenses, stopped employers from grabbing so much of the revenues from increased productivity, and adopted social welfare programs, the metric system and large denomination coins, and reasonable gun control legislation the USA would be far better able to lead a world in which it was not an exception to the rule.

Unfortunately, far too many people have become convinced that the USA cannot do any of those things because they will cost too much, cause disruption, and not work because the USA is so different. Yet the costs can be easily met from reductions in military spending, a return to the progressive taxation rates prior to 1970, and a combination end to subsidies for profitable corporations and imposition of a minimum alternative tax on corporations that currently escape from paying any or very few taxes.

Change is always disruptive, but it is inevitable and pervasive. The government actually stopped offering as much help to people losing their jobs in the 1980s when American industry was seeing its last gasps, making the transition even more disruptive. Fracking has transformed entire counties with almost no effort to soften the disruptions. However, the country doesn't seem to have had much problem changing over to smart phones, fluorescent light bulbs, Wi-Fi, interstate highways, jet travel, etc. It has always been just a matter of how the change was sold to people and how supportive the government and businesses were to making the change. As for the USA being different, it is different only because so few Americans have traveled extensively abroad.

Transformative projects do not have to be huge or costly to begin with. Deng Xiaoping let the four special economic zones develop for four years before expanding economic reforms to fourteen coastal cities in 1984. The experiment proved so successful, the rest of the country was clamoring for authority to negotiate contracts with foreign companies in less than two years.

Here are a few ideas that would quickly provide people with more money, time, and jobs, invigorating the economy and the tax base:

- Solar-powered electricity could be set up for the poor for free through federal grants.
- The work week could be reduced to 35 hours for non-exempt employees and overtime required for exempt employees who work over 40 hours per week, forcing employers to fully pay for the productivity they receive from employees.
- End the war on drugs by decriminalizing marijuana and making drug addiction a health issue. Treat drunk driving as a health issue. Offer grants for drug courts, rehabs, and counseling centers.
- Ban for-profit prisons.
- Return responsibility to classroom teachers for achieving grade level objectives measured by frequent and varied non-standardized assessment instruments.
- Require community colleges to assess the college skills of high school students in grades 9 and 10 to give them sufficient time to address deficiencies through programs designed by community college and high school faculty.
- Enforce full sex equality in the workplace in wages, access to promotions, and other benefits.
- Revise and impose realistic water use regulations in desert regions and prohibit further development.
- Ban the militarization of police forces and provide federal grants for community policing efforts that reduce the barriers between public safety officers and residents.
- Make domestic abuse, illiteracy, homelessness, unprepared parenting, malnutrition, childhood obesity, and mental illness the subject of grant programs that foster the sharing of best practices among grant awardees.

Of course many more ideas exist. None of them are impossible if people are shown why they save money, support a healthier society, and spring from rational and scientific analysis of policy issues rather than emotional opinions. People who are dismissive of change do not want to put in the effort. The difficulty is finding ways to motivate them to make that effort or at least let others make the effort. Their active opposition must be transformed into passive abstention. Otherwise, the United States will continue to see the income divide widen and the ability of most Americans to continue to be avid consumers diminish. At some point, apathy will overtake interest and the Republic will not be able to be restored.

Chapter 19—The United States of Plutocrats

SOME PEOPLE BELIEVE and often state that the United States of America is a republic not a democracy. They use as their source the constitutional requirement that the federal government guarantee that all states have a republican form of government. This is a straightforward example of the misuse of terminology. For nearly 225 years the United States of America was a democracy as well as a republic. Granted, the right to vote was restricted for several groups of adults until fully extended with the 26th Amendment in 1971 and has come under attack again with the spread of voter ID laws passed to combat unsubstantiated allegations of voter fraud. Nonetheless, the text of the Constitution clearly establishes a representative democracy in which citizens select from among themselves individuals to serve as legislators, chief executive, and back-up chief executive. While the structure is democratic, the actual practice can be less so or not at all. Remember, Freedom House, a reliable evaluator for this, considers only 60.5 percent of the 195 countries of the world practicing democracies even though 97.9 percent of them claim to be democratic. And yes, democracy like Catholicism, baseball, piano, and homosexuality requires practice.

As we have seen, voting was severely restricted in ancient Athens and that experiment continues to be upheld as the birth of democracy. The Roman Republic managed to lay the foundations for empire by having a Senate chosen from among patricians who chose two consuls each year. Eventually the plebs elected two tribunes who were inviolate and could veto any decision of the Senate. Other than women, the only adult Roman citizens left out of the loop were the equites, sort of a middle class. Ironically, Caesar Augustus, from an equites family, created political opportunities not only for them but also freed slaves while establishing a dictatorship using the façade of restoring the Republic after the civil wars. Even Great Britain, the progenitor of liberal democracy, only gradually extended the franchise. Nonetheless, the right of citizens to vote in meaningful elections (i.e., contested and fair) to select public office holders, to decide referenda, or to directly decide policies and laws is the hallmark of government by the *demos* (a Greek term that ironically translates in English into the title of an Oscar-winning film directed by Robert Redford about grief in a wealthy American family everyone is supposed to sympathize with because real tragedies happen to them, too). Funny how ordinary people are distinguished from celebrities and ordinary citizens are distinguished from politicians. Ordinary is not special, not connected, not preferred, not as good, not important, not many things that openly betray the idea of equality.

A republic is merely a state in which the legislature, head of government, and head of state are all elected. Even in Poland where the head of state was an elected king the official name of the country was *Najjaśniejsza Rzeczpospolita Polska* or Most Serene Republic of Poland. Who the electors are is not relevant just so long as there aren't so few "elector" becomes a title of nobility as in the Holy Roman Empire. Obviously, the Constitution establishes a republican state. Countries with royal heads of state, as in ten European countries and more than twenty others around the world, are monarchies, generally with elected heads of government (Saudi Arabia and Brunei being exceptions). Dictatorships may exist in states whose constitutions call them a republic or in which the name of the state includes the word "republic." That does not make them republics any more than calling an American bison a buffalo makes it a buffalo. Accuracy dictates that we look at the actual type of state.

For the same reason, we must look at who is actually empowered to elect representatives to decide the form of government. Three aspects of democracy help us to decide when we have one: if the elections are free and fair; if all legal citizens are equal under the laws; and if all full citizens are free to participate in all aspects of politics. Thus, if the electorate or true control over elections is restricted to the wealthy or landowners we have an oligarchy rather than a democracy. Indeed, we can say that the restrictions were so great in Britain at least until 1832 and in the United States until around the same time that both were oligarchies. And that is ignoring the rather large issue of denying the right to vote to female adult citizens.

This is why it is important to make a distinction between a legal citizen and full citizen. Many societies have held free and fair elections, granted equal protection under the laws, and permitted free participation while restricting who has the right to vote. All but the most radical political scientists will still call those societies democratic. They have even called societies democratic where the elections are officially free and fair but practically corrupted. The problem facing the United States at the moment, greater than all others save income inequality, is the abdication of citizens from their civic responsibilities. It sounds great blaming Super PACs, lobbyists, and wealthy donors for buying elections and mainstream media for failing to be honest, unbiased, and thorough. How did things get to be this way? Because citizens stopped participating, stopped becoming involved, and stopped demanding factual information.

Some things haven't changed and should. Because they haven't changed, the mindset has grown among voters that participation doesn't do any good. The deck is stacked in favor of the two major parties. For decades, voters have complained about holding their noses to vote for the lesser of two evils. It never occurs to them that their lack of activity or interest is why they end up with only two unsavory options, if that, and a sore snout. Thanks to gerrymandering, many congressional districts are so safe the opposing party doesn't bother to run candidates.

People complain day and night about television ads, robo-calls, and ever-larger campaign postcards. They should. Has anyone ever analyzed how effective any of these methods are at changing minds or making candidates visible? Does anyone know whether the positive results outweigh the negative reactions these invasions cause? Of course not. Who is going to spend the money conducting such an investigation? Maybe a grant-giving organization might fund some political scientist's interest, but the people who actually use these methods are never going to see the research results. Even without big money in campaigns, candidates rely on money for advertising and analytics far more than on volunteers for canvassing and telephone calls. Dr. Ben Carson raised more direct money from small donors than any other contender for the GOP nomination and used most of it on consultants. Technology long ago overtook the more human ways of reaching out to voters for support. Bernie Sanders was certainly trying to revive some of those methods. They are so unused in recent years he claimed they are revolutionary tactics.

Incumbency is by far the worst problem. Incumbents receive far more monetary and organizational support than challengers. For years, Congress had fewer turnovers than the Supreme Soviet or the Chinese People's Congress from session to session. Presidents are limited to two terms due to GOP animus toward FDR's popularity, popularity arising as much from the democratic socialist policies he put forward as from his wartime leadership. Many states limit consecutive terms as governor. Yet there are never any qualms about unlimited terms for legislators because supposedly longer tenure helps them be more knowledgeable and successful. Wouldn't that be true for executives also? Apparently not, although the history books are replete with the success stories of monarchies in which the monarchs had lengthy reigns. Entrenched politicians generate apathy unless they do something so egregious or are challenged by someone so popular from some other role before voters even begin to think they may need to replace an incumbent. Indeed, a fair number of incumbents have weathered scandals that sink others because they have become so closely identified with the job in their constituents' minds, meaning they have gotten a lot of money for their districts.

When State Senator Joe Bruno in New York was under investigation for corruption, the one thing supporters said over and over was how much good he had done for his district directing money for projects as Majority Leader. It never crossed their minds that perhaps other places in New York had more pressing needs but weren't even considered because their state senator was a Democrat or not among the favored Republicans under Bruno. His supporters were outright saying they had been bought off to love him, but since it was done with public money using the corrupt legislative process still in use in Albany that was okay. He was just representing their interests. Isn't that what a good legislator does? Should we ask Hillary Clinton about her Iraq War vote again?

Funding campaigns using private money, allowing donors to set up political action committees that can receive unrestricted money, and paying former elected and cabinet officials large sums of money for lobbying or speeches lead to one concern. The late Justice Antonin Scalia scoffed at the idea without glancing at the piles of evidence supporting it. Politicians benefiting from these arrangements are inclined to vote in the interests of the people providing the money more so than in the interests of their constituents. Individuals always have and always will become involved in politics for three reasons: enrichment, power, and duty.

One of the most interesting aspects of monarchies becoming constitutional over the last 200 years in most countries that retained monarchs has been the transformation of the role of monarch from being political to symbolic. Constitutional monarchs lost control of much of their wealth but remained wealthy. They lost almost all power except the moral kind that was demonstrated so clearly by King Juan Carlos of Spain actively denouncing an attempted coup against the early post-Franco democratic government. They have retained and generally made good use of publicly and frequently exemplifying the duty of all public officials to act in the name and for the benefit of the nation. Indeed, they sometimes do such a good job that they make elected officials look like venal, power-hungry animals with no sense of duty to the public whatsoever. Not that elected officials always need to be compared to a royal in order for them to be seen that way.

Hillary Clinton's poor response when she has been asked why she took so much money in speaking fees from Goldman Sachs illustrates the point. She has argued that she accepted the fees offered and knew they were not out of line with what former cabinet members have received or at least those from departments people easily remember exist. The going rate for former Secretaries of Labor to speak at corporate functions is apparently the meal served while they are talking.

Clinton has stated that receiving so much money as personal income cannot possibly contaminate any policies she would come up with to regulate Wall Street if she became President of the United States. She has defended receiving such large fees as evidence of how valuable her thoughts are. In effect she is saying this is a non-issue like Benghazi, private email servers, etc. Except this is not a non-issue like those others and those other secretaries of state did not decide to run for the Democratic presidential nomination. People who worked for her and her husband have publicly expressed their shock that Clinton could not come up with a coherent response that puts the question to rest even though she knows this is hanging over her head. It's as if she is using her excellent appearance before the Benghazi panel, which was a clearly political and vulgar attack on her, to say she doesn't need to respond any longer to questions about her character or decisions.

It is the exact same thing Nixon did with his Checkers speech in 1952. His enemies pointed at something that was perfectly ethical and responsible and he honestly responded that the only thing he and his wife had accepted as a personal gift was their dog Checkers. Patricia Nixon's solidly Republican cloth winter coat was proof since any self-respecting corrupt politician would demand a fur coat for his wife to keep her quiet. After that, he could always claim accurately that he had been a victim of a political effort to undermine his credibility and inaccurately that other attacks were equally spurious. Nixon used that incident successfully for 22 years. It has been about 24 years since Hillary Clinton was first attacked for her work with The Rose Law Firm, her law partner's suicide, and Whitewater. Is history repeating itself? At the very least, the Nixon example shows that just because a politician has inept political enemies does not mean the politician has done nothing wrong.

Nixon had an outstanding record as president with most of his foreign and domestic policies. Objectively speaking, his legislative agenda was very progressive. He was successful precisely because he was so good at politics. Clinton is similar in many ways and equally as admirable on many issues. Her supporters claimed she can get things done that Sanders or others can't because she is so good at politics. They are right about her skills but are denigrating the ways Sanders could achieve things through educating others rather than convincing others. It is the difference between Clinton stating what "I" will do versus Sanders saying what "we" will do during debates.

People who are very good at politics also are very good at deceiving people that they are doing nothing wrong. Convincing people to agree with you is the number one characteristic of a great politician. Almost all politicians act primarily to promote their own interests, not to represent the people who vote for them but to remain popular enough to get those votes again in the next election. They will do anything to succeed.

That is why Clinton even claimed that she made the speeches when she doubted she would ever seek elected office again and so they are not the speeches of a public person. Except if she had not been a public person who everyone thought would run in 2016 would her appearances have been so valuable? More importantly, she is indicating that the content of the speeches would have been different if she ever thought they were going to be subject to public scrutiny. And that is the whole point. Clinton wants to dismiss her closeness to Wall Street firms as something people like her do for valid reasons. She does not want her private views of Wall Street made public despite those views being relevant to her quest for the White House. Concealing that information is itself verging on corrupt activity. Withholding the transcripts only invites people to swoop in and voice their opinions on what are corrupt practices, what aren't, and whether politicians should avoid the appearance of impropriety even when they aren't doing anything technically illegal or corrupt. We come back to definitions.

One of the ways idiosyncratic definitions for what should be terms of art translate into structural issues is the impact they have on organizing to accomplish political aims. Progressives all want to have their own soap boxes rather than join forces to build larger, stronger organizations. Each activist or group of activists takes a specific angle on a problem and rolls it into a non-profit organization with its own small, underpaid staff, its sacred list of donors, and its own communications describing how the good fight will be fought once everyone chips in. Why are there six gun control groups or twelve wildlife groups or ten anti-hate groups sending requests for donations and asking for support? How many of these organizations have overlapping memberships? They are as duplicative and inefficient as the school districts and town governments in states that go further down than county level in the name of protecting local control when only a miniscule percentage of the residents ever bother to vote in town and school elections.

Unified action clearly is effective in making a stand on any issue. The Second Amendment is not stopping the US from adopting reasonable gun control legislation. The efforts of the National Rifle Association are. Just one organization has infiltrated the political system so thoroughly that nothing meaningful ever gets done about an issue that claims 34,000 lives a year and shatters many more lives. People favoring reasonable gun control measures have never come close to uniting so solidly. Gabby Giffords has done much to promote reasonable gun control measures. What she has not done is rally all of the people who have survived or been touched by gun violence but also recognize that limited gun ownership is fine for hunters and sports. Even James Brady and his wife were never able to pull together everyone affected by gun violence and demonstrate how pervasive the problem is. The people who advocate reasonable gun control due to personal experience never get added up and certainly never show themselves all in one place or a few locations so the country can recognize how great the problem is. There is no solid evidence of the great impact of gun violence, just anecdotes that are moving but less forceful because they are isolated.

Unlike the right wing, progressives haven't been good at collaborating, creating a consistent message, and uniting on issues. No one hears much about huge progressive events like the ones conservative organizations stage that attract GOP presidential nominees. The right wing can unite around saying "no" to change much easier than Democrats or progressives can unite around specific ideas to create change. Progressives don't want to be told what to do or to be led by strong leaders who define the agenda and the solutions. They will never get anywhere until they start working off of the same page the way social democrats did in Europe. Instead they argue over whether each position goes far enough or too far. How can they expect others to compromise if they can't compromise among themselves? How can they expect opponents or fence-straddlers to work with them when they can't even work with each other?

If Senator Sanders had won the Democratic presidential nomination, the Democratic Party was going to have a difficult time creating a suitable platform. The Democratic National Committee under Deborah Wasserstein-Schultz was doing everything in its power to rig the process in Clinton's favor. The Democratic establishment had no back-up plan if Clinton's policy positions were not the basis for the platform. Unlike the GOP, which has a ready set of policy positions that all of their candidates, even Donald Trump, support in one way or another, Sanders and Clinton differ substantially in areas that Clinton has not plagiarized from Sanders to undermine his candidacy. July proved rather late for the untidy progressives to finally get around to finding that elusive unity when also dealing with a large chunk of people disaffected by who was going to be nominated. Ironically, the most vocal and firm group among progressives was the Bernie or Bust crowd.

The Bernie or Bust crowd is the target audience for any further effort at creating an organization to do the groundwork for enacting revolutionary legislation. Some organizations already exist that could provide a body for a parasitic political revolution to use. Preferably, the organization can manage to bring other progressive organizations into the fold to coordinate efforts rather than duplicate them. The goal would be to create ways to attract support from those people also expecting significant change from this election who were not Sanders supporters. The organization would need to draw up plans for each of Sanders' policy proposals to accumulate as much sound evidence to support them, identify members of Congress to champion them, and unite non-profit organizations and state leaders and legislators in a team to promote them. The organization also would have to sort through all of the rules and diversions that can be used to block or slow down the legislation, assign people to remove as many of them as possible, and blunt the rest. That is a lot of work. It also is the only option short of going nuclear.

The nuclear option is to determine whether Congress has received the necessary requests from the states to call a constitutional convention. The requests have been sent and recorded as they straggled in. Enough interest was raised in the wake of the Occupy movement that Congress already had a study prepared on the subject. The study indicated that whoever might be deemed the best party of interest in the matter, the person or category of persons with legal standing, should insist Congress fulfill its constitutional duty to acknowledge the number of requests is sufficient and decide the terms under which a convention will be called. Failing that, a request for a writ from the federal district court requiring Congress to comply is needed.

A constitutional convention as contemplated by Article V of the Constitution has never been held and makes many people return to the Pandora's Box analogy. This approach can only be done if pre-emptive efforts are made to determine certain organizational aspects of a convention. For example, it would do little good to call a convention and have the state legislatures choose delegates mostly from among elected officials and well-connected others who have a stake in preventing much being done. Preferably, to avoid any appearance of self-interest, all delegates ought to have never held elective office at the federal or state level or be a member of a political party's national or state committees. The simplest procedure would be for voters to elect a delegate for their House district and two statewide delegates. To avoid too much unnecessary background preparation, candidates might need to pass a civics test prepared by officers of the American Political Science Association. Otherwise, there should be no hurdles for anyone to place his or her name on the ballot. Candidates could be provided with a set amount of advertising exposure to present themselves through a website, newspapers, or other public media source.

Given the atmosphere of political debate, it would be wise to follow the example of the original convention and treat the members as though they are a sequestered jury so that their deliberations are not influenced. Additionally, it would be wise to also give, as before, each state delegation one vote per motion based on the outcome of polling the members of the delegation. The delegates themselves would establish their rules of procedure. Since the essential structure of government is not at issue, it would be unwise to allow the delegates to write a wholly new constitution.

With that in mind, it would be wise to start with a list of proposed amendments just as the original convention started off with the Virginia Plan. Like the Virginia Plan, the point is not for it to remain as close to the original as possible but rather to focus attention on specific ideas that need to be addressed, revised, and voted that cover most of the subjects requiring deliberation. The primary point is to start from the same page. How about this page? The following are an exhaustive yet incomplete set of 14 amendments that address issues raised in this work aimed at restoring the Republic to a more vigorous form of democracy.

The Democracy Amendments

A. Elections for federal office shall be held on the first Saturday of November in even-numbered years. The only identification requirement for voting shall be a counter-signature to compare to the voter's signature in the voter registration rolls. If early voting is authorized by state statute, the early voting period shall be a minimum of twenty-eight (28) consecutive calendar days.

B. Any individual eligible under this Constitution to hold federal elective office shall be listed on the election ballot upon written request to the appropriate state authority. No requirement other than proof of eligibility shall be required.

C. Individuals elected to the House of Representatives shall serve no more than six (6) consecutive full terms in office. Individuals elected to the Senate shall serve no more than two (2) consecutive full terms in office. Individuals who have held federal elected office are prohibited from lobbying federal office holders, their employees, or any other federal employees for remuneration of any kind.

D. Congress is prohibited from making its members exempt from any law. Exemptions for members of Congress in existing laws are null and void.

E. A member of the Senate may hold the floor until he or she yields. Debate of any matter in the Senate shall be ended by a simple majority of the members present. Holds on any matter are prohibited. Advice and consent on appointments by the executive branch shall be given by the full Senate no later than ninety (90) calendar days after the appointment is submitted to the Senate.

F. All proposed legislation shall be given due consideration and a vote by committees established by each house of Congress. All proposed legislation approved by a majority of the members of a committee shall be introduced for debate to the full chamber. All proposed legislation not approved by a committee that receives support from at least ten (10) percent of the members of the chamber shall be introduced for debate to the full chamber. All proposed legislation introduced for debate to the full chamber shall have a yeah or nay vote if requested by at least twenty (20) percent of the members of the chamber. All amendments to proposed legislation must be reasonably construed and intended to relate to the main subject and purpose of the proposed legislation.

G. Districts established for members of the House of Representatives shall include no more than 600,000 residents as of the most recent decennial census. Districts shall be geographically rational along lines demarcating sub-state level government units whenever possible. All methods of establishing districts based on partisan concerns are prohibited.

H. Congress shall hold legislative sessions at least one hundred eighty (180) days per calendar year. Congress shall pass the next fiscal year's spending authorizations at least thirty (30) calendar days prior to the start of the new fiscal year. Failure to meet either or both of these requirements shall render all members of that Congress ineligible to stand for re-election when their term in office ends.

I. The District of Columbia and the Commonwealth of Puerto Rico shall be represented in Congress under the same terms as the states. Puerto Rico shall send voting representatives to the Electoral College.

J. Business entities and organizations established under state or federal statute or regulation are legal creations, not persons, whose rights, privileges, and obligations extend only as far as the statute or regulation under which they are created provides. The individual freedoms and liberties guaranteed to natural citizens and natural legal residents shall not extend to business entities or organizations established under state or federal statute or regulation. Business entities and organizations established under state or federal statute or regulation, and their representatives, except registered political parties, shall not provide any endorsement, support, or aid to any candidate for federal office and are prohibited from donating money, property, or services to any candidate for federal office.

K. Candidates for federal office may receive donations to fund political campaigns from natural citizens and natural legal residents of the United States only. Individuals, including the candidate, shall not donate more than $2,500 to any one candidate during the first election cycle after ratification of this amendment. The maximum donation per election cycle will increase $50 each subsequent election cycle. Congress shall designate and appropriate sufficient amounts for all candidates for federal office to apply to a non-partisan agency created by law to fund reasonable and directly relatable expenses for the purpose of campaigning for federal office.

L. Members of the Supreme Court shall adhere to the federal Judicial Code of Conduct. No federal judge at any level shall make speeches or publish any writing in any medium on any topic that was, is, or may be the subject of a case during their tenure.

M. Equality of rights under the law shall not be denied or abridged by the United States or by any state or jurisdiction within the United States on account of sex, sexual orientation, or sexual or gender identity. Congress shall have the power to enforce, by appropriate legislation, the provisions of this article.

N. Congress is empowered to pass legislation that supports the welfare of the natural citizens and natural legal residents of the United States, including, but not limited to, employment, housing, education, healthcare, healthcare insurance, food and nutrition, environmental health, transportation, sustainable energy, workplace safety, and urban renewal.

Chapter 20—Citizen Participation and the Fate of Democracy

DEMOCRACY EXISTS WHEREVER popular will and provisions for the welfare of all citizens are manifested in the policies and laws of a polity without infringing on equal protection of minorities of any sort. A handful of countries come very close to achieving this completely and they have the most contented populations in the world. Perfection, however, is not an option. Much as everyone loves labels, much as we have referred to democracies like we do classifiable species, democracy is not an "is or isn't" proposition. The noun "democracy" meaning a specific kind of political system should be discarded. Democracy is analogous to Christianity in this regard. One can say a political system is democratic, but that only places it in a broad category in which the practices, rites, and creeds vary substantially.

Democracy also can be viewed as the amount of sugar added to iced tea. More sugar means sweeter tea. Too little may turn people off from the unmasked tannins. Too much is overbearing. The more policies and laws mirror what the people want and need, the more democratic the polity. Too much democracy results in a tyranny of the majority. Too little makes citizens a bit bitter. Finding the right balance means citizens feel secure, contented, and optimistic as a result of what the government provides. Complaints arise from trivialities not the actual lack of anything other than maybe gratitude for what everyone has. The only requirement is the desire to participate and give one's due share in exchange for being treated equitably.

This is what Plato was getting at with his philosopher-king, the benevolent governor who addresses the concerns of every single one of the governed. It should not really matter how the government figures out what the popular will is just as long as the government can ascertain if it is hitting the mark or not. It should not matter what mechanisms and processes are used to provide for the welfare of all citizens just as long as those provisions do not discriminate among groups of citizens. It should not matter how minorities are given equal protection under the law as long the minorities themselves agree they are so protected. It is that simple.

By this standard, countries like China and Russia are far more democratic than they are given credit for. Ask Chinese or Russian citizens privately whether they are satisfied with how their governments look after the needs of average citizens. Do not ask those that seek out westerners, just anyone in a restaurant or on a bus, someone visiting the Great Wall or Catherine Palace the way Americans visit the Grand Canyon. A large majority will say they are satisfied. They are far more likely to feel secure about their basic needs being met than people in the US.

Do they have complaints? Yes! However, most of those are luxury problems compared to their complaints forty years ago. Now that those basic needs are being met and don't look like they are going to disappear, the Chinese in particular are looking for more. They want more access to the Internet. They want more options for travel. They want more supervision of local officials. They want more effort dedicated to protecting and cleaning the environment. Russians are heading in the same direction under Putin. Freedom is having fewer day-to-day things to worry about, the reverse of what has been happening to Americans since 1981.

This in no way ignores the fact that the governments of both of these countries are egregiously heavy handed when it comes to political dissent. Ever since Catherine the Great's time in Russia and the beginning of educational exchanges between China and western countries in the 1870s subjects and then citizens of those states have been introduced to and wanted to promote western political philosophies like liberal democracy and socialism. Russia in 1917 and China in 1949 saw those efforts pay off when Leninist parties embracing Marx-Engels communism took power. Japan had already embraced Prussian imperialism as a result of its contacts with the West.

While Japan was later forced to adopt liberal democracy, Russia and China had communism forced upon them, leaving them exhausted and ready in the 1980s for something different. However, just as Japan managed to turn western liberal democracy into a uniquely Japanese political system using one ruling party, China decided to forget about communism and embrace socialism with Chinese characteristics. Russia did essentially the same thing in creating a uniquely Russian political system while the other parts of the former Russian Empire/Soviet Union chose between old-fashioned autocracy and liberal democracy.

Small minorities in Russia and China wanted and still want to try liberal democracy with all of the accompanying freedoms of, to, and from whatever. Realists think that is a shoe that just won't fit. The dreamers receive support from overseas which does not strengthen their case. Foreign ideologies and interventions were the cause of so much pain in the past two centuries. The proponents of liberal democracy are seen as unpatriotic troublemakers by most of their fellow citizens as well as their governments.

The trend now seems to be for dissidents to do what they can to make enough money to immigrate to countries that have long acknowledged civil liberties. Self-imposed exile has as long a tradition as state-imposed internal exile. The governments of

Russia and China may yet learn that they are better off giving political dissidents a one-way ticket and a few parting gifts with the money currently spent on watching them and imprisoning them. After all, that is exactly what many right-wing people tell American democratic socialists (Denmark really is enchanting) and what some people said they would do if Donald Trump was elected and Canada didn't close the border. Robert Heinlein imagined that closed border in *Friday* and it did not seem that farfetched. Of course, how many people did jump ship? So few, it wasn't worth reporting apparently.

Through the lens of the Bill of Rights, Americans disparage China and Russia for being so harsh. But is the USA any better? We have had political prisoners and repression throughout our history. Eugene V. Debs was sent to prison for promoting socialist pacifism during World War I. He became ill there and that likely shortened his life. Quite a few careers in show business and government were ruined in the 1920s, 40s, and 50s merely because of alleged communist sympathies, too. The differences between how African-American protesters were treated in Ferguson and Baltimore *inter alia* compared to how the protests of the Bundy family and their supporters were handled provide one more clue. And let's not forget waterboarding, assassin drones, Guantanamo, Abu Ghraib, Edward Snowden, and Chelsea Manning. The USA has no business telling other sovereign states how they ought to act on the human or civil rights fronts.

Nor will that likely change. Hillary Clinton had the Secret Service remove someone who paid $500 like everyone else to attend an event just because the person interrupted her to stage a Black Lives Matter protest with a homemade banner. Clinton did nothing to reprimand the other, pinkish attendees from booing the protester. Similar incidents occurred on the campaign trail with Trump and other candidates. Exactly how is shouting down and ostracizing a minority voice consistent with claiming to be a free, democratic society? Such attacks on free speech in a setting that is supposed to provide at least some citizens able to pay the price of admission with access to a political candidate are not rare but are rarely reported by mainstream news sources. Indeed, why do candidates primarily interact with individual citizens at events with high price tags? Anyone want a picture of Mitt Romney as the Whore of Babylon? Sorry, we only have audio. Athenian democracy may not have been as great as advertised but at least for a while citizens were paid to participate rather than the other way round. Citizens prostituting themselves sounds better, right?

Most disturbing about dissenters at political campaign events being assaulted and removed is what this says about politicians and any interest they have in citizen participation in politics. As noted earlier, the USA is not a hotbed of political activity. Bernie Sanders said he wanted to promote new kinds of participation but so far has not found anything new to promote, just retreads of pre-PAC volunteerism. He didn't even do all of that. Certainly politicians like to see packed crowds at rallies, although again only crowds of supporters. They really like seeing packed crowds at fundraising events, although again only crowds of supporters.

Most candidates use that money to pay for mailings, television advertising, and robo-calls or professional call centers rather than fiddling with hiring people to organize volunteers to staff phone banks and canvas neighborhoods. One exception has been Democratic interest in registering voters on the demonstrated theory that the larger the electorate the better chance for Democrats. Aside from that, all candidates drool over their favorite form of citizen participation: accepting email messages begging for donations to meet the next FEC filing deadline, ramp up actions after a win (or a loss), or to celebrate a day ending in the letter "Y." Why? Because candidates have come to assume citizens are most helpful participating in elections by serving as ATMs. Oh, and voting.

The political revolution that can happen in the United

States of America in the next couple of years will happen provided that enough people do something other than complain or remain silent. The Occupy movement fumbled the ball with its insistence on direct democracy and leaderful decision making. A few people became energized enough to make a difference locally and even a bit more with Occupy Sandy meeting the needs of people hit hard by the superstorm and the Rolling Jubilee that has been successfully finding money and negotiating down people's medical bills. The moment and energy were lost to do anything nationally.

Bernie Sanders picked up the thread. Yet as energized as his supporters have been and as inspiring his rallies were, the final connection still was not being made. Far too many people were so disenchanted and so used to disappointment the best they could do was hit the donate button on the latest plea from Vermont. And the pleas from Vermont were literally telling those people that if they only would just hit that donate button right now Bernie Sanders would be sleeping in the White House next year and the revolution would have happened. Unbelievably, almost every single plea said that or some iteration of that cause and effect equation. And why does that equation sound so familiar?

Spending = speech. That's right. Even Bernie Sanders, the man who vowed to take money out of politics, continuously told people he needed money to get money out of politics. His supporters' donations speak for them. They say "End Citizens United" in a very rigid tone. What were we saying about how important it is to use terms as defined by experts? No higher authority than the Supreme Court of the United States defined speech to include spending money, specifically donating money to a political campaign. How do Bernie Sanders and a few progressive organizations say we can erase that definition from the books? By using that definition. Sanders' supporters vehemently defended this paradox by agreeing with him that the only possible way to change politics in the United States is to use the methods they want to change. That sentence should end with an interabang but pundits have used this year's crop reporting Donald Trump's tweets. Even WTF went Hollywood. We will have to settle for "say what again"?

Anyway, umm, folks.... Using methods you want to eliminate to eliminate them is not a revolution. That is maintaining the status quo. A revolution requires actions that use other methods to create change than those currently in place. Those methods do not have to be violent. They may involve using some of the structures in place like elections, political offices, the Constitution, and even existing political parties if they can be parasitically overtaken. We have said this before: electing one person to one very high political office using a grassroots campaign is not revolutionary. It may have been in 1828 when Andrew Jackson rode a populist wave into Washington. Nine score and ten years later, not so much.

The purpose of this political revolution is to restore the Republic to a point where a healthy majority of citizens are engaged enough with politics and their government that they take pride in paying attention to issues presented by professional, unbiased journalists, possibly help out in a local campaign or donate to a politician's war chest, feel fairly certain they understood what candidates promise to do if elected, acknowledge that family members or neighbors might hold different opinions but never think less of them because of that, know that contacting an elected official will get a personal response from someone, and vote even if neither candidate really represents the voter on every major issue. No hate. No demonization. No suspicions. No disgust. No surrender. All of that, every single point, places the responsibility for change squarely on the shoulders of citizens. Any change that is going to happen requires citizens to do something.

What about corporate personhood? What about Super PACs? What about those conniving party establishments? What about career politicians? What about every last, blasted corrupt feature of American politics? And how are we going to reduce income inequality? How are we going to take care of homeless veterans? How are we going make college affordable? How are we going to end Wall Street's manipulations? How are we going to deal with all of the issues no one has been dealing with for ten or thirty years?

Not one single thing can be done about any of those problems, issues, concerns, and nightmares until enough American citizens take action to indicate they will no longer tolerate the pettiness, hatred, lies, baiting, inaction, hostage-taking, selfishness, aggrandizement, lechery, gluttony, egotism, condescension, hypocrisy, et cetera. Enough American citizens must show they will no longer tolerate the Gordian fustercluck in Congress that makes the traffic on the Washington Beltway seem like a relaxed drive down one of the country's finest scenic byways. Enough American citizens must clearly announce they want a government that protects them not from ISIL, Will Ferrell movies, people who don't speak English, Russia, "illegals," gay marriage, darker skinned people (unless its John Boehner), or whatever is under the bed but from malnutrition, homelessness, joblessness, avoidable and treatable medical conditions, gun violence, decaying infrastructure, untreated mental illness, poor and incomplete education, unsafe water and corroding pipes, predatory lenders, banksters, discrimination, climate change, ignorance, under compensation and overwork, incarceration for addiction-related crimes, and all of the other things essential to preserving life, liberty, and the pursuit of happiness that are generally enjoyed in other western democracies.

The American people are responsible for allowing the terms of their social contract to be interpreted in a manner that gradually gave them less and less influence over their elected representatives. They bought the idea that government is bad. They bought the idea that every sovereign individual must take care of his or her selfish needs first without regard to the impact on others. They even bought the idea that there is no social contract. The more they bought, the lower they sank economically. The more they bought, the wealthier their employers and the owners of their employers became. They reached a point where their only hope left was to play the lottery and pray to magic Jesus. Then they bought again out of anger over terrorism coming from overseas. They bought out of denial about the domestic terrorism of bigots. They bought until almost all of what they had was in the hands of politicians, the major political parties, wealthy individuals, and corporations.

What can be done? That's easy enough: action.

- Action that cries out "stop and listen" just as clearly and effectively as one man standing in the way of a column of tanks or one woman raising a banner at a posh fundraising event.
- Action that hands grievances to the government, wealthy, and corporations.
- Action that provides the resources to take the steps necessary to correct the deficiencies that have arisen in the country.
- Action that obtains the means to rebuild communities.
- Action that meets everyone's essential needs.
- Action that seeks dignity and honor from labors.
- Action that guarantees peace, security, and fulfillment.

In return, citizens must offer more action. We must offer involvement in our cities, towns, and villages. We must offer engagement with those that need. We must offer ourselves to the betterment of our country and the future. We must offer participation in civic culture to be a defense against the weaknesses of apathy and self-absorption. We must offer to be participants in our own governance. We must offer to take responsibility for how our choices and actions affect others.

Enough people have rallied behind some of the last crop of candidates for the presidency for it to be clear that popular will is no longer reflected in the policies and laws promulgated by the federal government. The political establishment no longer is responsive to what people want and need. This is the new landscape. It has not faded since the summer of 2015; it has become clearer. The observations made here regarding the 2016 election were based on the data then available filtered through the principles and processes of political analysis. Almost everyone eventually realized what was readily apparent in late summer 2015 to anyone unhindered by prejudice: Donald Trump was going to be the GOP nominee and the Democratic establishment had the fix in to nominate Hillary Clinton. That second point guaranteed Trump the White House, with or without help from Russia.The result is what it is. Regardless, there is work to be done.

The United States cannot put off the political revolution that is possible. Sadly, Sanders showed no inclination to distinguish between the revolution and his election until after he lost the nomination. This work already reeks of hubris, so there isn't much point in laying out any further practical suggestions that will come off sounding like "the plan." If nothing else, readers should be aware by now that history is full of examples of how things can get done. Preaching to the choir at this point, but any active participation in the public sphere requires some knowledge of how politics work and some confidence in being able to use the facts at hand to figure out what is going on. The rest is a matter of taking action.

While any action already mentioned will do, one in particular can be rewarding and beneficial beyond measure. It requires talking with people to encourage them to become aware and do something. That's it. Share with others the enthusiasm and interest of being an engaged citizen. Talk about issues. Ask questions. Conduct research together. We have become afraid to talk about politics because everyone has those damned set-in-stone opinions or refuses to get involved. We have forgotten that politics is all about discovering the views of others and working together to solve problems affecting the layers of community to which we belong. Rather than only thinking about our own views, show an interest in the views of others, refuse to be judgmental, and find out how those views developed. The point of forming a community is to work together not to set out on our own paths but to pool resources, to contribute what we can, and to receive what we need.

This is not revolutionary. It is the first step to recommitting to our social contract and restoring the Republic. Speaking of steps, the *Daodejing* is a collection of 81 poems or entries that forms the basis for Daoism (Taoism), one of the most ancient ethical and political philosophies known. The reputed author, Laozi (meaning "Old One" or "Old Master"), was supposedly a functionary in one of the kingdoms of what is now China in the sixth century BCE. The *Daodejing* is the source for a well-known aphorism Mao Zedong frequently contemplated while sorting out how best to move forward with the revolution he led. As readers have probably guessed, the saying is "A journey of a thousand miles begins with a single step." However, the literal phrase is even more compelling because it emphasizes that one must first recognize and assess where one is presently before moving forward.

千里之行，始於足下

Qiān lǐ zhī xíng, shǐ yú zú xià

A journey of a thousand li starts beneath one's feet

Readers now know where we are as a country. We must all step forward together.

www.ingramcontent.com/pod-product-compliance
Lightning Source LLC
Chambersburg PA
CBHW031424270326
41930CB00007B/570
9781941071793